THE IRISH DRAMATIC MOVEMENT

THE IRISH
DRAMATIC MOVEMENT

by

UNA ELLIS-FERMOR

METHUEN & CO. LTD. LONDON
11, New Fetter Lane, E.C.4

First Published . . *November 9th 1939*
Second edition . .   *1954*
Reprinted   . .   *1964*

2·2

CATALOGUE NO. 2/3472/11

PRINTED IN GREAT BRITAIN

IN MEMORIAM

CONTENTS

PAGE

ACKNOWLEDGEMENTS   viii

PREFACE TO FIRST EDITION   ix

PREFACE TO SECOND EDITION   xv

Chapter 1. THE ORIGINS AND SIGNIFICANCE OF THE IRISH
            DRAMATIC MOVEMENT   1

Chapter 2. THE ENGLISH THEATRE IN THE NINETIES   18

Chapter 3. THE EARLY HISTORY OF THE MOVEMENT   33

Chapter 4. IDEALS IN THE WORKSHOP   59

Chapter 5. W. B. YEATS   91

Chapter 6. MARTYN AND MOORE   117

Chapter 7. LADY GREGORY   136

Chapter 8. JOHN MILLINGTON SYNGE   163

Chapter 9. CONCLUSION AND PROSPECT   187

Appendix 1. CHRONOLOGICAL TABLE OF THE MAIN EVENTS
             IN THE FIRST YEARS OF THE MOVEMENT   197

         2. SOME MATERIALS BEARING ON THE EARLY
            HISTORY OF THE MOVEMENT   207

         3. THE MAIN DATES CONNECTED WITH THE
            SPREAD OF IBSEN'S WORK AND THOUGHT   211

         4. A LIST OF PLAYS PRODUCED IN LONDON IN
            THE LAST DECADE OF THE NINETEENTH CEN-
            TURY   214

         5. A SUBJECT INDEX TO SOME OF THE MAIN
            CRITICAL OPINIONS OF W. B. YEATS AND
            LADY GREGORY   219

         6. A NOTE ON EDITIONS AND GENERAL WORKS
            OF REFERENCE   234

INDEX   237

ACKNOWLEDGEMENTS

I HAVE TO THANK the following for permission to include various quotations : Messrs George Allen and Unwin Ltd. for those from J. M. Synge's *Plays* and T. C. Murray's *Maurice Harte* ; Messrs. Ernest Benn Ltd. for those from Edward Martyn's *Tale of a Town* ; Messrs. Jonathan Cape Ltd. for those from Mr. Denis Gwynn's *EdwardMartyn* ; Mi. Padraic Colum for those from his play, *The Land* ; Messrs. Constable & Co., Ltd., for a passage from Kuno Meyer's *Ancient Irish Poetry* ; Messrs. Duckworth & Co., Ltd., for those from Edward Martyn's *Maeve* and *The Heather Field* ; Mr. Denis Gwynn for those from his book *EdwardMartyn* ; Messrs. Macmillan & Co., for those from the volumes *Plays, Plays and Controversies, Autobiographies and Essays* in The Collected Works of W. B. Yeats ; Mr. C. D. Medley for those from George Moore's *Hail and Farewell* and *The Bending of the Bough* ; Messrs. Putnam & Co., Ltd., for those from the works of the late Lady Gregory (*Cuchulain of Muirthemne, Irish Folk History Plays, New Comedies, Seven Short Plays, The Image, Three Wonder Plays, Three Last Plays*) ; Mr. Lennox Robinson for those from his play, *The Clancy Name* ; the late G. B. Shaw for a passage from the preface to his *Three Plays for Puritans* ; Miss Doris Arthur Jones for those from *The Foundations of a National Drama*, by her father, the late Henry Arthur Jones. I owe to many friends in Dublin the advantages of discussion and debate on subjects relating to the Irish drama and to the aesthetics of drama in general. Finally I would wish to express my great gratitude to Mrs. W. B. Yeats for her generous permission to use quotations from the works (mentioned above) of the late W. B. Yeats.

PREFACE TO THE FIRST EDITION

' THEY HAVE WON much praise for themselves and raised the dignity of Ireland.' It is not unfitting to begin this story with Lady Gregory's comment on the work of the company known through Europe and America as ' The Abbey Theatre '. The words she uses would be a fitting epitaph not only for the company but for the movement itself of which it was the outcome and to which this book is in small degree a tribute. Further, too, it is to those players that many of my readers, like myself, will have owed their first introduction to the modern Irish dramatists.

It was nearly thirty years ago that I first saw them in London and though I know that I saw four plays in all (of which *Riders to the Sea* must have been one), my deepest first impression was not made by the tragic genius of Synge but by the passionate nationalism of Yeats and Lady Gregory. It must have been in part at least an audience of Englishmen or Anglo-Irishmen that saw *Cathleen ni Houlihan* that day with Miss Sara Allgood in the part of Cathleen. A play was a real thing to me in those days as no play, alas, can ever be again, and I remember now recoiling from the wildness and the violence, the Old Woman with her boding, bringing her talk of war and death into the midst of ordinary things (this being before the average Englishman had learnt to accommodate this kind of thought in his mind). There was something as yet terrifying and savage about people who talked familiarly about it in the every-day setting of a homely cottage. The average Anglo-Irishman in the audience, meeting the play as most did for the first time, recoiled vigorously upon his English blood. Then came the quickening all over the stage, the exultation that was the secret of a people ' who believed so much in the soul and so little in anything else that they were never entirely certain that the earth was solid under the footsole ' :

'They that have red cheeks will have pale cheeks for my sake, and for all that, they will think they are well paid.
They shall be remembered for ever,
They shall be alive for ever,
They shall be speaking for ever,
The people shall hear them for ever.'

I think that then the Anglo-Irish part of the audience suffered that strange experience, the penetration and irradiation of the mind by something that appears to alter its constitution or its orientation and is called conversion. I can remember as if it were yesterday the swing over of sympathy, more sudden and complete than in any other play I have seen, the releasing of exultation and vision as the world of Edwardian London in which we had till then been reared was, suddenly, no longer 'solid under the footsole'. The race for whom a short life and a lonely death are outweighed by 'a story will be told for ever' had taken possession, and more than one half-hearted Irishman must have become whole-hearted from that out.

Curiously enough it was from this same play that, more than twenty years later, I learnt another lesson. This time it was in the class-room, not the theatre. I had been lecturing on the Irish drama, taking this play in its turn, off and on, for ten years, to large classes of English students to whom I generally read it aloud without shortening it. They were always deeply moved. Only at the end of the ten years, though, did I discover, when a small group of specialists plucked up courage to ask me to explain the allusions, that none of the references, not even the date '1798', had any meaning for them at all outside the play. It took me the best part of an hour to explain all they wanted, for a general outline of Irish history and literature had to be supplied. I blamed myself at the time for not realizing that Englishmen would have no associations, even with a name like Granuaile and needed to have it all explained. Afterwards I was not so sure. The play had been accepted for ten years on its merits as an expression of the worship of liberty and its own racial glory in a subject race and not of the nationalism of any particular people. Now I agree with what Lady Gregory says about *The Rising of the Moon* and again trust the play to take care of itself without explaining it.

x

PREFACE TO THE FIRST EDITION

This book arises naturally out of the experience implied or contained in those two episodes. It is an attempt to see the great Irish Dramatic Movement of the beginning of this century not as an Irishman sees it (that has been done beyond compare by the leaders of the movement themselves and by later Irish critics), but as an outsider sees it who comes to it reared in another culture yet willing to bring to it an intelligence as sympathetic as may be. For it is some such interpretation as this that must be made of all national art sooner or later, as it passes from the national to the international, from the exquisite flowering of a generation to that which belongs to the ages. Indeed, it is perhaps not untrue to say that the desire to talk about it is the most valid tribute the stranger can bring ; the proof, if proof were needed, that this piece of art has passed out of the keeping of its own race and has become the universal possession of mankind. In the American and English theatre and university world it has long been recognized that the work of Yeats, Lady Gregory, Synge and the group of men that supported and followed them at the Abbey Theatre must take its place in the world's drama, in that drama which contains already Euripides, Shakespeare and Molière. ' They have won much praise for themselves and have raised the dignity of Ireland.'

It is the leaders themselves that have left us the ' source books ' of the movement ; Lady Gregory, Moore, Yeats. Widely as the books differ—as widely as the minds that produced them—they have one thing in common. They are all, without exception, what one would most desire source-books to be ; autobiographic and immediate. Lady Gregory, in addition, records a large number of verifiable facts. It is true that, even under the firm benevolence of her instruction, one is sometimes bewildered by the completely contradictory dates or left suspended in a region of ' time out of mind '. ' (When can this have been ? thought my Uncle Toby).' And his modern descendant echoing his words finds nothing for it but the playbills in the files of the Abbey Theatre,[1] or reference to

---

[1] I should like to record here my debt to Mr. Lennox Robinson who drew my attention to these files and gave me many generous suggestions in conversation.

one of the later histories such as the careful and exhaustive work of Mr. Andrew Malone.

But the present book is not a history of the movement. To be its historian is a privilege reserved for the fellow-countrymen of the authors and players, for men who, like Mr. Andrew Malone, are closely acquainted with the circumstances in which this drama arose, the conditions, social, political and cultural from which it derived and in which it has since developed. Such a book as his, *The Irish Drama*,[1] has made superfluous the writing of any further exact histories, at least until such time as the continued growth of this still vigorous movement shall provide material for further record. He has made clear not only the earlier cultural history of Ireland, but the nature of the various political and nationalist movements and sentiments which took their part in shaping the early drama and are still, in modified forms, at work upon its descendants. And he has traced in clear detail the events which make up the history of the dramatic movement itself from 1899 onwards. I have not attempted to cover his ground again and I trust I have acknowledged at all points the considerable debt that I, and all students of this drama, owe to him.

Yet there is perhaps a certain service that the foreigner, if he be able, may render. He approaches the subject thinking that he has to till a small and easily compassable field in dramatic history—and, behold, it expands until it covers a mountainside. He begins with the modest intention of making his interpretation of the work of four or five playwrights and the little theatre that they instituted. He finds himself committed not only to this but to the disentangling of several profound and intricate aesthetic problems ; to the understanding of a race whose logical and imaginative processes are other than his own, as their relation to art is certainly other ; to the study of a great ancient civilization recalled and re-lived by the poets of a later age so that it became the inspiration of a national renascence. He finds, moreover, that the Irish Dramatic Movement whose early phase had seemed to fall easily into the years between 1899 and 1916 (or 1922) is a living organism which is still in full growth and development, of which one part cannot be separ-

[1] *The Irish Drama*. (Constable, 1929.)

ated from the others without great risk of destroying its life and its significance. He begins to realize that he will make but a poor thing of much of this interpreting and that if he had known fully what lay before him he would never have begun his exploration. Yet the Englishman's point of view remains a tribute which the Englishman alone can offer ; it is only the foreigner who can see this drama from outside and on the background of the world's dramatic history.

The greatest practical difficulty is that of deciding whether to attempt to cover the whole field from 1899 to the present day or to look for a point at which a first volume may suitably be concluded and at which a second may later take up the tale again. There is a sense in which the whole of this drama is a seamless texture, the early poetic movement changing gradually into the folk movement and that as gradually into the realistic and sometimes satiric tradition that followed, the preference for national and folk themes gradually extending, at the same time, until its scope covers all classes and no longer demands the background of a particular nation. But there is one part, the realistic movement which had its first beginnings in 1903 and reached its full strength from 1910 onward, which is more certainly indivisible than the movement as a whole. The realistic playwrights, who supersede the earlier group shortly after the death of Synge, form one continuous sequence which it would be practicably impossible to break in upon. And, at the same time, there is a kind of pausing place about 1910 or 1912 when the old tradition is just ceasing and the new just reaching its height, where a division may perhaps with least damage be made. To do this involves the anomaly of leaving the work of Colum, which all falls before this point, to be considered in the later volume with that of Robinson, Murray and their contemporaries. But the study of the early phases demands so much space that to do justice to these later authors on the same scale was impossible in one volume. To treat them on any other scale cannot be considered, so a pausing place is made somewhere in the years immediately after the death of Synge in 1910.

Another practical difficulty, though of quite a different kind, is that of including the Gaelic plays, of which there were several

xiii

in the early years of the movement written not merely for the Gaelic League but for the Irish Literary Theatre itself. Two reflections, that the Irish language is a difficult one to learn and that these plays fall, after the first years, mainly outside the province of the Abbey Theatre, induced me to pass over them; but for some idea of their significance and interest I would refer English readers in the first instance to the comments in W. B. Yeats's *Samhain* papers.[1]

There is still one individual tribute that may most fittingly be made here. I had hoped that the founder of the movement would himself have read and given his consent to at least the chapter on his own work, but this book was just ready for the press when the news came of the death of Mr. Yeats. So that most of what has been said here has never been submitted to him except in general discussion and conversation. Yet the book is, inevitably, more concerned with him than with any other one poet of the movement. Indeed, I sometimes think that I began to write a book about the Irish Dramatic Movement and ended by writing a book about Mr. Yeats. This happened inevitably. The more closely one studies the record of those years the more one grows aware of the courage and unflagging energy that carried the movement 'like a banner' through opposition, adversity and apparent frustration. This does not detract from the honour that is due to the other leaders of the movement. It is inevitable because, throughout, the major design was a direct emanation from one man's character and rooted in his poetic faith.

In conclusion I have to acknowledge, as always, a debt of gratitude to those whose help was generously given in many ways: to the late Dr. Lascelles Abercrombie for the first suggestion that the book should be written and for many conversations on the aesthetic problems that arose in the course of writing; to Dr. R. I. Best, Director of the National Library of Ireland, for placing at my disposal the unique records in his charge and for valuable comments; to Mr. Louis MacNeice for discussion, from the modern playwright's point of view, of the problems of poetic drama; to Professor Edna Purdie,

[1] Largely reprinted as *The Irish Dramatic Movement* in *Plays and Controversies*. (Macmillan.)

PREFACE TO THE FIRST EDITION

to Miss Olive Purser, to Mr. Lennox Robinson, to Mr. F. R. Higgins, to the Earl and Countess of Longford for suggestions on technical details ; to Miss Elizabeth Yeats for the generous loan of valuable original documents ; to Miss Lily Yeats for unfailing encouragement and for a store of illuminating memories, and to the late W. B. Yeats himself for discussions and conversations and for his benediction upon an Englishman's attempt to write the history of his work. If this book fails, and it does, for it is not the book I meant to make it, it is not for lack of generous help from these and from many others.

London.
March 17, 1939.

PREFACE TO THE SECOND EDITION

FOURTEEN YEARS HAVE PASSED since the first edition of this volume appeared and the steadily increasing study of the Irish Dramatic Movement, with the many contributions made to its history, have made the projected second volume unnecessary. But I did not want to let this study of the earlier movement go into a second edition without an attempt to link it with the Irish drama of the years immediately before the recent war. This link, which takes the form of a short extension of the final chapter, is the only alteration, apart from the correction of a few errors and misprints and some changes in the book-list at the end. The body of the book remains in its original form, for, although I should perhaps have modified a judgment here and there if I had been re-writing the whole, I have seen no reason to alter substantially what I then said. My enjoyment of this drama has suffered no diminution with the passage of the years nor has my faith in the quality of the Irish imagination grown dimmer.

London,
1953.

ABBREVIATIONS

The following abbreviations have been used in some of the footnotes and appendices :

Autob.	*Autobiographies* (W. B. Yeats), Macmillan's ed.
C.A.	*The Cutting of an Agate* (W. B. Yeats).
D.P.	*Dramatis Personae* (W. B. Yeats).
Ess.	*Essays* (W. B. Yeats), Macmillan's ed.
H.F. 1, 2, 3	*Hail and Farewell, Ave, Salve, Vale* (George Moore), ed. Heinemann, 1937
Hend.	W. A. Henderson's press-cuttings. (See Appendix 6.)
I.D.M.	*The Irish Dramatic Movement* (W. B. Yeats in *Plays and Controversies*).
I.F.H. 1, 2	*Irish Folk History Plays*, Vols. I and II (Lady Gregory).
I.L.T.	The Irish Literary Theatre.
Im.	*The Image and Other Plays* (Lady Gregory).
I.N.D.C.	The Irish National Dramatic Company.
I.N.T.S.	The Irish National Theatre Society.
L.P.	*Later Poems* (W. B. Yeats), Macmillan's ed.
Malone	A. Malone : *The Irish Theatre.*
N.I.C.	*New Irish Comedies* (Lady Gregory).
N.L.I.	The National Library of Ireland.
N.L.S.	The National Literary Society.
O.I.T.	*Our Irish Theatre* (Lady Gregory).
P.A.S.	*Per Amica Silentia Lunae* (W. B. Yeats).
Plays	The volume *Plays* in Macmillan's edition of the works of W. B. Yeats.
P.C.	*Plays and Controversies* (in the same edition).
Rev.	*Reveries over Childhood and Youth* (W. B. Yeats).
S.S.P.	*Seven Short Plays* (Lady Gregory).
T.L.P.	*Three Last Plays* (Lady Gregory).
T.V.	*The Trembling of the Veil* (W. B. Yeats).
T.W.P.	*Three Wonder Plays* (Lady Gregory).

CHAPTER I

THE ORIGIN AND SIGNIFICANCE OF THE IRISH DRAMATIC MOVEMENT

I

THIS BOOK is (as I have suggested in the Preface) an attempt to study the modern Irish drama, not historically, for that has been done, both by the leaders of the movement themselves and by other Irishmen better qualified for the task than a reader of another race and culture, but rather in the way in which alone an outside observer may be permitted to study it—in relation to the general achievement of drama and to the special history of the drama of the English-speaking world. This means that we must concern ourselves with essentials, not with accessories, with the nature and quality of this drama, and with such aspects of its influence and effects as are of vital enough importance to stand out in a general prospect over the whole art. And indeed this approach needs at the present day no apology. For to come down to essentials, the essentials of fact in practice and of the ' truths of the imagination ' in art and criticism, is our only chance. We must ask of all things we encounter, ' Quid hoc ad Æternitatem ? ' And if the story of Irish drama were merely a section of interesting and amusing theatre history we might feel to-day that the answer to that question was ' vanitas vanitatum '.

But it is not. For the Irish movement produced at least two great dramatic poets and so stands justified ' sub specie æternitatis ' in terms of one of the absolute values, poetic truth. Moreover, by some strange stirring of the spirit which in part eludes analysis, that poetic drama was a means of bringing back to the drama of the other English-speaking races the habit of high poetry which it had lost for two hundred years.

To understand the significance of this we must make a cast back into the history of the development of the English theatre from the time of Jacobean drama and a cast forward again into

I

the drama of Great Britain, Ireland and America at the present day, bearing always in mind as we do so that without great poetry, such as we find in the Greeks and in the Elizabethans, there will not be great drama. It is in these terms, then, that we are to consider this movement begun in Ireland at the end of the nineteenth century by Yeats and Lady Gregory and carried forward some few years later by Synge, in terms of its qualitative relations with the high dramatic achievement of other ages. If it could not in some way stand up to this comparison, we should not now be considering it.

The history of English drama (with which the Irish was, until the end of the nineteenth century, for practical purposes, identical)[1] is one of steady decadence from the end of the great Jacobean period until the middle of the nineteenth century. Many causes contributed to this, not all of which can be set down here. The habit of mistrusting artistic truth—often an accompaniment of Puritanism and from which we have seldom since been wholly free—did more in the mid-seventeenth century than its mere outward expression (the closing of the theatres) to check poetic experience in its dramatic form. The brilliant recovery at the Restoration, again, was more apparent than real, for it introduced fresh limiting factors both in comedy and in heroic drama, substituting a theatre of specialized tastes for the liberal fecundity of a drama that had been national in as full a sense as that of Athens. The Restoration drama, itself doomed to a short life by its very specialization, made it more difficult than ever for the English theatre to recover its position as an expression of God's plenty in the language of poetry and power. More accidents followed in the eighteenth century such as did not, in such damning combination, befall the drama of any of the great continental civilizations, with the possible exception of the Spanish. Opera became a rival instead of a co-operator by the introduction of a foreign king and court ; the novel, its second competitor, was from the outset in the hands of men of superlative ability and of one man, at least of first-rate genius ; the rise of the great actor-managers from Garrick onwards which brought back the popularity of the theatre did so at the expense of the drama (in spite of the appar-

[1] See, in more detail, *post*, Chap. 1, *The English Theatre in the Nineties*.

ent promise of Shakespearean revivals) by raising up audiences trained in the experience of histrionic skill and not in the exercise of the imagination. By the beginning of the nineteenth century, despite the effort of Goldsmith and Sheridan, this concatenation of mischances, not all of which befell any other contemporary drama, had reduced audiences, actors and managers alike to standards and assumptions which drove the poet out of the playhouse and made the writing of plays something like the supplying of scenario for the modern film. It became a business matter of sharking up melodrama, farce, comic opera or burlesque from materials that lay handy either in the author's fertile invention or in the rich supplies of German or French drama, English or foreign novels or modernizations of earlier plays. In nearly all these cases, it had nothing to do with artistic experience, whether from the author's or from the audience's point of view : nothing, that is, to do with poetry.

This state of decadence was psychologically more vicious than at first appears, for it involved that utter debasement of the imagination of the audience from which recovery, if possible at all, is slow and painful. Melodrama, with its substitution of sensation for emotion, situations for structure and spectacle for nearly everything, had taken the place of tragedy, while farce, which still kept a measure of artistic integrity in its alertness of construction, had thrown over its original observation of character and used easily recognized stock types no less than did the melodrama. Thus was induced that indolence of imagination—to which the majority of us are in any case prone —which is one of the worst effects of the modern cinema play upon some sections of the public to-day.

Such a condition of affairs is hard to redeem ; indeed there have been cases in the history of drama, such as the psychologically similar case of the Roman theatre, which have proved intractable to redemption. The poets, on the one hand, in whom the desire for dramatic expression cannot be utterly repressed, furnish a long list of poetic plays, from the late eighteenth to the late nineteenth century, in which fine dramatic material is so handled as to be unsuitable for treatment in the actual theatre, even had it been willing to receive them. Wordsworth, Coleridge, Keats, Shelley, Byron, Landor,

3

Beddoes, Browning and Tennyson[1] in their different ways offer a melancholy corroboration of the fundamental aesthetic law by which, if the final act of communication is thwarted, a complete artistic experience cannot be achieved, nor its result, a living work of art. Those come nearest to this achievement who, having least hope, write rather dramatic poems for the library than poetic drama for the stage. The men of the theatre, on the other hand, having all things in their control, reduce all to their own level ; we arrive at the position at which we have a theatre, but not a drama.

The difficulty, then, for any drama, of delivering itself from such a condition cannot be over-estimated. The poets are out of action and the men in action are unlikely, by tradition and training, to see what is wrong. Even did they see, they have a deadweight of economic, social and professional habit against them, and they give in or go out. The whole process of re-covery is too much like what used to be called in America lifting oneself by one's own boot-straps. Yet, after nearly two hundred years of decadence, a mild form of recovery did begin in the middle of the nineteenth century, starting in the only possible place, within the theatre itself, and consisting of a tendency, beginning in Lytton and steadily increasing in Robertson, to turn farce in the direction of comedy, technical conventions in the direction of realism. Robertson's fight for naturalism in character, dialogue and setting (delightfully re-corded by Pinero in *Trelawney of the Wells*) was taken up by Henry Arthur Jones, and undoubtedly a measure of artistic integrity—if no more than added seriousness and naturalism in the drama—would have been restored by them in any case. Whether it would have gone further than this, further than, say, Joanna Baillie had carried it in the early years of the century along a somewhat different line, is most doubtful.

The further redemption of English drama could, almost certainly, only have come as it did from outside. The first phase of this, which is generally known, in Jones's phrase, as the Renascence of English drama, came from Scandinavia, through the work of Ibsen ; the second and final phase, from the oppo-

[1] This is, of course, least true in the case of Tennyson, whose co-operation with Irving gave him a measure of practical success.

site point of the compass—indeed, ' Quod minime reris, Graia pandetur ab urbe '. . . .

It was perhaps inevitable that the English adoption of Ibsen should have certain marked peculiarities. The great figure of Ibsen gathered up for most readers and intelligent play-goers what was serious and vigorous, what had dignity and command in European drama of the second half of the nineteenth century. But the apostle of seriousness in the English theatre was Henry Arthur Jones, and his advocacy, if not precisely of Ibsen yet of something that immediately associated itself with Ibsen, was mainly occupied with the dramatist's right to handle serious and controversial topics in the theatre. It was a short step from that to the idea and habit of the problem play, and this, helped undoubtedly by the trend of the controversy of 1889–93 (fastening mainly on plays such as *A Doll's House* and *Ghosts*,) seems to have concentrated public attention upon Ibsen's social dramas to such an extent that knowledge of his work became limited to this relatively small section. There is no question that seriousness, as Henry Arthur Jones understood it, was needed in the English theatre ; indeed, it is hard to see how any growth could have come until dignity and earnestness were again associated in the public mind with the public stage. But it was undoubtedly a misfortune that, whatever the causes, the potent name of Ibsen, with all it carried of authority and command, should have been associated with the plays that treat specific social problems (generally with a remedial implication) rather than with those far greater plays whose psychological and spiritual problems lead to the implications of poetic truth.

In other words, the Ibsen that the English public discovered, when the stirring of the bones began in the late eighties, was the Ibsen who had, through the decade before, produced in succession *The Pillars of Society, A Doll's House, Ghosts* and *An Enemy of the People.*[1] Notwithstanding the work of the

[1] It is interesting and indicative that this predilection, revealed both by the newspaper criticism of the time and by the immediate trend of English problem plays and social drama, should have prevailed against both the enlightened early criticism of Gosse and his successors (from 1871 onwards) and the productions in the nineties of a number of the later, imaginative plays, under much the same conditions as those of the social plays in the eighties (*Rosmersholm, The Lady from the Sea* and *Hedda Gabler* in 1891, *The Master*

pioneer critics, led by Gosse, the imagination of the main theatre-going public of the nineties and after seems to have passed by the early poetic and romantic plays and the highly speculative *Brand*, *Peer Gynt* and *Emperor and Galilean*. None of these were, it must be admitted, eminently practical theatre plays, but the same indifference on the part of the general public seems to have remained towards that later phase to which Ibsen himself now passed, that of the partially or wholly symbolic plays, which run (with the single exception of *Hedda Gabler*) without a break from *The Wild Duck* to *When We Dead Awaken*.

Thus the choice of what, as it happens, is the least significant and least representative of the three main sections of Ibsen's work to represent on the English stage all that the potency and authority of his name conveyed, had the curious effect of settling the serious English drama, when it did emerge in the early twentieth century, in the prose form and the social-problem tradition. Ibsen, the greatest imaginative dramatist since the seventeenth century, came to be reverently represented, for the country which most needed his spirit in its full complexity, by a succession of dramatized Blue Books. And the paradox of this deep-rooted public and theatrical preference for the social plays is completed by the observation that on the other hand some of the finest critical analysis of the poetic genius of Ibsen was being produced at the same time in England or Ireland by Gosse, Archer, Wicksteed, Martyn and Shaw— most of whom were connected with the theatre.[1] The causes of this peculiar preference are, of course, far more complex than can be even indicated in such a summary, but the plain fact emerges that the English theatre, whether from incapacity, short-sight, bad luck or other obliquity, missed at one stride

---

Builder in 1893, *The Wild Duck* in 1894 and *Little Eyolf* in 1896). For purposes of comparison the reader is referred to Appendix 3, where the dates of Ibsen's plays and those of the more important episodes in the spread of Ibsenism in England are tabulated. It will be seen from this that the leaders of critical thought were in no way responsible for this arbitrary selection of the public's.

[1] See again Appendix 3 for the notable series of translations and articles, mainly by Gosse, between 1871 and 1879 where the emphasis is necessarily almost entirely on the non-social plays.

the poetry of its greatest contemporary poetic dramatist, restricting its experience of his mind to plays which, however noble their moral and however fine their art, could be read as treating of specific, limited and unspeculative issues.

It was thus left to the Irish Dramatic Movement to bring back to the English theatre the poetry that it had missed in Ibsen, presenting it, if not in terms of English society at least in a language which Englishmen could understand, and not leaving it to them to make either translations or selections. The direct influence of the Irish poetic drama upon the later English drama is less definite than was Ibsen's (except in so far as its body has become part of the composite body of the drama of the English tongue), but its indirect effect is hard to overestimate. For it demonstrated for the first time since the seventeenth century that poetic drama could also be living theatre material, and demonstrated it not only to the English audiences who saw its visiting companies from the early years of the twentieth century onwards, but to the group of young English poets then growing up, many of whom were profoundly affected by the experience. From the end of the first decade of the twentieth century, with the work of Masefield, Drinkwater, Abercrombie and others in England, the possibility of poetic drama as a working theatre form was again realized and, despite the interruption of the war years, this realization grew and spread through two English-speaking continents. If to-day we have in England and America a group of playwrights who can write poetic drama with the full and necessary confidence that it will find a hearing upon the stage, part at least of their recovery of their rightful privilege may be traced back to the fight of the early Irish pioneers. Without them and the impetus they gave to public opinion and to their immediate English successors we might not have had a range of poetic drama in prose and verse containing the work of writers as widely different as Mr. Eliot and Mr. O'Neill.

Nor has this impetus come to a stand in the country of its origin. The later development of the Irish drama from the first contributions of Boyle, Colum, Robinson and Murray on to the work of Macnamara, Shiels, O'Casey, Carroll, Teresa Deevy, Johnston, Higgins and O'Connor, has been

7

partly poetic, partly satiric, analytic or even iconoclastic in relation to the original movement. That is to say, it has been a vital and progressive growth neither imitative nor primarily reactionary but positive and individual. The relation between the two phases of the movement bears indeed some likeness to that between the two aspects of Jacobean drama, with high poetic tragedy on the one side and grim analytic social satire on the other. Both combine, in each case, with intermediate moods and positions to make a whole which is indivisible, a living and representative body of national drama which, by virtue of its scope and attitude, is also international.

II

But the Irish Dramatic Movement is significant not only because of the place which, by intrinsic and historic interest, it holds in the panorama of the world's drama but because of the light which can be thrown on fundamental aesthetic laws by a body of dramatic art comparable with the great drama of other ages, yet belonging to a period recent enough for the modern interest in artistic processes to have full play. In the records which those dramatists have themselves left as critics and historians, especially where they have defended their own intentions and design, there is laid bare, as for hardly any other drama before, the experiences of the dramatists themselves.[1] With Shakespeare and his contemporaries we reconstruct with great difficulty, through bibliographical and textual studies, through scientific analyses of the content of his imagery, some partial knowledge of the process to lay alongside the achievement. At the end of a long period of patient work, not unlike that which reveals the lines of an almost obliterated Egyptian temple, we may exclaim in triumph with one of his recent commentators, ' The door of Shakespeare's workshop stands ajar.' The Irish dramatists in their critical commentaries take us straight into a workshop which is not only theirs, but, in its essentials, that of dramatists at all times. Certain problems as to the process of collaboration, for instance, and the part played by the needs of the theatre in determining the form

[1] Among the few dramatists who have given us anything closely analogous to this body of evidence are Hebbel, Ibsen, Strindberg and Tcheckov.

of the drama can be illuminated by their evidence as by no other that we have received and, once illuminated, the process remains, not necessarily as a law to which all other artistic processes will conform, but certainly as a type which may explain cases upon which we have hitherto been uncertain.[1]

Much has been written and conjectured about both these practices in the Jacobean drama and to a certain extent in the Greek, but even in the case of Jacobean theatre history, of which we indeed know something, there is room for dispute and difference on the aesthetic effect of both practices. Now, for the Irish drama, our records on both points are indisputable and an aesthetic law or process once understood in terms of one body of art offers us at least the possibility of illumination for another similar body.

The evidence which Lady Gregory and W. B. Yeats give us points clearly to the fact that collaboration, often of a most intimate kind, was customary among several of these play-wrights and both the record of the process and the resulting work of art show that in certain cases artistic experience, often considered essentially an individual one, could be shared between two minds in all its phases. Collaboration, in art, may be defined as the combined work of two or more artists. But a distinction must be added immediately between mere co-operation and that true collaboration which gives to the product the artistic unity, harmony and congruence that we feel to be the distinctive quality of a work of art. Of mere professional co-operation there have always been plenty of examples and we have quite early records, such as the richly documented case of the lost Elizabethan play, *Keep the Widow Waking*, of the sharing out of work between several playwrights. But the results, at least judging by the large body of surviving Elizabethan plays belonging to several ' hands ', are not necessarily works of art. Quite a different situation, however, arises with the small group of plays upon which Beaumont and Fletcher worked together and with the equally interesting cases of *Eastward Ho* (Jonson, Chapman and Marston) and *The Witch of Edmonton* (Dekker, Rowley, Ford), and the Middleton-Rowley group. These plays, like those of Lady Gregory and W. B. Yeats, move

[1] Upon both these, see, in more detail, Chap. 4, *Ideals in the Workshop*.

9

at once into a different category from that of mere professional co-operation and it is for this comparatively rare artistic achievement that I should like to keep the term collaboration in its stricter sense.[1]

The test, if we look at it from the reader's point of view, is whether or not the result gives the effect of artistic unity as we recognize it in a work of art from the hands of a single man. (I think in all the plays that I have suggested above this is so.) The test from the artist's point of view is whether or not an artistic experience has been shared by two people simultaneously. And here again I think the aesthetic criticism of Lady Gregory and W. B. Yeats, helped by that of Moore, makes it clear that it is so. It will also be noticed that the resulting play (for it is to the dramatic side of the problem of collaboration that we are confined at the moment) is something different from the work of either of the dramatists separately and even from the sum of their separate qualities and capacities. It is, that is to say, analogous to a chemical compound in its relation to its component elements and not to a mixture.

If this be true and if genuine collaboration in artistic experience be possible, however rare, it opens a rather wider field of conjecture than has always been admitted in the case of anonymous plays of some distinction (such as *Two Noble Kinsmen*) which occur occasionally in our earlier drama. For it is no longer necessary to insist that any given author's presence as a collaborator must necessarily show itself in the precise characteristics familiar to us in his other works or that the presence of otherwise unfamiliar elements in any such play necessarily point to the existence of some hitherto unknown author of high distinction. The chemical compound resulting from this fusion of minds may dispose of both contentions. It would also, to my mind, free us for the future from the somewhat depressing task of trying to separate the portions that should be assigned to each playwright in such collaborations as those of Beaumont and Fletcher, for the presence of a new psychological factor of joint artistic experience would obviously so complicate the issue as to make failure a foregone conclusion.

[1] I have made a suggestion to this effect in my *Jacobean Drama*. (*Preface*).

It is the possibility of some such law as this that I think Lady Gregory and W. B. Yeats's records and achievements have established for us and this gives to their work a peculiar aesthetic interest, indicating the presence of a factor capable of wider application.[1]

The testimony of the Irish group is of no less interest when they touch upon the more general question of the relations of the theatre, its conditions and demands, and the work of the dramatic artist.[2] Here it has always been possible to know more or to conjecture more reliably ; we have but to reconstruct in our minds the physical conditions and customs of the theatre, Greek, Elizabethan and so forth, which we are studying, and our imaginations will trace for us the operation of some at least of these factors in modifying the form and character of the plays that have survived. But here again the actual testimony of the artists themselves has a definite value, for what working playwrights have done in one generation they are likely to have done in another, and when Yeats describes his attention to the audience's response and his willingness to modify his expression in certain cases to get more necessary theatrical effectiveness there is certain support given to our conviction that the major dramatists of all ages have probably been willing to treat the theatre as in part at least their workshop. All these things are significant, not merely for the light they may throw on obscure passages of our earlier dramatic history, but because they may cure us of unprofitable and unrealistic conjecture

---

[1] Certain modern dramatists are putting this method into practice again at the present day, and have great faith in the possibilities both of collaboration as a mode of artistic experience and of the influence of theatre conditions upon the living work of art. Whether in all contemporary examples it is so successful as in the cases of Beaumont and Fletcher, Yeats and Lady Gregory, is at least doubtful. When the process miscarries, even if two sound artists are concerned, it is liable to result in an elimination of all but the qualities common to both (as one subtracts, not *adds*, its spectral rays by superimposing a light filter of one colour upon that of another). This is, of course, what one would expect on *a priori* grounds. All I am trying to establish here is the fact that the other, the peculiar chemical union, can and does occur and must therefore be accepted as one of the possible modes of artistic experience. And it is the Irish dramatists who guide us to this conclusion.

[2] See again Chap. 4, *Ideals in the Workshop*, Section II.

upon the artistic processes of the great dramatists in ages which have not recorded them. What Yeats and his colleagues came to adopt as their practice may have had its equivalent in the practice of Shakespeare and his contemporaries, of Aeschylus and his.

III

The Irish Dramatic Movement, in addition to the aesthetic value of its drama and to the critical value of its records, brings certain points of interest to the notice of the historian and of the linguistic philosopher. This is not perhaps the place, nor have I, certainly, the equipment to consider in detail the significance of the re-vivifying of the ideals of the ancient Irish civilization, interesting as such an attempt must be in the light of certain rather different modern experiments in this direction. Nor do I feel competent to analyse as would a linguistic expert the full significance of Mr. Yeats's concept of the 'living language' and its relation to poetry.[1] But at the heart of the original movement (whatever difference of orientation there may have been after the later satiric and realistic movement set in), there was this double inspiration, the vitality of the undying, self-renewing legends surviving from the old Irish civilization or from the pre-Christian heroic age, and the faith in the spoken English of the Irish countryside as the vehicle of poetry. Both are, to an Englishman at least, symptomatic of one desire and that a sane and procreative one, not the desire to turn back to the past or to fix ideas in a negative and inhibitive way, but the desire to restore the Irish mind to its own habitat, to free it from the distracting and falsifying pressure of an alien artistic culture. It is not, then, an artificial or purely romantic return to the past and an arbitrary selection of a mode of expression, but a clearing away of later, intrusive growth to preserve and give room for the native spirit. In a recent volume,[2] Yeats, referring to Berkeley's early consciousness of the distinction between the English and the Irish mode of thought, says that he ' fought the Salamis of the Irish intellect '. Just so, in the last years of the nineteenth century, Yeats and

[1] See also *post*, Chap. 4, *Ideals in the Workshop*.
[2] *Wheels and Butterflies*, 1934 (p. 12).

his colleagues set out to fight the Marathon of the Irish artistic imagination. For that it is a different intellectual process from the English, and a different imaginative process, no one, I think, is long in doubt who has affiliations with both races. It is part of the purpose of this book to indicate how and on what terms that wholly different culture began to revive as one side of the wider Irish national movement.

For it is in the national movement itself that it begins ; that movement which was at once political, economic, historical, linguistic, literary and theatrical ; which had begun, along certain of these lines, with the Fenian movement and was associated, in successive ways, with the names of John O'Leary, John F. Taylor, Charles Gavan Duffy, Maud Gonne, George Russell, Standish O'Grady, Kuno Meyer, Whitley Stokes, Douglas Hyde, George Moore, Lionel Johnson, G. B. Shaw and Oscar Wilde ; from which at last the Irish Literary Society emerged in 1891 and grew in due course into the Irish Literary Theatre and so into the dramatic movement. And these sides, the political, the economic, the historical, the linguistic and the literary were so closely associated in the early days of the Irish theatre that it was a task of no little difficulty, asking no mean skill, to preserve the integrity of the artistic movement without cutting its connection with these roots and making it sterile. It is hard, indeed to think of any other group of Irishmen of that day who could have accomplished this task if it had not devolved upon Yeats and Lady Gregory, supported by Russell and Martyn. For all of them, especially the two leaders, brought, as well as their fervent nationalism, a cosmopolitanism that was an infallible test for distinguishing vital and enduring nationalism from the parochialism which was always at hand to threaten it. Their standards and their outlook were Irish, as far removed as could be from the traditions of art that had, up to then, been habitually imported from England. But the leaders of the new art, turning to native material as their immediate cultural predecessors had not done, yet proclaimed an Irish revival in broad and sane terms such as no limited nationalism could have done. For it was clear that the development of a great Irish drama could come neither from the parochialism of Ireland nor from the parochialism of England. Their experience, their mood, their wisdom was cosmopolitan ; they had been reared in European culture, social and artistic, and thus could give to the new art the thing it needed most, nationalism informed by cosmopolitanism.

This led, inevitably, to some stormy years at the outset and to some curious, paradoxical positions : Martyn, in religious and cultural convictions a European, dropped out on the issue of nationalism, probably because he was not at heart cosmopolitan enough and could not approach nationalism through internationalism ; Yeats, who was giving the drama the best service it could receive through his power of unifying the two, was attacked at first in the antagonistic press for unorthodoxy and lack of patriotism ; they had probably perceived (no less surely because unconsciously) that his culture was not so parochial as their own.[1]

Some parts of the general movement were of course incorporated with the dramatic and preserved by it, and names like A.E.'s (George Russell) and Douglas Hyde's combine the economic, the historico-legendary, the linguistic and the literary-theatrical aspects. All the early leaders, indeed, were profoundly interested in the ' heroic literature of Ireland and the imagination of the folk ', or in the poetry deriving from those days when, as Dr. Johnson had put it, ' Ireland was the school of the West, the quiet habitation of sanctity and learning '. And they were no less concerned with the two-fold linguistic issue, the revival of the Gaelic tongue and the preservation, as the vehicle of poetry and dialogue of the living language, of the English used by the native Irish speakers.

The interest in the ancient civilization of Ireland and in the body of history, poetry, legend or saga that survived from it was there from the first. Lady Gregory's two volumes of saga material, *Cuchulain of Muirthemne* and *Gods and Fighting Men*, translations of the two great bodies of heroic legend surrounding Cuchulain and Finn, were published in 1902 and 1904. They, even more than the earlier translations of Whitley Stokes, Kuno Meyer and O'Curry, or even Standish O'Grady's, became a storehouse from which were drawn the materials

[1] Indeed, in the earliest press notices, it is never excess but always defect of nationalism that is attacked.

for some of Lady Gregory's own *Irish Folk History Plays*, for Yeats's sequence of Cuchulain plays, for his, George Russell's[1] and Synge's three dramatic versions of the Deirdre legend and for his and George Moore's *Diarmuid and Grania*. To Yeats, moreover, the existence of a ' body of story ' was not a mere matter of practical convenience ; he, to some degree like A.E. found in it high kingly traditions of undying beauty that linked the ancient myth and the life of the folk and saw in the ancient way of life the source from which living Irish culture and imaginative growth should derive.[2] Free from Martyn's nostalgia for a dead past, they might yet, all three of them, have echoed, each in his own terms, Martyn's belief that ' the Empire of the Gael is in Tir n'an Og ' ; only, for them it was a ' Third Empire ', not a dead one.

Language, which came second only in importance to the ' body of story ', was also bound up with an enlightened nationalism in the beliefs of Yeats, Lady Gregory, A.E., Hyde and the leaders of the Gaelic League. On the one hand there was the living Gaelic, rapidly being revived as a vehicle of literature, by the Gaelic plays of Douglas Hyde and his followers, a movement primarily national, perhaps even political, but at the same time of great importance in spreading dramatic experience among audiences in the country districts, especially in the West. On the other hand was the gradual adoption of the English speech of the people, in the work of Lady Gregory, Yeats and Synge, as the medium of poetic drama, whether in prose or verse. For Yeats at least this became a matter of first aesthetic significance ; since to him the centre of dramatic art was speech, and life itself, no less than literature, was the product of language, ' all literature was but the perfection of an art that everybody practised ', and the ' living language ' became far more than an effective medium for vigorous dialogue—

---

[1] Of the three, George Russell's (A.E.'s) version of *Deirdre* is perhaps most independent of the version in *Cuchulain of Muirthemne*, but A.E. had his own peculiar relations with and interpretation of the early literature of Ireland and drew upon many sources.

[2] The references, and they are many, to the heroic literature and saga material in the prose works of Yeats and Lady Gregory will be found in Appendix 5 (*Critical Opinions*). They are too numerous to cite here.

became, indeed, ' the delicate movement of living speech that is the chief garment of life '.[1]

The literary movement (of which the dramatic was itself an offshoot) was the last phase of the national movement to be clearly defined and it had, in consequence, a hard fight to establish its place. This was on one side only part of the battle for liberal nationalism, but it had to combat not only political prejudice but a general backwardness in the necessary cultural experience among all but a small part of the people. It was not imagination or intellectual vivacity that were lacking ; these qualities have seldom, perhaps, existed together in so large a proportion of any race as they do in the Irish. The trouble was that their powers had been diverted to other, mainly to political, interests and that the general experience of art, literature and drama was slight. This was perhaps less difficult to alter than the ingrained habit of cheap theatrical taste that faced the reformers of the English stage,[2] but hard work was needed to familiarize even so strong and so responsive a race with good art. Yeats himself has left us several pictures of the cultural background of the Ireland of the nineties and shown us the double conflict of art with limited nationalism upon the one hand and with sheer inexperience upon the other. Fortunately the common people, in whom the leaders of the dramatic movement had rested so much faith, did not fail them ; even when, later, the stalls of the Abbey Theatre wanted prose comedy, the sixpenny gallery applauded the poetic plays. (Truly, a race worth working for!) These vicissitudes are reflected in detail in the newspaper comments of the time, in many passages in *Samhain*[3] and in Yeats's *Autobiographies*. Perhaps the position may be best summed up in the following extracts from letters written in 1903 in defence of Synge's *Shadow of the Glen* against the extreme national party :

A community that is opinion-ridden, even when those opinions are in themselves noble, is likely to put its creative mind into some

[1] For these references also, see Appendix 5 and for a fuller account, Chap. 4.
[2] See *post*, Chap. 2.
[3] The organ of the Irish Literary Theatre and the Abbey Theatre Company from 1901 to 1908 under the editorship of Yeats. See Appendix 6.

sort of a prison. If creative minds preoccupy themselves with incidents from the political history of Ireland, so much the better, but we must not enforce them to select those incidents. If, in the sincere working-out of their plot, they alight on a moral that is obviously and directly serviceable to the National cause, so much the better, but we must not force that moral upon them. I am a Nationalist, and certain of my intimate friends have made Irish politics the business of their lives, and this made certain thoughts habitual with me, and an accident made these thoughts take fire in such a way that I could give them dramatic expression. I had a very vivid dream one night, and I made *Cathleen ni Houlihan* out of this dream. But if some external necessity had forced me to write nothing but drama with an obviously patriotic intention, instead of letting my work shape itself under the casual impulses of dreams and daily thoughts, I would have lost, in a short time, the power to write movingly upon any theme. I could have aroused opinion ; but I could not have touched the heart, for I would have been busy at the oakum-picking that is not the less journalism for being in the dramatic form. . . .

I would sooner our theatre failed through the indifference or hostility of our audiences than gained an immense popularity by any loss of freedom. I ask nothing that my masters have not asked for, but I ask all that they were given. I ask no help that would limit our freedom from either official or patriotic hands, though I am glad of the help of any who love the arts so dearly that they would not bring them into even honourable captivity. A good Nationalist is, I suppose, one who is ready to give up a great deal that he may preserve to his country whatever part of her possessions he is best fitted to guard, and that theatre where the capricious spirit that bloweth as it listeth has for a moment found a dwelling-place, has good right to call itself a National Theatre.[1]

[1] W. B. Yeats, *An Irish National Theatre* (*Plays and Controversies*, pp. 56–9).

CHAPTER 2

THE ENGLISH THEATRE IN THE NINETIES

[The English dramatic renascence and the phases which led up
to it have been touched on briefly in the Introduction, where the
part played in the history of the English drama by the Irish movement has been outlined. A certain amount is repeated here in
more detail and from a slightly different angle in order to give
those readers who wish it a picture of the English theatre which
at first influenced the conservative Irish stage and was later influenced
itself by the new Irish stage created by the literary theatre. For those
readers who do not need this particular side-light upon the relations
of the two bodies of drama, this chapter can be omitted without loss
of continuity.]

THE DRAMA of the Irish movement was, though utterly national
in its origins, material, resources and methods, in no way
limited to Ireland in its effects. Before it was four years old
it was beginning to be known in England[1] and its international
reputation was well established before the American tour of
1911-12. To English audiences in London and the provinces,
both plays and actors were an entirely new experience and
although English dramatists for the rest of the decade followed
for the most part the lines laid down by their own renascence
of the eighties and the nineties and were mainly inspired,
directly or indirectly, by Ibsen, the English return to poetic
drama in the years before the European war was, if not directly
prompted or inspired, at least encouraged by the elder move-

[1] Leaving aside the production of W. B. Yeats's *Land of Heart's Desire*
in 1894 (Avenue) and Edward Martyn's *Heather Field* in 1899 (Terry's)
as independent events, the visits of the company to England (with its own
plays) begin surprisingly soon with the flying visit of Saturday, May 2, 1903
at the Queen's Gate Hall, S. Kensington (see Appendix 1, under date).
In the following year were two visits, to the Royalty and the Court Theatre,
and from then onwards they continued steadily. (See, for a description
of these visits, Lady Gregory : *Our Irish Theatre*, 37-8 and W. B. Yeats :
The Irish Dramatic Movement (Plays and Controversies, pp. 38-9).

ment in Dublin. While remembering—as who would not ?—its nationalism, we do well to remember also its internationalism : the one a matter of origins, the other of results.

Moreover, in the years immediately before the rise of the Irish Literary Theatre, the Dublin stage was in many ways a kind of provincial English stage. English companies visited Dublin and produced there some of the plays that were appearing in London. For no inconsiderable part of its theatrical experience the Dublin public depended upon English material and followed English taste. Its audiences during the nineties were educated by English drama in English stage traditions.[1]

For both these reasons, the English and the Irish stage are closely related, the Irish dependent upon the English at the beginning of the story, the English indebted in less definite but more fruitful way to the Irish movement down to the present day. The dramatic history of the two countries is in many ways one at the outset, and the story of the Irish development can only be understood in its full significance if we remind ourselves of the development of the common drama up to that date in England.

A Renascence of the English drama, to adopt Henry Arthur Jones's name for it, began to be noticed in the middle eighties, though in fact there had been a steadily increasing promise of new life from the days when the Bancrofts produced T. W. Robertson's successful plays in the sixties. Some historians would even wish to put the beginnings further back and see in Lytton's *Money* (1840) the germ of a hopeful naturalism. Certainly, from the sixties onward, something was troubling the drama. The old automatic acceptance of melodrama on the one hand, farce on the other and spectacle on every side was passing away, and though it was long till melodrama was reborn as tragedy there were signs that farce would soon be lifted again into the comedy from which it had fallen. The earliest was the rebellion of Robertson and the Bancrofts against certain of the dead conventions of characterization, theme and setting, but the first definition of the new direction was given by the added seriousness and growing artistic integrity

[1] For a further description of theatrical conditions in Ireland before 1900, see A. E. Malone *The Irish Drama*, Chap. I.

of Jones, and afterwards Pinero, in the theatre itself and the steadily spreading interest in Ibsen among the reading public and the men of letters from the early seventies onward. William Archer's adaptation of *The Pillars of Society* was produced in 1881,[1] Henry Arthur Jones's own *Saints and Sinners* in 1884 and a healthy body of discussion, opposition and defence, developed through the late eighties.[2] The translations of Ibsen and the prefaces or articles on him by Edmund Gosse and William Archer were followed by the productions of the plays in London, by the furious controversy that broke out upon them from 1889 to 1893 or 1894 and by the lifelong crusade of Henry Arthur Jones for a serious drama, a drama-reading public and an audience educated in respect for the theatre. Side by side with this crusade Jones himself, from the time of *Saints and Sinners* onward, was writing plays of serious content, attempting to reclaim for the drama the long lost themes of religion, ethics and all which could concern a whole man, and in so doing make the drama a living force. In this he was followed immediately by Arthur Wing Pinero and later by Shaw, so that the serious drama, akin to, where it was not derived from, Ibsen, passed on by natural stages through the ' problem play ' into the hands of Galsworthy, Barker, Hankin and Houghton in the first decade of the twentieth century, and the battle for the rehabilitation of the English stage was won.

That it was won in strictly limited terms and those terms the succession to Ibsen has already been noticed. It is significant in that the return to the paths of poetry and power was delayed for the time, partly by the ethical grounds on which the battle had been fought, partly by the inherent preference of his English

[1] *Quicksands, or the Pillars of Society* adapted from Ibsen's play by Wm. Archer and produced at the Gaiety Theatre on Dec. 15, 1881. (See Clement Scott : *Drama of To-day and Yesterday.* Appendix.)

[2] A brief account of the early stages of Ibsen's progress in England and of the contributions made by critics, translators, dramatists, actors and theatre-managers will be found in Halvdan Koht *The Life of Ibsen* (English translation, 1931, Vol. II, pp. 114-15 and 266-70). The men and women most concerned are, of course, well known : Edmund Gosse, William Archer, Janet Achurch, Walter Scott the publisher, Mrs. Marx-Aveling, G. B. Shaw, J. T. Grein, Elizabeth Robins. For an outline of the main phases of this piece of stage history, see Appendix 3.

followers for the social and non-poetical drama of Ibsen's middle period over the great poetic drama of his earlier and the no less great symbolical and psychological drama of his later years. It was inevitable in so far as the rehabilitation of the theatre as a serious force was the matter of greatest moment ; until that was achieved the divorce of literature and the theatre was like to remain as complete as in the earlier years of the nineteenth century, when farce and spectacle and melodrama possessed the stage and the plays of Wordsworth, Byron, Shelley and Landor only the library.

To Henry Arthur Jones, its first historian, the English dramatic renascence did not appear so simple as has perhaps been conveyed in this summary. It may be urged that he, like many a pioneer, began as a voice crying in the wilderness and ended preaching all unwittingly to ninety and nine just men who needed no repentance ; yet there was, about the year 1894-5, a kind of relapse. This, to judge from his later writings, seems to have thrown him into a despair not altogether justified by the facts and certainly not at all by the event. In 1883 he writes : ' We have ready to our hands in abundance every element of a great dramatic renascence—except good plays '[1] and we agree with him. In 1893, ' We have travelled far the last ten years. This improvement in the intelligence and in the critical faculties, and in the insight and judgement of the great play-going public is, I think, likely to continue in an increased ratio. There is almost certain to be within the next few years a decided raising of the standard of dramatic entertainment all round '[2] and we, wise after the event, applaud his prophetic insight. But in 1903 his tone is different and we, looking back upon the growing respect for Ibsen and upon the body of work already produced by G. B. Shaw (and having the advantage of knowing the body of work, not yet produced, but about to be, by Galsworthy) wonder whether he has lost his understanding of current dramatic tendencies or whether the renascence did indeed nearly founder in a reaction against the conduct of some of Ibsen's more foolish adherents. Both elements are undoubtedly present, the new religion did not spread rapidly

[1] *The Theatre and the Mob.* (*Nineteenth Century Review*, Sept. 1883.)
[2] *The Future of the English Drama.* (*The New Review*, 1893.)

enough to satisfy the ardent apostle, and there is at the same time evidence that the Ibsenites themselves (satirized, for instance, in Shaw's *Philanderer*) were discrediting Ibsen and his serious followers with the general public. But Jones, not knowing at that time the recovery that was to follow, took the relapse in earnest :

The ink in my pen had hardly dried (after announcing *The Renascence of the English Drama* in 1893) when a series of letters appeared in the English newspapers assailing the leaders of the English dramatic movement as subverters of English morality. . . . Very little was heard of the English drama for the next two or three years. . . . To sum up the last ten dramatic years in one sentence, we may say that we have passed from the raptures of ardent morbidity in 1894 to the graces of soppy sentimentality in 1903 ; we have exchanged a dose of drastic purgative for a stick of barley sugar. Now neither black draught nor barley sugar can long furnish the staple diet of man ; neither ardent morbidity nor soppy sentimentality can give forth a great spirit to possess and inform a national drama.[1]

To see how much there is of truth in this and to remind ourselves what the material was upon which the London theatre, and at a few removes that of Dublin,[2] fed during the nineties, it is well to make a list of the main London productions during that decade. To do this in the body of this chapter would be intolerable, and I refer those readers who ask for a fuller (not necessarily a complete) list of plays to the Appendix, where I have cited some three hundred.[3] I throw into one paragraph here some hundred of these, which seem to me best worth bearing in mind either as signs of things to come or as representatives of the actual average taste of the time. It should, of course, be borne in mind that, in making this selection,

---

[1] *Literary Critics and the Drama* (1903). (*Foundations*, 248–9.)

[2] To come nearer an impression of the characteristic Irish theatre-fare in these years, we must lay emphasis upon the plays of certain writers such as Boucicault who, though still popular enough on the English stage for occasional revivals (such as that of *London Assurance* in November 1890) drew crowded audiences in the Irish theatres and were far more often produced there than in London. (See, for more detail, A. E. Malone, *op. cit.*, Chap. 1.)

[3] Appendix 4.

I have included all or nearly all the most enterprising and novel productions of the decade and that the reducing has been entirely at the expense of the mass of supposedly normal, dull or old-fashioned work. The proportions are thus completely unrepresentative of the body of drama actually produced during these ten years ; for a more nearly just impression of this, the Appendix will better serve :

[1889. *A Doll's House, Pillars of Society.*]

1890. *Clarissa* (from Richardson's novel), *A Pair of Spectacles* (Grundy from the French), *The Cabinet Minister* (Arthur Wing Pinero), *A Village Priest* (Grundy from the French), *Judah* (Henry Arthur Jones), *Sweet Will* (Henry Arthur Jones), *The Deacon* (Henry Arthur Jones), *Ravenswood* (Merivale, from Scott's *Bride of Lammermoor* with Irving in the main part), *Beau Austin* (W. Henley and Robert Louis Stevenson), *London Assurance* (Dion Boucicault, revival).

1891. *The Dancing Girl* (H.A.J.), *Rosmersholm* (Ibsen), *Ghosts* (Ibsen), *Hedda Gabler* (Ibsen), *Ibsen's Ghost* (J. M. Barrie), *Lady Bountiful* (Arthur Wing Pinero), *The Streets of London* (Boucicault, revival), *The Lady from the Sea* (Ibsen), *The Times* (Arthur Wing Pinero), *The Crusaders* (H.A.J.), *Alone in London* (Buchanan and Jay).

1892. *The Intruder* (Maeterlinck), *Lady Windermere's Fan* (Oscar Wilde), *The Magistrate* (A.W.P.), *Richelieu* (Lytton, revival), *Virginius* (Knowles, revival), *Haddon Hall* (Grundy), *Hoodman Blind* (H.A.J.), *Charley's Aunt* (Brandon Thomas).

1893 *The Bauble Shop* (H.A.J.), *A White Lie* (Grundy), *Becket* (Tennyson, with Irving in the main part), *The Masterbuilder* (Ibsen), *The Amazons* (A.W.P.), *A Woman of No Importance* (Oscar Wilde), *The Second Mrs. Tanqueray* (A.W.P.), *An Enemy of the People* (Ibsen), *The Tempter* (H.A.J.), *The Foresters* (Tennyson), *A Gaiety Girl* (Owen Hall), *Sowing the Wind* (Grundy), *Widowers' Houses* (George Bernard Shaw).

1894. *The Cotton King* (Sutton Vane), *Arms and the Man* (G.B.S.), *A Bunch of Violets* (Grundy from the French), *The Masqueraders* (H.A.J.), *The Wild Duck* (Ibsen), *Journeys end in Lovers meeting* (Hobbes and G. Moore), *The Professor's Love Story* (Barrie), *The Case of Rebellious Susan* (H.A.J.), *The New Woman* (Grundy), *The Slaves of the Ring* (Grundy).

1895. *An Ideal Husband* (Wilde), *King Arthur* (Comyns Carr, Irving in the title), *The Notorious Mrs. Ebbsmith* (A.W.P.), *The Prude's Progress* (Jerome and Philpotts), *A Story of Waterloo* (Conan Doyle, Irving in the chief part), *The Triumph of the Philistines* (H.A.J.), *Harmony* (H.A.J.), *The Manxman* (from Hall Caine).

1896. *Michael and his Lost Angel* (H.A.J.), *The Prisoner of Zenda* (Rose and Hope), *The Sign of the Cross* (Wilson Barrett), *The Geisha* (Owen Hall), *The Rogue's Comedy* (H.A.J.), *A School for Saints* (John Oliver Hobbes), *The Greatest of These* (Grundy), *Magda* (Sudermann), *In Sight of Saint Paul's* (Sutton Vane), *The Strike* (Boucicault, revival), *Under the Red Robe* (Rose and Weyman), *Little Eyolf* (Ibsen), *The Late Mr. Costello* (Grundy).

1897. *The Sorrows of Satan* (from Marie Corelli), *The Physician* (H.A.J.), *The Princess and the Butterfly* (A.W.P.), *The Seats of the Mighty* (G. Parker), *A Marriage of Convenience* (Grundy from Dumas), *The Silver Key* (Grundy), *The Liars* (H.A.J.), *Admiral Guinea* (Henley and R.L.S.), *The Pilgrim's Progress* (from Bunyan).

1898. *The Belle of New York* (Hugh Morton), *Pelleas and Melisande* (Maeterlinck), *Three Musketeers* (Hamilton from Dumas), *When a Man's in Love* (Hope and Rose), *The Musketeers* (Grundy from Dumas).

1899. *What Will the World Say?* (G. P. Bancroft), *The Only Way* (from Dickens), *Ours* (Robertson, revival), *Carnac Sahib* (H.A.J.), *The Gay Lord Quex* (A.W.P.), *Halves* (Conan Doyle), *The Degenerates* (Grundy), *The Silver King* (H.A.J., rev.).

(To these should be added the list, between three and four times as long as this, of the apparently less interesting or less representative plays,[1] a constant succession of music-hall entertainments, of light opera (of which the best were still those of Gilbert and Sullivan) and, most important of all, Irving's Shakespeare productions at the Lyceum.)

If we were to assume the theatre-going public to be one indivisible entity, an undiscriminating but somewhat loveable gusto would be indicated by the combination of all these groups. Actually, they indicate instead divergent lines of taste all more or less provided for, though the entry of a play of

[1] Appendix 4.

Ibsen's generally stands for a few productions (in some cases only one) and that of a play by one of the favourites, Henry Arthur Jones, Arthur Wing Pinero or Sidney Grundy, generally means a long run.[1] What is, I think, beyond dispute is that there can be traced through the decade a growing body of serious drama neither necessarily sentimental nor conventional. At first this seems to be mainly in the hands of Jones himself. But after the year 1891, the year of the great Ibsen controversy that saw more of his plays produced than any other, there seems a gradual increase of 'seriousness'. The year 1893 saw both *The Second Mrs. Tanqueray* and *Widowers' Houses* besides two more Ibsens ; the year 1894, *Arms and the Man* and *The Wild Duck*. The relapse of 1894 which was still keeping Jones in despondency in 1903 did not prevent the production of *The Notorious Mrs. Ebbsmith* in 1895, *Michael and His Lost Angel*, *Magda* and *Little Eyolf* in 1896, an adaptation of *The Pilgrim's Progress* in 1897 or *Pelleas and Melisande* in the following year. Plays that were either serious in treatment or intrinsically valuable as literature (or both) were in fact put on the boards ; it is true that some of the most original were still coming from Norway, Germany and Belgium, but, as against this, Shaw was writing a good deal that, though not always produced, was in many cases published.

The theatre appetite of the eighteen-nineties appears, then, somewhat miscellaneous. (So does that of the fifteen-nineties ; and neither of them can compete with that of the present day for sheer omnivorousness.) But that does not, I think, justify Jones's despair. Seriousness, purposefulness and the problem-play had settled in London for a somewhat lengthy visit, and already the younger generation in Ireland saw this clearly enough to make their movement in part a reaction against it.

But by then the voice of Henry Arthur Jones was no longer crying in a wilderness. By the year 1898 it was the leader of a sizeable choir and even so eminent an individualist as Shaw is found agreeing in part at least with his lamentation over the inertia of the English stage. He, however, does not recognize any signs of a renascence before the late nineties

[1] *The Liars*, for example, ran for 291 nights. (See Doris Arthur Jones : *Life and Letters of Henry Arthur Jones*, p. 186.)

and describes his experiences as a dramatic critic between 1894 and 1898 as typical of all late nineteenth-century drama—up to the advent of Shaw :

> The theatre struck me down like the veriest weakling. I sank under it like a baby fed on starch. . . . The doctors said : This man has not eaten meat for twenty years : he must eat it or die. I said : This man has been going to the London theatres for three years ; and the soul of him has become inane and is feeding unnaturally on his body. . . .
>
> Why was this ? What is the matter with the theatre, that a strong man can die of it ? . . .
>
> I did not find that matters were improved by the lady pretending to be ' a woman with a past ', violently oversexed, or the play being called a problem play, even when the manager, and sometimes, I suspect, the very author, firmly believed the word problem to be the latest euphemism for what Justice Shallow called a bona roba, and certainly would not either of them have staked a farthing on the interest of a genuine problem. In fact these so-called problem plays invariably depended for their dramatic interest on foregone conclusions of the most heartwearying conventionality concerning sexual morality. The authors had no problematic views : all they wanted was to capture some of the fascination of Ibsen. It seemed to them that most of Ibsen's heroines were naughty ladies. And they tried to produce Ibsen plays by making their heroines naughty. But they took care to make them pretty and expensively dressed. Thus the pseudo-Ibsen play was nothing but the ordinary sensuous ritual of the stage become as frankly pornographic as good manners allowed.[1]

About the same time a mind as different from either of these as they were from each other was discovering, though not in public, the same complaints. In the case of Edward Martyn who was not an Englishman—indeed, very consciously not an Englishman—there is less concern with the need, or indeed possibility, of reform on the English stage and a readier tendency to attribute the low taste of the English public to ineradicable characteristics of the English temperament. But his record, though he draws from it different conclusions, points to the same experience as that of Jones and Shaw. And his affinities

[1] *Three Plays for Puritans.* (Standard ed., p. xii.)

with continental drama and familiarity with French and German theatres make his comparison worth listening to :

There must, after all, be two publics—one for the good and one for the bad. And this would seem to apply in a measure to other countries also, [beside Germany] but not to England. There the public is wholly for bad modern drama, and for bad art in general, for the most part. That is why, I suppose, when returning to England from the Continent, it has always seemed to me like entering a comparatively half-civilised country.

The contrast has always struck me as peculiar between the upholstered, drawing-room-like shapelessness of an English theatre, designed for an addled, overfed audience, who loathe, above all things, any performance on the stage that would appeal to a lofty and aesthetic sense in humanity, and the grand lines and noble austerity of some foreign theatres like, let us say, the Théâtre Français, where the first consideration is not materialism but art.[1]

The Irish verdicts upon the condition of the English theatre at the turn of the century and at the beginning of their own revival, then, confirm those of the leading English critics and dramatists of the time, though the application and the moral drawn from them are different and the pessimism is deeper. This is no doubt due in part to an Irishman's natural despondency when faced with the manifestations of English art ; he has, of course, simultaneously, the consolation of knowing that his ' is another journey ' and that the task of rousing the English public, inspiring the English theatre and calling into being English playwrights rests not upon him but upon that gallant fighter, Henry Arthur Jones. Thus Yeats, looking back, in the year 1906, upon the naturalistic drama of the post-Ibsen school, sees as perhaps no Englishman could see the poetic poverty, and puts his finger neatly, wittily and quite unerringly upon the weaknesses if not of Ibsen (as he thinks) yet certainly of Ibsen's followers :

Of all artistic forms that have had a large share of the world's attention, the worst is the play about modern educated people. Except where it is superficial or deliberately argumentative it fills one's soul with a sense of commonness as with dust. It has one mortal ailment. It cannot become impassioned, that is to say,

[1] Martyn papers, 1899, quoted Denis Gwynn : *Edward Martyn* (p. 140).

vital, without making somebody gushing and sentimental. Educated and well-bred people do not wear their hearts upon their sleeve, and they have no artistic and charming language except light persiflage and no powerful language at all, and when they are deeply moved they look silently into the fireplace. Again and again I have watched some play of this sort . . . wondering why the chief character, the man who is to bear the burden of fate, is gushing, sentimental and quite without ideas. Then the great scene comes and I understand that he cannot be well-bred or self-possessed or intellectual, for if he were he would draw a chair to the fire and there would be no duologue at the end of the third act. Ibsen understood the difficulty and made all his characters a little provincial that they might not put each other out of countenance. . . . One only understands that this manner, deliberately adopted one doubts not, had gone into his soul and filled it with dust, when one has noticed that he could no longer create a man of genius. . . . Put the man who has no knowledge of literature before a play of this kind and he will say, as he has said in some form or other in every age at the first shock of naturalism, ' Why should I leave my home to hear but the words I have used there when talking of the rates ? ' And he will prefer to it any play where there is visible beauty or mirth, where life is exciting, at high tide as it were. It is not his fault that he will prefer in all likelihood a worse play, though its kind may be greater, for we have been following the lure of science for generations and forgotten him and his.[1]

And over against this is the voice of the enthusiastic English theatre critic of the old school, with his worship of Irving (and not much power of distinguishing the comparative virtues of any of the materials that Irving handled), with a loyalty to the ideal and the beautiful which reads perilously like an extract from a famous scene in one of Shaw's most distinguished plays, and his obviously genuine and unassumed distress at the wave of diabolic Ibsenity then passing over England. It may stand as representative of a host of similar outcries and will serve to show both the reactionary attitude that threw Jones into despair and the easy, elevated sentimentalism that precipitated Shaw's scorn :

The Ibsen reaction, with its unloveliness, its want of faith ; its hopeless, despairing creed ; its worship of the ugly in art ; its grim

[1] *Discoveries*, 1906. (*Cutting of an Agate*, 1919, pp. 77–80 *passim*.)

and repulsive reality, regret it as we will, is a solemn and resistless fact. At the outset, some of us, conscientiously and in the interests of the art we loved, and had followed with such persistency, tried to laugh it out of court. But the time came when the laugh was on the other side. I own it ; I admit it. . . .

Society has accepted the satire, and our dramatists of the first class have one after the other broken away from the beautiful, the helpful, and the ideal, and coquetted with the distorted, the tainted, and the poisonous in life. Any appeal to them in the name of art is vain.[1]

This revelation of English taste and standards should, in fairness, be balanced by a similar testimony to purity of taste from Dublin. The conservatism of the public and its average leaders was at least as pronounced there, though perhaps it stood on different grounds, and the general artistic level was apparently considerably lower. Avoiding the vituperations of the contemporary press on the first plays of the Irish Dramatic Movement (for most of these are so much entangled with the political and religious controversies of that time and place as to lose much of their force for the present-day Englishman) I offer, for its intrinsic worth, the following extract from a volume which gave the Dublin public a selection of certain (carefully expurgated) famous Elizabethan plays. The level of prudery is worse than that shown by the corresponding English publications and by the London theatre productions in the eighties and nineties, but the disinterested desire for elevation of tone is close to Clement Scott's and gives one a sharp impression of how the drama reading public of Dublin was prepared for the crusade of Yeats and Lady Gregory :

It is much to be regretted that the dramatic masterpieces of Shakspere's contemporaries, *in their entirety,* are wholly unfitted for general reading. The reason is obvious ; the plays in question abound in strong pictures of gross subjects, many passages being absolutely inconsistent with the delicacy of the present day, and some of the very finest scenes being polluted by occasional coarseness

---

[1] Clement Scott : *The Drama of Yesterday and To-day* (1899). Preface, pp. x-xi.

of language. Consequently they are totally unknown to the vast majority of readers, and are also necessarily excluded from all educational courses.[1]

These, together with numerous other comments which could be cited[2] will perhaps have served to throw some light on the public taste in the two countries and on the standards which those publics demanded (and got) from dramatists and actors. But they serve also to indicate both the sharp cleavage between the ideals of men of letters and contemporary theatre standards in each country, and at the same time the difference between the ideals of the two groups of leaders ; the English, led, perhaps not uncharacteristically, by a Welsh Dissenter and an Irish agnostic, seeking a higher intellectual and moral standard ; the Irish, as presented confusedly in Martyn's work but distinctly in Yeats's, seeking for a new poetic birth, a drama ' where there is visible beauty or mirth, where life is exciting, at high tide '.

The English plays that went to Ireland on tour were generally of the older school but, frivolous as this material was and unworthy of the Irish artistic imagination that Yeats meant to feed, there was nothing that suited his purposes any better in the best that could have been had from England, for that best was directly or indirectly derived from Ibsen. ' In the theatre of Ibsen we are not flattered spectators killing an idle hour with an ingenious and amusing entertainment ; we are " guilty creatures, sitting at a play " ; ' a fine enough statement of what Shaw wanted to emphasise, but not the language to use to the poets and makers of the new Irish spirit. It was not only the conscious nationalism of the Irish Dramatic Movement, but the inborn racial quality of the men themselves, that made the moral severity of English Ibsenism barren for their purposes. And so the Irish Dramatic Movement becomes, on its negative side (which is slight compared with its creative ardour), the first reaction against Ibsen, setting in long before the corresponding movement is perceptible in England in the works of the poetic dramatists of the years immediately before the first World War.

[1] H. M. FitzGibbon. Dublin, Sept. 1889. (Preface to *Famous Elizabethan Plays.* London, 1890.)

[2] See, for more detail, the note at the end of this chapter.

They had everything to create without precedent, for precedent could only have harmed either their national or their artistic integrity.

[NOTE.—The body of commentary on the state of the drama and the theatre at the end of the nineteenth century and in the early years of the twentieth is far more considerable than can be suggested in this chapter. I have therefore left it to this note to indicate, to those readers who wish to follow the matter further, some of the main topics discussed and the articles, reviews, etc., in which they can most readily be studied. (I omit of course the bulk of the serious articles on Ibsen and prefaces to the translations of his works ; a brief list of these will be found in Appendix 3 and further information in Dr. Halvdan Koht's life of Ibsen.) Henry Arthur Jones's campaign to raise the literary and moral quality of working theatre productions is best summed up in articles such as *Religion and the Stage* (*The Nineteenth Century Review*, Jan. 1885) and the Preface to the 1891 edition of *Saints and Sinners; The Theatre and the Mob* (*The Nineteenth Century Review*, 1883) and *The Future of the English Drama* (*The New Review*, 1893), both these being reprinted in *The Renascence of the English Drama* (1895), a volume containing some sane and solid criticism of the position ; *An Introduction to . . . Filon's ' The English Stage '* (Introd. 1896, translation 1897) ; *Literary Critics and the Drama* (1903) and *The foundations of a National Theatre* (1904), both reproduced in the volume *The Foundations . . .* (1913). G. B. Shaw's commentary is mainly to be found in *Our Theatres in the Nineties*, which contains his dramatic criticism written for the *Saturday Review* between 1895 and 1898, in *The Quintessence of Ibsenism* (1891, 1913, 1926), in the play *The Philanderer* (1893) and in the preface to *Three Plays for Puritans* (1900). Clement Scott's collection of his notices and his survey of the theatre of his time throw considerable light both on the conditions of his day and on the taste of a representative and popular dramatic critic (*From ' The Bells ' to ' King Arthur ' : A critical record of the first-night productions at the Lyceum theatre from 1871 to 1895* (1896) and *The Drama of Yesterday and To-day* (2 vols. 1899,) with its valuable appendix, a ' list of important plays produced in London between 1830 . . . and the end of the century '). The newspaper discussions and reviews in general during the last decade of the century are essential and the most important comments on one aspect, the reception of Ibsen, are summarized and quoted by Shaw in *Quintessence*. To these much might be added, but we may here mention Auguste Filon's *The English Stage* (translated 1897, with a preface by Henry

Arthur Jones), William Archer's *Theatrical World* (1893–7) and some illuminating passages in Denis Gwynn's *Edward Martyn* (1930) which give a picture of the average theatre manager's attitude to an ' advanced ' playwright (pp. 119–20) and some interesting extracts from the Martyn papers on theatrical taste in England (p. 140 seq.).]

CHAPTER 3

THE EARLY HISTORY OF THE MOVEMENT[1]

' We went on giving what we thought good until it became popular.'   LADY GREGORY.

' Literature must take the responsibility of its power and keep all its freedom.'   W. B. YEATS.

THE HISTORY of the Irish Dramatic Movement is well known and it has been well told by the original leaders and founders. Lady Gregory and W. B. Yeats both wrote accounts of various parts of it and George Moore contributed surprisingly full description of certain episodes, though his impression of events does not necessarily tally with theirs. Yet a brief account of the main course must be given again here, if only to show the nature of the conflict stirred up by it and the small, half-casual, half-heroic beginnings it had.

W. B. Yeats founded the Irish Literary Society in London in 1891[2] and the National Literary Society in Dublin in 1892. This was followed in 1893 by the Gaelic League (founded by Dr. Hyde and other Gaelic scholars) and in January 1899 by the Irish Literary Theatre. In the interval between 1892 and 1899 Yeats had discussed with many people the possibilities of finding a small theatre in London or Dublin, with Florence Farr, with George Moore, with Edward Martyn and, finally and fruitfully, with that fine, practical genius, Augusta, Lady Gregory.[3] ' Things seemed to grow possible as we talked,'

[1] This is an account of those episodes and aspects of the movement which appear most significant to an English onlooker. For an account which describes fully the relations of the movement to Irish history and culture, the reader is again referred to Mr. A. E. Malone's *The Irish Drama*, especially the first five chapters.

[2] W. B. Yeats gave a clear account of this part of the movement in *Dramatis Personae* (13–18 Cuala ed.) and the relations of the three groups in the early nineties were summarized by Lady Gregory in *Our Irish Theatre* (76).

[3] *O.I.T.* 6–7.

she says ; and we can believe it. ' Things '—whether the founding of a theatre, the writing of plays, the obtaining of a licence to act in Dublin, the obtaining of a patent for the Abbey Theatre Company, the vanquishing of the hostility of the United Irish Societies of America or of the witnesses in the Judges Court of Philadelphia—all seem to have become possible when Lady Gregory talked. Her own book, *Our Irish Theatre,* is a continuous, unconscious revelation of the power of her tenacious persuasiveness, no less than of the fighting courage of Yeats. Each appreciated to the full the spirit and capacity of the other and the two collaborators, taking Edward Martyn into their counsels in the summer of 1898, set the Irish Theatre upon its way.

Two plays were chosen for production, Edward Martyn's *Heather Field,* already published and under consideration for production in Germany, and Yeats's *Countess Cathleen,* also published but not yet produced.[1] The money needed was guaranteed by a subscription list, but this was not used in the end, as the deficit was paid by Martyn. The Irish Literary Theatre was founded (Jan. 16, 1899) and the first performances announced for the coming spring. The plays were put into rehearsal in London, as it was only there that a company could be gathered and rehearsed. George Moore was then drawn in, almost inevitably, since one of the plays was by his life-long friend Edward Martyn, and assumed sudden and violent control. According to his own account, which occupies upwards of thirty pages in *Ave.,* he reconstituted the cast, which he found hopelessly unsuitable, revised the method and conduct of rehearsals, overcame the artistic scruples of Yeats and the religious scruples of Martyn, put, with his unique knowledge of theatre politics,[2] the whole thing on a sound, practical,

---

[1] *The Heather Field* and *Maeve* were published in 1890 and the *Countess Cathleen* in 1892. Two plays by writers connected (or shortly to be connected) with the movement had already been produced by Grein's Independent Theatre in London in 1894 : George Moore's *The Strike at Arlingford* and W. B. Yeats's *The Land of Heart's Desire.* (The first of these was not produced by the Abbey, but the second in a revised form was played in 1911.)

[2] This he really had. ' I doubt if (our work) could have been done at all without his knowledge of the stage.' (*Samhain,* 1901.)

working basis and packed the company off to Ireland on the eve
of the production with the grateful consciousness of having,
by a prodigious expenditure of energy, saved the situation,
the company, and even, it might be, the honour of Ireland.

Or, as Lady Gregory more abstemiously puts it, ' Mr. George
Moore gave excellent help in finding actors, and the plays were
rehearsed in London.'[1]

Meanwhile the political and religious forces in Dublin society,
which played so great a part in the history of this company
in Ireland and America for the next twelve or fourteen years,
had got to work. A pamphlet, *Souls for Gold*,[2] which attacked
Countess Cathleen for supposed blasphemy in some of the
speeches and stage directions, was circulated and stirred up a
sharp controversy. This in itself would not have been so bad ;
Irishmen are perhaps better endowed than Englishmen for
riding out political and religious storms. But the tender
conscience of Edward Martyn, a deeply religious man and much
addicted to the clergy, was disturbed, not so much by the
pamphlet as by the attitude of certain of the clergy to it, and he
threatened to remove his financial backing if the play were
indeed shown to be heretical. It was quickly submitted to the
judgement of ' two good churchmen', Father Finlay and Father
Barry, both of whom declared themselves satisfied with its
intention, the latter in rather interesting terms.[3] Lady Gregory's hand appears again for a moment here for, as Yeats tells
us, ' Martyn agreed to accept the verdict, and Lady Gregory
made Moore promise silence for a fortnight.'[4] (The second

---

[1] Experience of the work of both writers leads one, when in doubt, to
follow Lady Gregory's version.

[2] This pamphlet (see Appendix 2) attacks the play on two counts, heresy
and blasphemy on the one hand and pseudo-Celticism on the other. It is not
a particularly interesting piece of work to read to-day, but it obviously carried
a heavy charge of dynamite in 1899. The author attacks all Irishmen who
act or watch this monstrous play, particularly the actor of the part of Shemus,
' And as he kicks to pieces the Holy Virgin's image in Catholic Dublin, has
he secured beforehand an escort of Cromwellians and a life insurance policy ? '
(p. 10). This episode, as it happens, is one of those which Yeats removed
before production.

[3] See *O.I.T.* 21–2, and *D.P.* 36.

[4] *D.P.* 36.

would appear to have been the more formidable task.) Not
that she was altogether successful, for, though he was restrained
from public utterance on this already difficult problem, Moore
was deeply disappointed at the loss of what he could not fail
to see was a superb biographical opportunity :

He had meant to write an article called ' Edward Martyn and his
soul '. He said : ' It was the best opportunity I ever had. What
a sensation it would have made. Nobody has ever written that way
about his most intimate friend. What a chance. It would have
been heard of everywhere.' As Florence Farr and I sat at breakfast
in a Dublin hotel, having just arrived by the mail boat to make some
final arrangements, Martyn came wiping the perspiration from his
face in great excitement, his first sentence was : ' I withdraw again.'
He had just received by post ' Edward Martyn and his soul ' in the
form of a letter.[1]

But Moore was at least partially silenced, Martyn at least
partially reassured ; Yeats and Lady Gregory kept their heads
and the play went forward. Yeats's own description is perhaps
the best at this point. It reveals unconsciously what appears
in crisis after crisis in the history of this movement, the rare
combination of courage and flexibility with which he met
and surmounted them. Seeing that a riot was imminent,
he ' asked for police protection, and found twenty or thirty
police awaiting (his) arrival ' at the theatre. Having thus
ensured that the play should have a reasonable chance of being
played, he listened attentively to its reception and, not wanting it
to degenerate into an anti-clerical demonstration, altered certain
details hard for the audience to stomach and not essential to his
main purpose. Years later, speaking of the different versions
of *Countess Cathleen* he says, ' Every alteration was tested by
performance.'[2] There was a practical objectivity in his attitude
which is rare in a poet watching the audience's response to his
own poetry, but this same adaptability, unusual in itself, is rarer
still in combination with his peculiar fighting courage. It was
upon such qualities as these that the success of the movement in
the early years turned. This pair of productions was a success, if

[1] W. B. Yeats, *D.P.* (37, Cuala ed.).
[2] *D.P.* 39.

a stormy one, though the *Heather Field*, less controversial, was the more universally acceptable.

The first series of productions ran from May 8th to 13th of 1899 at the Ancient Concert Rooms in Great Brunswick Street[1] and though the opposition of certain political and religious factions ran high, strong support came from such men as T. P. Gill, whose *Daily Express* had been backing the movement steadily all the season.[2] The other Irish reviews are copious and vigorous if not always of a nice discrimination. After the first night a number of London critics were sent over, including Max Beerbohm, who gave a good report of the venture.[3] The theatre had in fact lived up to the claim made in its preliminary announcement : ' The Irish Literary Drama will appeal rather to the intellect and spirit than to the senses. It will eventually, it is hoped, furnish a vehicle for the literary expression of the national thought and ideals of Ireland such as has not hitherto been in existence.'[4]

One effect of the success, especially that of the *Heather Field*, was to convince the leaders of the movement that they had a promising playwright in its author. The place for the discussion of Martyn's capacities as a dramatist is not here,[5] but it is difficult for a later reader to believe, and must have been impossible for his contemporaries to foresee, that a man who began his career so competently and with so apparently sound a sense of the theatre as appears in the *Heather Field* and *Maeve* was to decline steadily from that success. ' Though we had not seen his unfinished play, we engaged the Gaiety Theatre for a week in 1900. His play, understood to be satirical and topical, was to be the main event. *Maeve,* originally published with

---

[1] For details, see Appendix 1.

[2] Moore describes at considerable length the dinner given by Gill in honour of the I.L.T. after the first set of productions (See *H.F.* i, 121, 134–64). Yeats, writing some twenty years later, dryly remarks that he and Moore remembered it rather differently. (*D.P.* 45.)

[3] For extracts from these notices, see *Beltaine* I. For Max Beerbohm's notice, see *The Saturday Review,* May 13, 1899. Others of interest are those in *The Express, The Nation, The Freeman,* and a later one (Sept. 30, 1899) in *The Saturday Review* on ' Literary Ideals in Ireland '.

[4] Preliminary announcement (leaflet), Hend. 1. 21.

[5] See *post,* Chap. 5.

the *Heather Field,* would accompany it.'[1]   With the published version of *Maeve* and the production of the *Heather Field* to go upon, who would have predicted *The Tale of a Town* ?

The summer of 1899 must have been a long drawn-out tragical farce. Martyn completed *The Tale of a Town.* Yeats and Lady Gregory read it ; Moore read it. Each has recounted the episode in his own way. Moore's is the longest.[2] Yeats's goes straightest to the point : ' Lady Gregory and I . . . read it. It seemed to us crude throughout, childish in parts, a play to make our movement and ourselves ridiculous.'[3] The thing could not be put better. And in some such form as this, for it was no case for softening the blow, it had to be put to Martyn ; one gathers that the task fell to Yeats. In the upshot Moore and he re-planned the play and Moore re-wròte it. Moore was not reticent, either during or after, and it would appear that the process was freely discussed in the presence of the victim. Martyn's exasperation is intelligible.[4] In a year or two his other interests, especially Church music, superseded that of the Irish Literary Theatre and he began to take less and less part in it, though he continued to write plays which were produced by other dramatic societies in Dublin. But the next set of productions in February 1900[5] gave him a measure of success still. Though Moore's adaptation, *The Bending of the Bough,* was more completely successful, his own *Maeve* appealed to something in the audience which even the leaders of the movement had not foreseen. Both plays, in fact, turned out to be unexpectedly nationalist. *The Bending of the Bough* achieved, what indeed that raw and misproportioned effort, *The Tale of a Town,* had aimed at ; it was ' the first play dealing with a vital Irish question

---

[1] *D.P.* 49.

[2] *H.F.* I *passim,* esp. 270–5.

[3] *D.P.* 51.

[4] J. Hone, *Life of George Moore* (1936), p. 222, says in this connection : ' Unquestionably Martyn suffered. But it would seem from his correspondence and unpublished manuscripts that he bore more resentment against Yeats and Lady Gregory than against Moore.' Unfortunately Hone does not quote any of the MSS. that bear on this point.

[5] See, for details, Appendix 1.

[6] *O.I.T.* 27. For W. B. Yeats's contributions to the play, see *D.P.* 51.

that had appeared in Ireland.[6] And *Maeve* appeared, in the hands
of its audience, to be charged with implications of which the
English actors knew nothing and Martyn himself not much.
The bewilderment of everybody is lightly indicated by Lady
Gregory,[1] but they grasped the fruits of their success and
promptly planned an October season.

The third set of plays, at the Gaiety Theatre towards the end
of October, were played by ' Mr. F. R. Benson's Shakespearean
Company'.[2] That is to say, *Diarmuid and Grania*, written
in collaboration by Yeats and Moore, was produced by Benson,
and Douglas Hyde's *Casad-an-Sugan*, the first play in Irish
produced in any Dublin theatre, was played by the amateurs
of the Gaelic League.[3] The collaboration is described by Yeats
in *Dramatis Personae*[4] and a fantasia on the same theme is provided by Moore,[5] but it was difficult from either of these to
reconstruct an impression of the play until the manuscript
came to light in 1946, in the possession of the late Miss Lily
Yeats.[6]

---

[1] ' The Gaelic League in great force sang *Fainne Gael an Lae* between the
acts, and *The Wearing of the Green* in Irish ! And when " author " could
not appear, there were cries of " An Craoibhin " and cheers were given for
Hyde.' (Founder and president of the Gaelic League.) ' The actors say
they never played to so appreciative an audience, but were a little puzzled
at the applause, not understanding the political allusions. Curiously *Maeve*,
which we didn't think a nationalist play at all, has turned out to be one. . . .
There is such applause at ' I am only an old woman, but I tell you that Erin
will never be subdued ' that Lady ——, who was at a performance, reported
to the Castle that they had better boycott it, which they have done. G.M.
(George Moore) ' is, I think, a little puzzled by his present political position,
but I tell him and E. Martyn we are not working for Home Rule, we are
preparing for it.' (*O.I.T.* 27-8.)
[2] See, for details, Appendix 1.
[3] See *O.I.T.* 28-9, 261, and *Samhain*, 1901 and 1902. By the end of the
third season, there were, as W. B. Yeats says, ' Excellent Gaelic plays by
Dr. Douglas Hyde, by Father O'Leary, by Father Dineen, and by Mr.
MacGinlay ', *Samhain*, 1901.
[4] 60-5, 67, 70.
[5] *H.F.* i. 346 *seq.*
[6] The reviews, on the whole, spent a good deal of their time objecting
(and perhaps justifiably) to English actors in such a play, but most of them
seemed to think the play itself effective. One reviewer (Hend. i, 111), who

One thing began to be clear at the end of this season. For three years English actors had been brought over for the plays of the Irish Literary Theatre and it was time that a regular company, English or Irish, should be built up.[1] Moore believed in a stock company, English trained, perhaps under Benson's supervision ; Benson hesitated to accept this. Martyn became restive about paying any longer for a company that did not produce his plays. It seemed as though a certain confusion were entering the affairs of the company. It was at this point that Yeats characteristically took a decisive line. He was the one member of the management with positive aesthetic ideals, and he needed, more than any of the others, actors who understood his design in gesture, staging and verse-speaking. He happened at this time upon the work of William and Frank Fay, amateur producers who, with a little company of working men and women acting in their spare-time, ' had been in the habit of playing little farces in coffee palaces and such like '.[2] Yeats saw them play Miss Milligan's *Red Hugh,* a play of the old rattle-trap type, and saw also that their acting transformed it. The fact that they were amateurs counted for and not against them with him, their enthusiasm for the material of the Irish Literary Theatre was as great as his, and he offered them his *Cathleen ni Houlihan.* George Russell (A.E.) had already promised them his *Deirdre* : ' I hope,' he said, ' I shall not suffer too much in the process, but I prefer them to English actors as they are in love with their story.'[3]

This was the end of the original Irish Literary Theatre, for Lady Gregory, Yeats and A.E. all joined or gave their support to the Fays' society[4] and performances were planned for April

---

quoted five lines, compared the handling of the story with that of the old tale. Yeats comments on all this in his *Samhain* (1902) (see *P.C.* 18). An edition of the text by W. Becker is in preparation.

[1] On this, see *Samhain,* 1901 (*P.C.* 5–9).

[2] *O.I.T.* 30 (cf. *Samhain,* 1901). For a fuller account of this part of the history, see Malone, *The Irish Theatre,* Chaps. 2, 4 and 5, and an unpublished doctoral thesis by Alan Cole, Trinity College, Dublin.

[3] Letter from George Russell to Lady Gregory, quoted *O.I.T.* 30–1.

[4] Martyn and Moore dropped out at this point and did not join the new Society.

at St. Teresa's Hall in Clarendon Street. The society was re-born as the Irish National Dramatic Company which almost immediately afterwards became known as the Irish National Theatre Society.[1] It was founded, as a leaflet later explained, ' to continue—if possible on a more permanent basis—the work begun by the Irish Literary Theatre'.[2] W. B. Yeats was made President and A.E. Vice-President and a famous period of producing and playwriting was begun.

The first series of the Irish National Theatre Society's[3] plays took place at St. Teresa's Hall in Clarendon Street in April 1902.[4] George Russell's *Deirdre* was immediately successful. Yeats says that the audiences took to it from the first. It was a well-constructed play and though Russell did not, as Yeats expected, write a number of other plays, he often gave plots or incidents that suggested plots to other dramatists.[5] Yeats himself disliked the play at first and would not stay in the theatre ; it seemed to him superficial and sentimental. But later he came to like it, especially what he regarded as the absence of ' character ', a virtue in tragedy to which he often refers in his critical works.[6] *Cathleen ni Houlihan* had its deserved success as soon as the audience grasped the transition from the humour of the opening passages to the tragic exaltation of the end. Both plays were repeated with others at the October series and *Cathleen ni Houlihan* continued to be one of the most popular short plays in the company's repertory.

At this next series, in October 1902[7] at the Ancient Concert Rooms, two new playwrights came in, Seumas O'Cuisin (James Cousins) and Fred Ryan ; O'Cuisin with *The Sleep of the King* and *The Racing Lug* and Ryan with *The Laying of the*

[1] See Appendix 1.
[2] Leaflet of the I.N.T.S. Hend. i. 322.
[3] The programme is headed ' Mr.W. G. Fay's Irish National Dramatic Company ' in April, but, by the following December, ' The Irish National Theatre Society '. I have kept the same title throughout as the change seems rather one of terminology than of constitution or personnel.
[4] See, for details, Appendix 1.
[5] *D.P.* 78–9.
[6] See *post* Chap. 4, *Ideals in the Workshop.*
[7] See Appendix 1.

Foundations.[1] Yeats and Lady Gregory's *Pot of Broth*, hardly less popular in the long run than *Cathleen ni Houlihan*, was also added. Some of these were repeated in the December series at the Camden Street Playhouse[2] and there were a number of isolated performances in the following January and February in and around Dublin.[3] By the time of the fourth series, in March 1903, the company was working well together. Yeats's *Hour Glass* and Lady Gregory's *Twenty-Five* were added to the stock and the productions were followed by a lecture by Yeats on 'The Reform of the Theatre'. In May of the same year the company went to London for the first time, playing, at the Queen's Gate Hall in South Kensington, *The Hour Glass, Twenty-Five, Cathleen ni Houlihan, The Pot of Broth* and *The Laying of the Foundations*. This London visit was of great importance. Not only were the plays a notable success and the reviews full of praise, but the literary world of England awoke to the significance of the Irish Dramatic Movement and this led to the interest and help of Miss Horniman in setting up, little more than a year later, the Abbey Theatre Company.

Of what kind, then, was the movement, and the company that represented it, in this, perhaps the first phase in which it can be said to have been clearly itself ? For by the year 1903, when W. B. Yeats, Lady Gregory and the Fays were working together, when the principles and theories were already defined or defining themselves and beginning to find their way into practice in sympathetic hands, the essentials of the later famous Abbey Theatre (The National Theatre Society Ltd.) were already to be seen. We are concerned here, of course, with the traditions of the company in acting, producing, setting ; the dramatic theories and practices of the leaders of the movement belong to other chapters.

The policy of the company and its leaders may be summed up in Lady Gregory's words at the head of this chapter, ' We went on giving what we thought good until it became popular.'

[1] The MS. of *The Foundations* is apparently lost (Hend. 1. 102, article by W. A. Henderson), but the *Racing Lug* was published as a supplement to *The United Irishmen* (Hend. i. 209).

[2] See Appendix 1.

[3] *Ibid.*

In this, as has been pointed out,[1] they cut clean across the theatre traditions of both Dublin and London. They had in fact no traditions, except the age-old one of service to a high imaginative idea, and they joined to this an exceptional capacity for translating poetic intention in terms of gesture, voice, verse-speaking and setting. Yeats knew what he wanted in all these ways. The two Fays knew that what Yeats wanted, even if it had never been heard or seen on any stage, was right. They produced it—often with a few yards of sacking and a cauldron of dye, but they produced it. And everyone was continually on the watch, like people who see their world for the first time every day, so that everything they did was original. That is, they drew it from its origins in their own imaginative conception, and their spontaneity and unself-conscious rightness, which later took not only Ireland but England and America by storm, was assured :

'It seemed to me,' Yeats once wrote to Lady Gregory of the Odéon,[2] 'that a representation so traditional in its type as that at the Odéon has got too far from life, as we see it, to give the full natural pleasure of comedy. It was much more farcical than anything we have ever done. I have recorded several pieces of new business and noted costumes which were sometimes amusing.' And, six years earlier, writing of the production of A.E.'s *Deirdre* by Fay, ' It was acted with great simplicity ; the actors kept very quiet, often merely posing and speaking. The result was curiously dreamlike and gentle.'[3]

It was inevitably a world of continual experiment ; the whole theatrical art seems to have been tested and built up again from its beginning by these people. And the zest with which they watched their own and others' experiments come to fulfilment was itself a part of their reward :

The Hour Glass dresses were purple played against a green curtain. It was our first attempt at the decorative staging long demanded by Mr. Yeats. Mr. Yeats says, in *Samhain*, 1905, ' Our staging of *Kincora*, the work of Mr. Robert Gregory, was beautiful, with a high grave dignity and that strangeness which Ben Jonson thought to be

[1] Chap. I.
[2] A letter of Dec. 19, 1908, quoted *O.I.T.* 97–8.
[3] *D.P.* 80.

a part of all excellent beauty.' The first acts of the play are laid in King Brian's great hall at Kincora. It was hung with green curtains, there were shields embossed with designs in gold upon the walls, and heavy mouldings over the doors. The last act showed Brian's tent at Clontarf ; a great orange curtain filled the background, and it is hard to forget the effect at the end of three figures standing against it, in green, in red, in grey. For a front scene there was a curtain—we use it still in its dimness and age—with a pattern of tree stems interlaced and of leaves edged with gold. This was the most costly staging we had yet attempted : it came with the costumes to £30. A great deal of unpaid labour went into it.[1]

The same attack on tradition was made in the speaking of verse and in the producing of verse plays. W. B. Yeats, who had ' never ceased attacking the methods of the ordinary theatre . . . in the speaking of verse ',[2] slowly trained the speakers who could be trusted with his and with A.E.'s verse plays, and a native school of acting grew up. And players and producers were enthusiastic, both for the plays and for the new method which was growing in their hands. 'The players themselves work in them with delight. . . . W. Fay most enthusiastic, says you are a wonderful man, and keeps repeating lines. He says, " There is nothing like that being written in London." '[3] And gradually the public itself became sound. ' The well-to-do people in our stalls sometimes say, " We have had enough of verse plays, give us comedy." But the people in the sixpenny places do not say they get too much of them.'[4] What was good was becoming popular.

But the conditions under which they worked were not easy and like many good things, the native Irish theatre grew up on a spare and strenuous diet.

' Often near midnight,' says Lady Gregory, ' after the theatre had closed, I have gone round to the newspaper offices, asking as a favour that notices might be put in, for we could pay for but few advertisements and it was not always thought worth

[1] O.I.T. 107. And compare the description of the setting of *Shadowy Waters* (O.I.T. 108).

[2] O.I.T. 29.

[3] Letter of Lady Gregory to W. B. Yeats on the rehearsing of *On Baile's Strand*, O.I.T. 79.

[4] O.I.T. 78-9.

while to send a critic to our plays. Often I have gone out by the stage door when the curtain was up, and come round into the auditorium by the front hall, hoping that in the dimness I might pass for a new arrival and so encourage the few, scattered people in the stalls.'[1]

Back of the stage the conditions were much the same :

Mr. Fay discovered a method of making papier mâché, a chief part of which seemed to be the boiling down of large quantities of our old programmes, for the mouldings and for the shields. I have often seen the designer himself on his knees by a great iron pot— one we use in cottage scenes—dyeing pieces of sacking, or up high on a ladder painting his forests or leaves. His staging of *The Shadowy Waters* was almost more beautiful ; the whole stage is the sloping deck of a galley, blue and dim, the sails and dresses are green, the ornaments all of copper. He staged for us also, for love of his art and of the work, my own plays *The White Cockade*, *The Image*, *Dervorgilla*, and Mr. Yeats's *On Baile's Strand* with the great bronze gates used in other plays as well, in Lord Dunsany's *Glittering Gate* and in *The Countess Cathleen*. It was by him the scenery for Mr. Yeats's *Deirdre* was designed and painted, and for Synge's *Deirdre of the Sorrows*. I am proud to think how much ' excellent beauty ' he has brought to the help of our work.[2]

Years later, at the beginning of the prosperous American tour of 1911, Lady Gregory was to look back on these days when nothing was certain, no success assured and failure of all but ideals and determination threatened : ' And that evening I went to the Plymouth Theatre (in Boston) and found a large audience, and a very enthusiastic one, listening to the plays. I could not but feel moved when I saw this, and remembered our small beginnings and the years of effort and discouragement.'[3]

But in 1903 the small beginnings were still in their infancy[4]

[1] *O.I.T.* 46–7.

[2] *O.I.T.* 108. Yeats gives the same kind of picture in his *Samhain*, 1904 : ' It has been forced to perform in halls without proper lights for the stage, and almost without dressing-rooms, and with level floors in the auditorium that prevented all but the people in the front row from seeing properly.'

[3] *O.I.T.* 173–4.

[4] Though they were growing rapidly : ' I cannot describe the various dramatic adventures of the year,' Yeats says in *Samhain*, 1903, ' with as much' detail as I did last year, mainly because the movement has got beyond us.'

and the effort and discouragement was to last for a long time yet.
Indeed, the main stages in the history of the company can best
be summed up from this point onward by an account of the
chief crises through which it passed in establishing its right
to play what was ' good ' and to make it ' popular ', disregarding
utterly that form of unpopularity that it earnt, now from
Dublin Castle, now from the Clan-na-Gael. The significant
dates in the history of the company's growth and adjustment
are the granting of the Abbey Theatre Patent and the forming
of the National Theatre Society with the generous financial help
of Miss Horniman, in 1904 ; the fight with certain groups
of nationalists and patriots over the production of *The Playboy
of the Western World* in 1907, the last and fiercest of a long series
of battles over Synge's interpretation of Ireland ; the somewhat
different fight, this time with Dublin Castle, over the production
of *Blanco Posnet* in 1909 ; and the significant first American tour
in 1911 when these earlier controversies were finally fought
to a finish and the artistic supremacy of the company established.

The founding of the Abbey Theatre grew from the first
London visit in May 1903, made possible by an almost incredible
effort of the actors. ' It was hard for the actors to get away.
They had their own work to do. But they asked their
employers for a whole Saturday holiday. They left Dublin
on Friday night ' (one did not sleep aboard the Mail at Holyhead
or Dun Laoghaire till 7.0 in the morning in those days),
' arrived in London on the Saturday morning, played in the
afternoon, and again in the evening, at the Queen's Gate Hall,
and were back at work in Dublin on Monday morning.'[1]
But it was worth it. For this was the beginning of their
reputation in England and, more important, of the interest
which led that generous patron of the drama, Miss Horniman,
to build the Abbey Theatre and give the company the free use
of it for a period long enough to set them on their feet. This
was indeed all they needed. Their own genius and indomitable
courage did, as she had foreseen, the rest.

But before a new theatre could be opened in Dublin a new
Patent under the Crown had to be obtained, much as in London

[1] *O.I.T.* 37. See also Yeats's *Samhain*, 1904, *passim* for the history of this
period.

in the eighteenth century. The building of the theatre and the negotiating for the Patent went on simultaneously. The Patent was settled first, the inquiry being held on August 4th, 1904 and the Patent granted to Dame Augusta Gregory ; the building was ready for rehearsal a month or so later. The Company opened there on December 27th. There was very little conflict at either moment,[1] the record of this important metamorphosis is peaceful and curiously unlike those of the earlier and later years. Indeed, the only stormy moment in the life of the Patent itself came later, when its withdrawal was threatened at the production of *Blanco Posnet* in 1909.

Both negotiations had their inevitable diversions. The inquiry before the Privy Council made good reading if only because of the incredible ignorance of contemporary drama revealed unwittingly by the official guardians of its chastity.[2] And the building of the Abbey Theatre by the conversion of the Mechanics' Institute and the old morgue provides, in Yeats's account, at least one interesting episode. ' The other day, while digging up some old rubbish in the Morgue, which is being used for dressing-rooms, they found human bones. The workmen thought they had hit on a murder, but the caretaker said, " Oh, I remember, we lost a body about seven years ago. When the time for the inquest came, it couldn't be found." '[3] (An incident which could, perhaps, hardly have occurred in London. . . .) The theatre was never, from the first, devoid of character.

Only the final stage of transmutation remained. And in 1905 the Irish National Theatre Society, playing under Lady Gregory's Patent at the Abbey Theatre, became the National Theatre Society Limited, known more familiarly as ' the Abbey '. From this point onward the most interesting side of its history, to the dramatic historian, lies in its determined production of plays that were judged good by the leaders, whether their

---

[1] This, of course, by comparison. The Patent was violently opposed by three Dublin theatres, The Gaiety, The Theatre Royal and the Queen's and, in consequence, did not at first allow of the performance of English plays (*Samhain*, 1904).

[2] See also Yeats's account (*Samhain*, 1904).

[3] Letter to Lady Gregory, Aug. 1904. Quoted *O.I.T.* 43.

judgement were confirmed or not by the extreme Irish Nationalists, English or Irish moralists[1] or English censors. This
judgement, in the first instance that of people of genius, had
never been perverted or conventionalized by looking to com-
mercial or popular effects. And their training in regarding the
whole of theatrical and dramatic art as something to be built
again from its beginning had made independence and firmness
of judgement an almost unconscious habit, like technical pro-
ficiency or physical skill. There was perhaps nowhere in
Europe a group of people qualified as were these by their genius
and by the discipline they had accepted from their genius,
to bring into being again a living theatre and a poetic drama,
and supported by actors and theatre workers whose appreciation
was such that they went on giving their services free. How
much all that has followed in English drama from the beginning
of the century to the present owes to their indefatigable courage
and utter originality will never easily be estimated.

The first[2] characteristic fight of this kind came with Synge's
Shadow of the Glen[3] in 1903, but it was mainly a newspaper
battle, led by the *Independent* and others who were outraged by
the picture of Ireland's womanhood. As Shaw put it later,
the ' Clan-na-Gael . . . suddenly struck out the brilliant idea
that to satirise the follies of humanity is to insult the Irish nation,
because the Irish nation is, in fact, the human race, and has no
follies, and stands there pure and beautiful and saintly to be
eternally oppressed by England and collected for by the Clan '.[4]
The company, of course, continued to produce this play,
though an anti-Synge party was growing, and with sound

[1] Perhaps the most interesting comment on this aspect of the problem
is Yeats's short article on ' Moral and Immoral Plays ' in *Samhain*,
1903.

[2] This is not counting the battle over *The Countess Cathleen*, which, as Lady
Gregory says, in 1913, ' was not a very real one '. (*O.I.T.* 25.) Of course,
by 1913, she had herself seen ' hills in comparison with which you'd call *that*
a valley '.

[3] The controversy is conveniently summed up, for those who do not want
to search the files of *The Independent* and *The United Irishman*, by Yeats in
two short articles, reproductions of letters written to the Press at the time,
in *P.C.*, 54–65.

[4] Interview for the New York *Evening Sun* (1912). Quoted *O.I.T.* 300.

judgement refrained from producing the *Tinker's Wedding*.[1]
The grumbling disaffection broke openly in 1907 with the production of *The Playboy of the Western World*.[2]

The story of the week of rioting that followed its production
on January 26th, 1907, is well known from Lady Gregory's
inimitable description, but the causes are hard for an Englishman to understand. Undoubtedly Shaw's malicious account of
them, quoted above, covers one aspect of the case and Lady
Gregory sums up, ' It was a definite fight for freedom from mob
censorship.'[3] What follows had better be given in her own
words, for it condenses into brief statement a long and tangled
succession of factors and a confusing interplay of forces :

A part of the new National movement had been, and rightly,
an attack on the stage Irishman, the vulgar and unnatural butt given
on the English stage. We had the destroying of that scarecrow
in mind among other things in setting up our Theatre. But the
societies were impatient. They began to dictate here and there
what should or should not be played. Mr. Colum's plays and Mr.
Boyle's were found too harsh in their presentment of life. I see in a
letter about a tour we were arranging : ' Limerick has not yet come
to terms. They have asked for copies of proposed plays that they
may " place same before the branch of the Gaelic League there " '
. . . . Finally, a company was only allowed to produce a play after
it had been cut and re-arranged by a local committee, made up of
the shopkeepers of the town. We would not submit Mr. Synge's
work or any of the work we put on to such a test, nor would we
allow any part of our audience to make itself final judge through
preventing others from hearing and judging for themselves. We
have been justified, for Synge's name has gone round the world, and

[1] This and *Where There is Nothing* were never produced by the Abbey
Company. The good sense of the directors knew where the line must be
drawn, just as well as they knew that, once drawn, it must not be drawn
back. They no more attempted to force these two plays on Catholic Dublin
than they consented to withdraw *The Playboy*.

[2] ' *The United Irishman* . . . from that on has attacked almost every play
produced at our theatre, and the suspicion it managed to arouse among the
political clubs against Mr. Synge, especially, led a few years later to the
organized attempt to drive *The Playboy of the Western World* from the stage.
—W.B.Y. 1908 ' (*P.C.* 54, note).

[3] See also W. B. Yeats's account in *The Arrow* (Feb. 1907), reprinted with
a note *P.C.* 192–3.

we should have been ashamed for ever if we had not insisted on a hearing for his most important work.[1]

But the insistence cost something at the time :

There was a battle of a week. Every night protestors with their trumpets came and raised a din. Every night the police carried some of them off to the police courts. Every afternoon the paper gave reports of the trial before a magistrate who had not heard or read the play and who insisted on being given details of its incidents by the accused and by the police.[2] (Curiously like the old theatre-riots of mid-eighteenth century London—except for the part played by the police.) There was a very large audience on the first night, a Saturday, January 26th. Synge was there, but Mr. Yeats was giving a lecture in Scotland. The first act got its applause, and the second, though one felt the audience were a little puzzled, a little shocked at the wild language.[3] Near the end of the third act there was some hissing. We had sent a telegram to Mr. Yeats after the first act 'Play great success'; but at the end we sent another— 'Audience broke up in disorder at the word shift.'[4] . . . On the Monday night . . . I noticed on one side of the pit a large group of men sitting together, not a woman among them. I told Synge I thought it a sign of some organized disturbance and he telephoned to have the police at hand. The first part of the first act went undisturbed. Then suddenly an uproar began. The group of men I had noticed booed, hooted, blew tin trumpets. . . . It was impossible to hear a word of the play. The curtain came down for a minute, but I went round and told the actors to go on playing to the end, even if not a word could be heard. . . . The disturbance lasted to the end of the evening, not one word had been heard after the first ten minutes.[5]

I have quoted Lady Gregory's account at some length if only

[1] *O.I.T.* 115–17 *passim.*   [2] *O.I.T.* 115.

[3] Compare also W. B. Yeats's description (*The Cutting of an Agate*, p. 130).

[4] The notorious but, to modern ears, innocuous line is now received without protest : 'A drift of chosen females, standing in their shifts itself, maybe from this place to the Eastern world.'

[5] *O.I.T.* 112–13. See also W. B. Yeats : *P.C.* 193, note. He adds, 'On the last night of the play there were, I believe, five hundred police keeping order in the theatre and in its neighbourhood. Some days later our enemies, though beaten so far as the play was concerned, crowded into the cheaper seats for a debate on the freedom of the stage. They were very excited and kept up the discussion till near twelve.'

because events such as these, surmounted by the Irish players, lie somewhat outside the experience of the average English playwright, actor or theatregoer and nearly, it may be, outside his imagination. (*Ghosts* itself was received in London in 1891 with less physical demonstration, if hardly with less verbal hysteria.) It is essential to add that at the last performance of that week, the curtain fell, according to *The Sunday Independent*, amid ' thunders of applause '.[1]

The other celebrated fight of the early years of the company was of an entirely different kind, and the directors of the theatre who had proved themselves equal to ejecting rioters with the help of the police, now found themselves wrapped in a cloud of confused subtleties of official and diplomatic evasion. They, however, were not evasive. One of the most humorous pieces of dialogue Lady Gregory has ever written is that, presumably fairly close to fact, in which she and Yeats, jointly and severally, discomfort a succession of Dublin Castle officials.[2]

The situation, as Shaw said later, was bound from the first to determine in their favour. Yet at the time it appeared as though they had to choose between endangering the hard-worn Patent and forgoing their principle of playing whatever they thought aesthetically fine under legally permissible conditions.

Blanco Posnet had been printed but not published. It had already been rejected by the censor in England, but he had no jurisdiction in Ireland,[3] so that when Shaw offered the play to the Abbey, they accepted it and put it into rehearsal. And then the trouble began.

Lady Gregory, who was in Dublin superintending the rehearsals, had a letter from Dublin Castle pointing out that, ' His Excellency, after the most careful consideration, has arrived at the conclusion that in its original form the play is not in accordance either with the assurances given by those interested when the Patent was applied for, or with the conditions

[1] Quoted by Yeats in his opening speech at the debate at the Abbey Theatre on Feb. 4, 1907 (see *P.C.* 195).

[2] *O.I.T.* 145–62.

[3] ' The Theatrical law of Ireland was made by the Irish Parliament, and . . . we must be grateful to that ruling caste of free spirits, that being free themselves they left the theatre in freedom,' as Yeats had already pointed out in *Samhain* in 1904.

and restrictions contained in the Patent as granted by the Crown.[1]   On August 12th, she interviewed an official at the Castle to explore the question of the production, the Lord Lieutenant's position and the possible forfeiture of the Abbey Theatre Patent if the directors persisted.   On August 13th Yeats had arrived from Galway and he and Lady Gregory, taking it seriously, discussed their position with a solicitor.   But they decided that it was their business to go forward with the play, even if it meant forfeiture.   They interviewed the official again, exchanged letters and telegrams with Shaw, met more officials, explained the principles involved and described their own early fights with the nationalists on the one hand and the Church on the other.   On August 20th they interviewed the Lord Lieutenant himself, and yet other officials, and still the Patent seemed in danger.   On August 21st they received a letter from the Castle saying that a legal document forbidding the performance of the play would reach them at once.   They wrote a statement, rather like a death-speech from a political or religious scaffold, and went on with the rehearsals, now fully prepared for this to be the end of the Abbey Theatre, but declaring their principles of freedom to the last.   Shaw also declared his. . . .   The directors were more concerned with freedom from the censorship of the mob and of the Castle, he with the root principle of the nature of blasphemy.   But they were at one in their way of meeting this crisis.   ' In any case,' Shaw had written on the 12th of August, ' do not threaten them with a contraband performance.   Threaten that we shall be suppressed ; that we shall be made martyrs of ; that we shall suffer as much and as publicly as possible.   Tell them that they can depend on me to burn with a brighter blaze and louder yells than all Foxe's martyrs.'[2]

On August 25th the play was produced to a crowded house.[3]

[1] *O.I.T.* 144.   [2] *O.I.T.* 152.

[3] (A friend, who was in the audience that night, tells me that there was heavy booking from England to see the play the censor had forbidden and sad disappointment among many of the visitors who were unable, with the best will in the world, to find anything pornographical in it. This is an interesting comment on the English theatre public in 1909, the conduct and reputation of the censor, the reputation of Shaw, and a number of other things. . . .)

' There were no protests made on any side. And the play, though still forbidden in England, is still played by us, and always with success.'[1]   The description of the evening itself is characteristic :

The play began, and till near the end it was received in perfect silence. Perhaps the audience were waiting for the wicked bits to begin. Then, at the end, there was a tremendous burst of cheering, and we knew we had won. Some stranger outside asked what was going on in the theatre. ' They are defying the Lord Lieutenant ' was the answer ; and when the crowd heard the cheering, they took it up and it went far out through the streets.[2]

The Castle had capitulated without protest. They had not had, as a matter of fact, a leg to stand on, but their bluff had given them the appearance of a centipede.   Shaw, when it was all over, summed up the successive and simultaneous blunders in their tactics as a ' proof of the danger of transacting import- ant business at the Castle when all the responsible officials are away bathing.'[3]

The deputies found themselves confronted by a matter which required tactful handling and careful going. They did their best ; but they broke down rather badly in point of law, in point of diplomatic etiquette, and in point of common knowledge.

They committed the indiscretion of practically conspiring with an English official who has no jurisdiction in Ireland in an attempt to intimidate an Irish theatre . . . they assumed that this official acts as the agent of the King . . . they assumed that the Lord Lieutenant is the servant of the King. . . .

In conclusion, may I say that from the moment when the Castle made its first blunder I never had any doubt of the result, and that I kept away from Dublin, in order that our national theatre might have the entire credit of handling and producing a new play without assistance from the author or from any other person trained in the English theatres.[4]

[1] *O.I.T.* 168 (1913). It is to this day one of the most brilliant perform- ances in the Abbey repertory.

[2] *O.I.T.* 168.

[3] Letter from George Bernard Shaw to Lady Gregory. Aug. 27, 1909. Quoted *O.I.T.* 274–9.

[4] *Ibid.*

He might have added that he had also left them the credit of handling Dublin Castle equally without assistance and with equal success.

Little remains to add of the history of the growth of the company.[1] The main formative influences had done their work by 1909 and the thing that had ' seemed to grow possible as we talked ' at Duras eleven years before had become something of European fame needing only a few more years of growth along the same lines to be established for ever as the central and significant dramatic revival of the early twentieth century. The tour in the United States in the winter of 1911–12 marks the end of the characteristic early conflicts, at once the fiercest and the last. The Irish nationalists in America mobilized every force they could touch to boycott the plays throughout the Eastern States. The fight took much the same form everywhere, though it was fiercer in some towns than in others. It started in a prejudice, not the less violent for its ignorance and generally among the members of the Gaelic League, against the picture of Irish life and morals which the plays of the new school were said to give. The general prejudice was entangled with and sometimes manipulated by political prepossessions of a far-reaching and almost infinitely complex kind. And mingled again with both was the religious prejudice of some sections at least of the Church. The results of such an agglomeration of confused passions were unpredictable in any individual case, and the career of the players was dogged with startling and unexpected episodes. Much of the prejudice seems to have come from genuine, misguided stupidity and total ignorance of what the plays actually were (' What did you really think,' said one Philadelphia lady to another, ' of Lady Gregory's play, *The Cowboy of the Western World* ? ')[2] But some, like that of the article in *America*,[3] whose author bases his attack on *The Tinker's Wedding* and *Where There is Nothing*, which were never played by the company in America or else-

---

[1] Lists of the plays produced, which themselves give a fair indication of its later activities, can be found in *O.I.T.* (Appendix 1) and, extending to the year 1928, in Malone : *The Irish Drama* (Appendix 2).

[2] See *O.I.T.* 215. For other instances see *O.I.T.* 188.

[3] Nov. 4, 1911. Quoted *O.I.T.* 306–7.

where, point to a deliberately unscrupulous choice of weapon. 'The details,' this writer points out, 'which are even more shocking than those of the *Playboy*, are too indecent for citation . . . may not be even outlined by a self-respecting pen. . . .'[1] Less vindictive, but still deeply disturbed, some of the nationalist reviewers plead for the true, old ideals of Ireland as the only remedy against this insidious horror : ' Brothers and Sisters everywhere, place a little history of Ireland in the hands of each little boy and little girl of the ancient race, and all the Lady Gregories in the world will not be able to destroy an atom of our splendid heritage.'[2]

Reviews like these, and there are several between September 1911 and March 1912, are as incredible to a generation accustomed to an element of aesthetic judgement, even of logic, in its dramatic criticism, as is that noble utterance which, in 1891, dispatched *Ghosts* as 'Just a wicked nightmare.' But in 1911 they were not only customary and familiar, they led to action of the directest kind, the kind dear to Irish-American nationalists.

The fate of the players varied, as has been said, from town to town. In New York the nationalists half-wrecked one performance of *The Playboy* (it was generally *The Playboy* that they fastened on), in Philadelphia they succeeded in having the company arrested and brought up successively in the magistrates' and judges' Courts, while the chief feature of the Chicago nationalists' welcome was the threatening letter assuring Lady Gregory that her doom was sealed and tastefully symbolizing the statement with illustrations of a gun (species indeterminate), a coffin, some nails and a hammer.[3] Lady Gregory herself dispatches this last most briefly of all : ' I have been walking to the theatre every night as usual in spite of that threatening letter. I don't feel anxious, for I don't think from the drawing that the sender has much practical knowledge of firearms.'[4]

---

[1] I have never come upon the details he refers to. I think perhaps he must be in the position of the lady who, speaking of a famous line in *The Playboy* in 1907, said that, ' the word omitted but understood was one she would blush to use even when she was alone '. (See *O.I.T.* 112 and 306–7.)

[2] *The National Hibernian.* Quoted *O.I.T.* 313.

[3] Facsimile, *O.I.T.* 296.

[4] Extract from a letter of Feb. 12, 1912. *O.I.T.* 252.

It was not, of course, for nothing that Mr. Shaw said she was
' the greatest living Irishwoman '.

It was in New York and Philadelphia that the victories were
won, and in the many American towns where the players were
received with enthusiasm, and there was no disturbance at all ;
in the Universities, which already had lecture courses on their
plays ; in the societies, where Lady Gregory discovered that
she was, in addition to everything else, a born platform speaker.
Up and down the Eastern States the ' true Ireland ', as Yeats
said, was ' fighting the false '.[1] And whether the victory
was won in the theatre, in the judge's court or on the lecture
platform, it was done so thoroughly that in the next winter's
tour to America, ' there were no riots and we were of the happy
people who have no history, unless it be of the continued kindness of America, and of the growing kindness and better understanding on the part of our own countrymen '.[2] What was
' good ' had become ' popular '.

It is hard to leave the American episodes without a few at least
of Lady Gregory's descriptions. The first night of *The Playboy*
in New York (Nov. 28, 1911) is characteristic of the type of
disorder they outrode :

> Very soon after the curtain went up on *The Playboy* the interrup-
> tions began . . . and the disturbance was let go on nearly all through
> the first act. I went round, when the disturbance began, and knelt
> in the opening of the hearth, calling to every actor who came within
> earshot that they must not stop for a moment but must spare their
> voices, as they could not be heard, and we should do the whole act
> over again. At the end Tyler came round and I was delighted when
> he shouted that it should be played again. O'Donovan announced
> this and there were great cheers from the audience. And the whole
> play was given then in perfect peace and quiet. . . . In the box
> office this morning they have a collection of spoils left by the enemy
> (chiefly stink-pots and rosaries).[3]

And in the same way, on the first night of the same play in
Philadelphia :

[1] Letter to Lady Gregory. Dublin, Dec. 3. Quoted *O.I.T.* 211.
[2] *O.I.T.* 253.
[3] *O.I.T.* 203–4.

We had a little trouble last night, the first of *The Playboy*. . . .
Two (men) were arrested for assault. Nothing was thrown but
a slice of currant cake, which hit Sinclair, and two or three eggs,
which missed him—he says they were fresh ones. . . . I gave eight
tickets to be given to athletes among the Pennsylvania students
as A.D.C.'s for me tonight. They would have been very useful
putting out offenders and taking messages to the stage.[1]

The 'greatest living Irishwoman' was no stickler for legal
formalities—no more than Queen Elizabeth.

The scenes in the Philadelphia Magistrates' and Judges'
Courts were characteristic of the tangle of prejudice and mis-
representation and the triumphant emergence of the company,
of whom Shaw was so sure : ' You will beat the Clan na Gael
as you beat the Castle.' By the prompt and skilful assistance
of John Quinn, the New York lawyer, the whole thing was
cleared up in the minimum time and the company set out,
vindicated, upon its way.

'J.Q. asked one witness if anything immoral had happened
on the stage, and he answered, " Not while the curtain was up ! "
I think it was the same witness who said, " A theatre is no place
for a sense of humour." The players beamed and the audience
enjoyed themselves.'[2]

The effect of all this at home was, of course, admirable. ' I
think for the moment it has made us rather popular here in
Dublin, for no matter how much evil people wish for the
Directors, they feel amiable towards the players. If only Miss
Allgood could get a fortnight, I think the pit would love even
The Playboy.'[3]

From this time on the company and the movement were
established throughout both continents. Their acting and
theatre technique were become a source of delight to connois-
seurs wherever they had played and were seriously discussed
and compared with the great styles of the main continental
theatres and of the past. Their leaders' names were familiar
wherever the English-speaking theatre was known or spoken of.
Their drama had been recognized as the most individual body

---

[1] *O.I.T.* 218–19.
[2] *O.I.T.* 229–30.
[3] *O.I.T.* 235.

of plays in verse or poetic prose written in the English language since the seventeenth century and had been included in the curricula of American Universities. They had 'won much praise for themselves and had raised the dignity of Ireland'.

The story does not end in 1912 ; it has not ended in 1953. But with the end of the work of Synge and with its acceptance the actual revival of poetic drama had been completed. This book is the story of the revival, of the bringing back of the habit of poetry to the theatre ; so that work and its acceptance marks a place where we may well pause.[1]

We have been the first to create a true ' People's Theatre ', and we have succeeded because it is not an exploitation of local colour, or of a limited form of drama possessing a temporary novelty, but the first doing of something for which the world is ripe, something that will be done all over the world and done more and more perfectly ; the making articulate of all the dumb classes each with its own knowledge of the world.[2]

And this was also what the poetic drama had done in England in the Elizabethan and Jacobean age.

---

[1] What follows is, as I have indicated, of equal interest and of enduring vitality, but it would need another volume to consider fairly its place in the history of drama. For the subsequent history of the movement and for an account of the various lines along which the drama developed the reader is referred to the full and thorough account of A. E. Malone, in *The Irish Drama*, to which I myself am much indebted.

[2] W. B. Yeats, *A People's Theatre* (published in *The Irish Statesman*, 1919, republished, *P.C.* 199–218).

CHAPTER 4

IDEALS IN THE WORKSHOP

' What we wanted was to create for Ireland a theatre with a base of realism, with an apex of beauty.'

I

THE MOVEMENT which created a living drama in Ireland sprang, as I have indicated, from the poetic faith of one man. Through the rough-and-tumble of the early years described in the last chapter, the managers of the theatre, the actors and the dramatists alike carried through unbroken the ideals of imaginative reality and of poetic truth. It is perhaps worth while, before describing the achievement of each dramatist as an individual, to pause and look at the history of the whole movement, not in terms of event but of intention ; to see how intention met or created event and how far event tempered intention. For the leaders of the movement began with ideals, carried them heroically into the workshop of the theatre, let them prove themselves there (in the full assurance that they would prove sound), and in their later reflections upon the conflict, set down certain of their ideals again in terms of proven dramatic theory. Looked at this way, the story of the Irish drama seems to offer an unusually lucid exposition of what one feels to be after all the normal sequence : poetic faith, poetic practice and poetic theory. The faith is most clearly to be seen in the early critical writings of Yeats, the tempering of this faith in the historical accounts of Lady Gregory, the practice in the body of drama left by Yeats, Martyn, Lady Gregory, A.E., Synge and their successors, and the theory again in the later critical works of Yeats. We are driven, to find a parallel at all close, to the works of individual men rather than to the records of a whole movement, to Ibsen, or perhaps better still to Hebbel, the body of whose drama is backed by a continuous record of his ideals, his experience and his theories in the form of critical writings, letters and the *Tagebücher*.[1] For the major dramatic movements of other times we have either an insufficient record of original intention (as for the Greek) or too long and too slow a period of development for intention to be conscious (as with the Medieval drama of Western Europe) or a borrowed theory followed by a totally different practice upon which the great leaders left little record (as with the Elizabethan) or, as with the English nineteenth-century renascence, the ideals and the fulfilment in the hands of different men.

But the Irish drama is brought to life, as it were, under our eyes, by people who were not, when they began the movement, already active dramatists. They were young men full of ideals who had read drama, thought about it and discussed it far more than they had as yet practised it. Moore had a good outfit of theories, though it is not so clear what were his ideals. Martyn's were inspired by the continental theatrical standards, higher all round than the English, and by the nobility and severity of Ibsen's art and he would have given to Ireland a theatre which should make it free of these. The ideals of Yeats were original and creative ; such as make a new phase of art out of nothing and breathe the breath of life into it. And he and Lady Gregory were not content to construct a viaduct between Dublin and Christiania.

It was, from the first, Yeats who was the main reservoir of these ideals ; and though not everyone, either at the beginning or later in the company's history, agreed with him, those who did not seceded and were absorbed in other movements and other activities, like Martyn and Moore, while those who sympathized came gradually into closer and closer alliance, as did Lady Gregory and Synge. Not all his ideals were practical down to the last detail—there were Lady Gregory and the Fays to adjust the balance there—but all were sound as ideals and a far greater number than at first appears possible became workable in the end. He himself has left the fullest statement of

[1] I am indebted to my friend, Professor Edna Purdie, for indicating to me in the first instance the closeness of the parallel here. For a full account of the interaction of theory and practice in the work of Hebbel, the reader is referred to her volume, *Friedrich Hebbel*, and especially to the chapters on *Dramatic Technique* (VIII) and *Conception of Tragedy* (IX).

their early form in the *Samhain* papers and certain lectures and articles which he afterwards collected, together with these, under the name of *The Irish Dramatic Movement*.[1] It is noticeable that Lady Gregory's writings contribute very little to this part of the question, but that on the second phase of the experience, the modification or triumphant justification of the ideals in the workshop of the theatre, she gives us, in *Our Irish Theatre* and in the notes on her plays, an invaluable insight into the processes by which the ideals became workable. Finally, in Yeats's later prose works, the tested ideals develop into dramatic theories, most of which, especially when most disputable, are of great aesthetic interest and significance. *The Cutting of an Agate, Per Amica Silentia Lunae, The Trembling of the Veil, Dramatis Personae* and the annotations to the later editions of the plays contain the scattered indications of a body of theory, even if it is never actually gathered into a system.

What, then, are these ideals which clothed themselves with the Irish Dramatic revival and can be seen working upon and worked upon by it until they become identical with its spirit and with their creator's achievement ?

Before everything they are poetic. Against a background of English drama following Ibsen in the serious prose discussion play or degrading him in the automatic problem play, following the Elizabethans at long distance in the pseudo-poetic play or continuing the more recent traditions of farce, domestic melodrama or the French '*pièce bien faite*', stands the figure of Yeats, the man who from his own innate wisdom and with no help from any dramatic tradition then at work in Europe, led the drama of the English-speaking people back to the paths of poetry and power, making way, in both countries, for the first body of plays which can seriously compare with the Elizabethans. To do this by imitation was impossible ; he knew, no less than Ben Jonson, that ' likeness is always on this side truth '. It must be raised again from the earth, not in its material or its form or its language only (though he provided for all of these) but in the spirit. His determination to return to the thought

---

[1] *Plays and Controversies.* Macmillan, 1927. With these should be considered also various articles and speeches, especially in *Beltaine, The Arrow* and the contemporary press.

and speech of the people was more than a wise appreciation of a hitherto unexplored field, it was an instinctive recognition of the roots of poetic truth. He believed that the drama must be born again or perish utterly, for it had reached the phase known to contemporary biologists as ' the old age of the species '.

He began, then, with the belief that poetry, a spirit and an unassailable essence, lived still in the Irish peasants whose attitude to common life was like that of the great ages, of Chaucer, of the Italian renascence, of Greece, of the Elizabethans, and that this spirit revealed itself in the living language which they alone still spoke, and in their love of the heroic and homely in legend and in daily life : ' That conversation of the people which is so full of riches because it is so full of leisure, or ... those old stories of the folk which were made by men who believed so much in the soul, and so little in anything else, that they were never entirely certain that the earth was solid under the foot-sole.' [1]

In the same way, before newspapers and second-rate books had ' driven the living imagination out of the world ' and ' when the imagination turned to life itself for excitement ' there had been a world of men in whom the root of poetry lived, unconscious and untouched :

Everything that their minds ran on came to them vivid with the colour of the senses, and when they wrote it was out of their own rich experience, and they found their symbols of expression in things that they had known all their life long. Their very words were more vigorous than ours, for their phrases came from a common mint, from the market, or the tavern, or from the great poets of a still older time. . . . Yesterday I went out to see the reddening apples in the garden, and they faded from my imagination sooner than they would have from the imagination of that old poet, who made the songs of the seasons for the Fianna, or out of Chaucer's, that celebrated so many trees.[2]

Just such was the living speech of the people of Ireland in his own day, the unconscious and spontaneous revelation of the living imagination.

[1] *Samhain,* 1904. (*P.C.* 123.)
[2] *Samhain,* 1904. (*P.C.* 97.)

One can write well in that country idiom without much thought about one's words ; the emotion will bring the right word itself, for there everything is old and everything is alive and nothing common or threadbare.[1]

With the ' living imagination ' then for guide, and allowing no other interfering or conflicting loyalty, aesthetic, moral, social or political, Yeats began to clothe his belief ; and the principles of dramatic subject, form and language, even the practical details of setting, acting and speech defined themselves in harmony with that fundamental principle. Often this meant the widest freedom and a refusal of rule, often the strictest discipline ; bit by bit it became the basic principle of that movement which culminated in the work of Synge. The scope allowed was unlimited, from poetic tragedy to prose comedy, from heroic legend and history play to tales of the daily life of peasants or tiny plays as slender as shapely bubbles of high, frothing talk. Its discipline was severe, but it was the positive discipline of the artist that says ' Thou shalt ', not the negative discipline that says ' Thou shalt not '. All these dramatists believed or came to believe that the theatre itself was the workshop in which the drama must be formed and, if need be, modified ; that the study of the masters of drama was essential for the novice, not that it might be imitated, but for the growth of understanding ; that its function was the highest : ' that they might have life and . . . have it more abundantly '. All believed in simplicity, naturalness and economy in acting and in setting, and Yeats, beyond this, believed in the virtue of re-moteness, itself a mode of simplicity, in the setting and acting of heroic or poetic plays. All resisted steadily any attempt to interfere with their policy whether from above (as in Lady Gregory's fight with Dublin Castle) or from below as when they fought through the lean first years, refusing to lower their standards to a possible box-office success. From the first they set themselves against subsidies that would mean deference to some controlling factor other than their own principles and they accepted none until Miss Horniman's was given in virtue of what they had already become and to let them go forward in being themselves.

[1] *Samhain,* 1902. (*P.C.* 30.)

The notice called ' *Advice to Playwrights* ' (which, after a few years, they began to circulate to intending dramatists whose plays they were obliged to return unused), sums up many of these intentions and indicates at once the nature of their demands and the elasticity admitted within these :

Advice to Playwrights[1]

. . . A play to be suitable for performance at the Abbey should contain some criticism of life, founded on the experience or personal observation of the writer, or some vision of life, of Irish life by preference, important from its beauty or from some excellence of style ; and this intellectual quality is not more necessary to tragedy than to the gayest comedy. . . .

The dramatist should also banish from his mind the thought that there are some ingredients, the love-making of the popular stage for instance, especially fitted to give dramatic pleasure ; for any knot of events, where there is passionate emotion and clash of will, can be made the subject matter of a play, and the less like a play it is at the first sight the better play may come of it in the end. Young writers should remember that they must get all their effects from the logical expression of their subject, and not by the addition of extraneous incidents ; and that a work of art can have but one subject. A work of art, though it must have the effect of nature, is art because it is not nature, as Goethe said : and it must possess a unity unlike the accidental profusion of nature.

The Abbey Theatre is continually sent plays which show that their writers have not understood that the attainment of this unity by what is usually a long shaping and reshaping of the plot, is the principal labour of the dramatist, and not the writing of the dialogue.

But some of these ideals demand a more detailed account than this. Yeats has given us, especially in his early work, some clear and firm descriptions of the function he assigned to the drama of the living imagination, as firm, though hardly as reiterative as those with which Henry Arthur Jones was supporting his campaign for ' serious ' drama on the other side of St. George's Channel. The contrast between the two is of great interest. It is the contrast between the vision of an artist, intellectually defined, and the opinions of a man of good principle who has a high regard for the arts.

[1] Quoted by Lady Gregory : *O.I.T.* 100-2.

We have to write or find plays that will make the theatre a place of intellectual excitement—a place where the mind goes to be liberated as it was liberated by the theatres of Greece and England and France at certain great movements of their history, and as it is liberated in Scandinavia to-day. If we are to do this we must learn that beauty and truth are always justified of themselves, and that their creation is a greater service to our country than writing that compromises either in the seeming service of a cause. We will doubtless come more easily to truth and beauty because we love some cause with all but all our heart ; but we must remember when truth and beauty open their mouths to speak, that all other mouths should be silent as Finn bade the son of Lugaidh be in the houses of the great. Truth and beauty judge and are above judgement. They justify and have no need of justification.[1]

This idea of drama, firm-rooted but elastic, did not of its nature lead to the proscription of one kind of material or the recommendation of another, as so often in the contemporary English drama, but certain ideas on its nature and essence gradually emerged. There is a conception of tragedy, for example, learned first by Yeats in the course of his own experience and re-applied and accepted by Lady Gregory in hers, which is a working ideal long before it becomes a theory regarded from a distance :

The arts are at their greatest when they seek for a life growing always more scornful of everything that is not itself and passing into its own fullness, as it were, ever more completely as all that is created out of the passing mode of society slips from it ; and attaining that fullness, perfectly it may be—and from this is tragic joy and the perfectness of tragedy—when the world itself has slipped away in death.[2]

There was from the first in his ideal of tragedy a desire for that remoteness, for that distance from actuality and nearness to imaginative reality, which led him later to a theory of tragedy in which ' character ' was an interference and a limitation. The full expression of this did not come until later[3] but already, in

[1] *Samhain*, 1903. (*P.C.* 45-6.) cf. also *P.C.* 57-8, 60, 61-3, *Samhain,* 1904 (*P.C.* 101-4, 123), *Samhain,* 1906 (*P.C.* 177).
[2] *Samhain*, 1904. (*P.C.* 124.)
[3] See *The Tragic Theatre* (1910) in *The Cutting of an Agate.* (And see *post*, Section III.)

the service of ' that tragic ecstasy which is the best that art—
perhaps that life—can give ', he can perceive an error in ' trying
for too much character '[1] and his praise of A.E.'s *Deirdre* both
in the *Samhain* papers and in the reminiscences of the *Dramatis*
Personae is for the ' absence of character . . . like the absence of
individual expression in wall decoration '.[2]

Curiously enough, Lady Gregory agrees with him here, but
she adds some illuminating corollaries to the main proposition,
the chief of them being some clear distinctions, born of her own
experience, between the function of character in tragedy and
in comedy :

> In a lecture I gave last year on playwriting I said I had been forced
> to write comedy because it was wanted for our theatre, to put on at
> the end of the verse plays, but that I think tragedy is easier. For, I
> said, tragedy shows humanity in the grip of circumstance, of fate, of
> what our people call ' the thing will happen ', ' the Woman in the
> Stars that does all '. . . . Well, you put your actor in the grip of this
> woman, in the claws of the cat. Once in that grip you know what
> the end must be. You may let your hero kick or struggle, but he is
> in the claws all the time, it is a mere question as to how nearly you
> will let him escape, and when you will allow the pounce. Fate
> itself is the protagonist, your actor cannot carry much character, it is
> out of place. You do not want to know the character of a wrestler
> you see trying his strength at a show.
>
> In writing a little tragedy, *The Gaol Gate*, I made the scenario in
> three lines, ' He is an informer ; he is dead ; he is hanged.' I wrote
> that play very quickly. My two poor women were in the clutch
> of the Woman in the Stars. . . . I knew what I was going to do and
> I was able to keep within those three lines. But in comedy it is
> different. Character comes in, and why it is so I cannot explain,
> but as soon as one creates a character, he begins to put out little feet
> of his own and take his own way.[3]

There is a shock in the naïve and fearless statement, ' I think
tragedy is easier.' Perhaps no one but Lady Gregory, to whom
playwriting was a craft that she explored in delighted fascination, not a cult to be worshipped in paralysed stupefaction,
could have written those words in the year 1913. But within

[1] *O.I.T.* 106. Letter quoted by Lady Gregory.
[2] *D.P.* 80.
[3] *New Irish Comedies* (notes, pp. 158–9).

the limits of the contrast which she is defining here, they are true. And there is the evidence not only of *The Gaol Gate* but of the longer tragic or semi-tragic legend and history plays (*Grania, Kincora, Dervorgilla*), to show that she had put the ideal of a form of tragedy in which ' your actor cannot carry much character' into honourable practice.

But the ideals never so hardened that they were not ready to say at any moment, ' It is to intuition we must turn for new discoveries ', or, looking back upon the process, ' But when it came to writing the scene, I suppose it was either intuition or experience that took the pen and brought it to its present end '.[1] Intuition and experience, one merged into the other, and to distinguish them or dispute about them was no part of the business.

From this it almost necessarily follows that heroic or legendary material will play the same part in their serious plays as the daily life of the west of Ireland peasant in their comedies. Yeats was early conscious of this, before he wrote the plays on the Cuchulain cycle and while Lady Gregory was translating the legends that gave the matter for these (and for many of her own *Irish Folk History Plays*) into *Gods and Fighting Men* and *Cuchulain of Muirthemne* :

Our movement is a return to the people. . . . The play that is to give them a quite natural pleasure should tell them either of their own life, or of that life of poetry where every man can see his own image, because there alone does human nature escape from arbitrary conditions. . . . If you would ennoble the man of the roads you must write about the roads, or about the people of romance, or about great historical people.[2]

The scientific movement is ebbing a little everywhere, and here in Ireland it has never been in flood at all. And I am certain that everywhere literature will return once more to its old extravagant fantastical expression, for in literature, unlike science, there are no discoveries, and it is always the old that returns. Everything in Ireland urges us to this return, and it may be that we shall be the first to recover after the fifty years of mistake.[3]

[1] *The Image and other plays.* (*Notes to Shanwalla*, 222, 223.)
[2] *Samhain*, 2. (*P.C.* 32.)
[3] *Samhain*, 1905. (*P.C.* 158.) (See also pp. 155–9 *passim*, and at intervals throughout the *I.D.M.* papers.)

Guided by the living imagination, then, the drama found its own forms, or, as Yeats was the first to admit, brought to life again the ancient forms. Upon this no specific principles were laid down beyond those in the *Advice to Playwrights* which is concerned rather with causes, the positive self-discipline of the artist, than with the effects and kinds to be achieved. But upon one subject, that of language, Yeats had something more to say, for the ideal of the living language, though it derives immediately from their first principle, might have been neglected without some reminder that here, as ever, the style was the man.

Yeats began in the belief that the experience of the living imagination could only be revealed in a language as living as itself and that that, for the English-speaking peoples, meant a language that had not been contaminated by the daily newspaper and the cheap Press, a language, that is, spoken by people who had not only never read these things themselves but did not inherit their speech from those who had. It was perhaps hard for him to accept the use of the English language at all, but he early saw that Irish (which, in any case, he did not write himself) had its own and limited function in the new movement and could not be substituted for English for those Irishmen who were not Irish speakers. The only way then to give the ideal actuality was to use a form of English which had somehow escaped contamination, and this, for Ireland, meant the language of the Irish-speaking people of the west, when they translated their native syntax and imagery into English ; for to them, though they were nearly bilingual in both, English was generally the second language. The acclimatizing of this language on the stage, so that it should be still a natural and not an artificial or an imitative thing, was more arduous than might be guessed and here Lady Gregory and Douglas Hyde (themselves bilingual) were the main resources. Her translations and the training she gave Yeats in the spoken idiom were the base of the tradition. But the ideal was his, before ever he possessed the instrument, and by reason of this ideal, this instinctive choice of a language old and honest and alive, he achieved two great things ; he gave a vital direction to the tradition of Abbey Theatre dialogue in the early years and, later, he rescued from the sterile task of French art criticism the master genius of the movement, sending Synge to the Aran islands to learn Irish and become a playwright.

That idiom of the Irish-thinking people of the west . . . is the only good English spoken by any large number of Irish people to-day, and we must found good literature on a living speech, seeing ' the difference between dead and living words, between words that meant something years ago and words tha. have the only thing that gives literary quality—personality, the breath of men's mouths '.[1] Falstaff gives one the sensation of reality, and when one remembers the abundant vocabulary of a time when all but everything present to the mind was present to the senses, one imagines that his words were but little magnified from the words of such a man in real life. Language was alive then, alive as it is in Gaelic to-day, as it is in English-speaking Ireland where the schoolmaster or the newspaper has not corrupted it. I know that we are at the mere beginning laboriously learning our craft, trying our hands in little plays for the most part, that we may not venture too boldly in our ignorance ; but I never hear the vivid, picturesque, ever-varied language of Mr. Synge's persons without feeling that the great collaborateur has his finger in our business. May it not be that the only realistic play that will live as Shakespeare has lived, as Calderon has lived, as the Greeks have lived, will arise out of the common life, where language is as much alive as if it were new come out of Eden ?[2]

Looking back upon this from the year 1935, he added a word upon these early ideals in language, ' I was fresh from my struggle with Victorian rhetoric. I began to test my poetical inventions by translating them into like speech. Lady Gregory had already, I think, without knowing it, begun a transformation of her whole mind into the mind of the people, begun " to think like a wise man " but to express herself like " the common people".'[3]

But just as ' the only thing that gives literary quality ' to language is ' the breath of men's mouths ', the common use

[1] *Samhain*, 1902. (*P.C.* 29, 31.) cf. also *Samhain*, 1903 (*P.C.* 46–7) and *Samhain*, 1906 (*P.C.* 168–70).

[2] *Samhain*, 1904. (*P.C.* 119–20.) See also, for comparison with these early ideals, the illuminating comments on the language of Moore's, Hyde's and his own dramatic dialogue, *D.P.* 60–7.

[3] *D.P.* 67.

that means life, so the new drama must live in terms of *its* common life, the theatre. That the theatre made the drama they all in different ways believed, and from the start even Yeats himself would watch the reception of a play, as he did that of *Countess Cathleen* [1] and alter it time and again, ' every alteration tested by performance', and Synge, planning the *Playboy* would recast the whole first act so that it might fit the limitations of the Abbey stage. This was more than a concession to expediency ; it was a fundamental principle of the movement, an ideal of practised discipline as steadily held as those that directed their policy and the practice of acting, speech and setting. The ' workshop' aspect of their experience (which must be considered separately in the next section of this chapter) was also a conscious part of their ideal.

As the living imagination inspired the play and the theatre moulded it, so the acting and the setting were to serve as subsidiary arts, to bring it forth with simplicity, naturalness and, if need be, ' remoteness'. In two of the *Samhain* papers, Yeats sets down clearly his idea of the function and of the kind of acting and setting he desired. The first, the significant article of 1903, which helped to bring Miss Horniman's sympathy and help, begins with the uncompromising declaration, ' I think the theatre must be reformed in its plays, its speaking, its acting, and its scenery', for ' there is nothing good about it at present'. The second, a year later, announces Miss Horniman's offer of the Abbey Theatre and repeats his claims in a slightly fuller form, but with unchanged intention.[2]

In speech, gesture and setting he would have simplification of everything that might detract from or interfere with the verse or prose cadences of the words and the intensity of the emotion ; speech accompanying the words without being their rival, gesture in the same way accompanying speech, and setting, simple in form and colour, deferring to both. ' There must be nothing unnecessary, nothing that will distract the attention,' no ' restless mimicries of the surface of life '.

Speech, and especially verse speech, must be both audible

---

[1] See *D.P.* 39, and notes to the play in *P.C.* (290–1).
[2] *Samhain*, 1903 (*P.C.* 45–9) and *Samhain*, 1904 (*P.C.* 116–37). cf. also *P.C.* 20–4, 68–9, 71–2, 179–86, 205, 300, *D.P.* 80, and *O.I.T.* 35–6, 98.

and musical—the sacrifice of either to the other (and both were possible in 1904 as both are in one way or another to-day) he found intolerable. But the musical speaking of verse so that it should at the same time be audible and simple was an art which had to be raised again from nothing and the prose works of Yeats are full of references to the experiments of Mr. Dolmetsch and Miss Florence Farr and to his own and Frank Fay's applications or additions :

An actor must so understand how to discriminate cadence from cadence, and so cherish the musical lineaments of verse or prose, that he delights the ear with a continual varied music. . . . When one wishes to make the voice immortal and passionless, as in the Angel's part in my *Hour Glass*, one finds it desirable for the player to speak always upon pure musical notes, written out beforehand and carefully rehearsed. On the one occasion when I heard the Angel's part spoken in this way with entire success, the contrast between the crystalline quality of the pure notes and the more confused and passionate speaking of the Wise Man was a new dramatic effect of great value.[1]

But next to speech in importance, and of great possible help or hindrance to it, is gesture, and again and again Yeats argues against the fidgety 'business' of the professional or semi-professional actor of his time, praises the stillness of amateurs who did not move about much because no one had ever taught them that they ought to, and builds up the new tradition, at least for poetic, romantic and tragic drama, from this foundation :

That we may throw emphasis on the words in poetical drama, above all where the words are remote from real life as well as in themselves exacting and difficult, the actors must move, for the most part, slowly and quietly, and not very much, and there should be something in their movements decorative and rhythmical as if they were paintings on a frieze. . . . Then, too, one must be content to have long quiet moments, long grey spaces, long level reaches, as it were—the leisure that is in all fine life—for what we may call the business-will in a high state of activity is not everything, although contemporary drama knows of little else.[2]

---

[1] *Samhain*, 1904. (*P.C.* 128–9.) Compare the later comments in the notes to the volume *Plays*, especially that on the music for the plays (pp. 433–5).

[2] *Samhain*, 1904. (*P.C.* 132–3.)

This repeats almost exactly the ideal expressed in an earlier paper (*Samhain*, 1902) [1] where Yeats describes the Fays' production of A.E.'s *Deirdre*.

If Yeats was ' the advocate of the poetry as against the actor ', he was equally ' the advocate of the actor as against the scenery ', seeing justly the ascending importance of these three in the dramatic hierarchy. Half an hour spent with photographs of settings or designs for settings made during the nineties or the early years of the twentieth century will put the reader in a position to appreciate the tradition that Yeats had to fight. In England certainly and often even on the Continent, elaboration of detail in setting and background confused the impression of the play, and even in some of the most beautiful picture effects of, say, Reinhardt's early period, the effect of the picture is so rich that the actor can only be an intrusion upon it or be lost in it.[2]

The whole of Yeats's passage upon this is extremely interesting and contains much wholesome admonition, by no means dead or useless to-day. I quote a part of it :

The background should be of as little importance as the background of a portrait-group, and it should, when possible, be of one colour or of one tint, that the persons on the stage, wherever they stand may harmonise with it or contrast with it and preoccupy our attention. Their outline should be clear and not broken up into the outline of windows and wainscotting, or lost into the edges of colours.

This is true even of ' a play which copies the surface of life in its

---

[1] ' They showed plenty of inexperience, especially in the minor characters, but it was the first performance I had seen since I understood these things in which the actors kept still enough to give poetical writing its full effect upon the stage. I had imagined such acting, though I had not seen it, and had once asked a dramatic company to let me rehearse them in barrels that they might forget gesture and have their minds free to think of speech for a while. The barrels, I thought, might be on castors, so that I could shove them about with a pole when the action required it.' *Samhain*, 1902. (*P.C.* 20.)

[2] In England one might instance the Irving and the Tree settings, from the eighteen-eighties to the period of the European war. Excellent examples of the early Reinhardt designs will be found in his settings of *The Merchant of Venice* (1905) in such a volume as Fuerst and Hume's *Twentieth Century Stage Decoration*, 1928.

dialogue '. But the settings of poetic drama must be handled more imaginatively. For poetic drama,

We should be content to suggest a scene upon a canvas, whose vertical flatness we accept and use, as the decorator of pottery accepts the roundness of a bowl or a jug. Having chosen the distance from naturalism, which will keep one's composition from competing with the illusion created by the actor, who belongs to a world with depth as well as height and breadth, one must keep this distance without flinching. The distance will vary according to the distance the playwright has chosen, and especially in poetry, which is more remote and idealistic than prose, one will insist on schemes of colour and simplicity of form, for every sign of deliberate order gives remoteness and ideality.

Such a decoration,

will not only give us a scenic art that will be a true art because peculiar to the stage, but it will give the imagination liberty and without returning to the bareness of the Elizabethan stage. The poet cannot evoke a picture to the mind's eye if a second-rate painter has set his imagination of it before the bodily eye ; but decoration and suggestion will accompany our moods, and turn our minds to meditation, and yet never become obtrusive or wearisome. The actor and the words put into his mouth are always the one thing that matters, and the scene should never mean anything to the imagination until the actor is in front of it.[1]

This expression of the true relation of producer to dramatist —the fullest exercise of the imagination in a high degree of reverence—had never been more clearly understood in that generation.

Thus was conceived the theatre ' with a base of realism and an apex of beauty '.

II

Such, then, were the ideals which were carried into the workshop.

---

[1] *Samhain*, 1904. (*P.C.* 133–5 *passim*.) A belief emphasized again in our own day by Wilson Knight in his *Principles of Shakespearian Production* (1936). Yeats is abreast of the contemporary Parisian movement, as he shows in his comment on Appia and Fortuni at the end of this same article. There is much, though, in his ideal that points forward still further, to the work of to-day (or yesterday) in the studios of Fuerst, Baty, Pitoëff or St. Denis.

Just as, in outlining these, we drew mainly upon the early prose commentaries of Yeats, so now, in watching the triumphant emergence of these ideals from the theatre workshop, we must draw chiefly upon Lady Gregory's records. For the contributions that she was able to make to our knowledge of their methods of playwriting depend upon a certain eager, exploring naïveness in her approach to the experience. She had never thought of writing plays before and so had no defined ideals ; she had not even (as she tells us) taken much interest in the theatre, and so had no theories. Suddenly she found herself immersed in the affairs of a small theatre where everyone took a hand in everything and, in an incredibly short time, discovered that she was one of its playwrights. No wonder that the experience was startling, and no wonder, with her practical temperament, that her interest, in so far as she had leisure for reflexion at all, fastened on *how* she did it. It was a matter for delighted speculation and, with that simple directness in which lay a great part of her power, she continued through most of her career as a dramatist to make comments (all too brief) on the strange process at work in her. Being utterly unpreoccupied with herself, she was free to consider it with a detachment that makes her records read like a case-book :

I began by writing bits of dialogue, when wanted. Mr. Yeats used to dictate parts of *Diarmuid and Grania* to me, and I would suggest a sentence here and there. Then I, as well as another, helped to fill in spaces in *Where There is Nothing.* . . . Later in the year we wrote together *Kathleen ni Houlihan.* . . . For *The Pot of Broth* also I wrote dialogue and I worked as well at the plot and the construction of some of the poetic plays, especially *The King's Threshold* and *Deirdre* ; for I had learned by this time a good deal about playwriting to which I had never given thought before.[1]

Thus Lady Gregory slid imperceptibly into playwriting, with an intermediate stage of drafting scenarios for Douglas Hyde.[2] Once started, there was no holding her back, for the ' desire for experiment is like fire in the blood ', and with a soundness of

[1] *O.I.T.* 80–3 *passim.*
[2] For *The Marriage* and *The Poorhouse.* (See *O.I.T.* 83.) *The Poorhouse* was afterwards re-written in English by Lady Gregory and became the well-known *Workhouse Ward.*

dramatic instinct amazing in a woman who had taken no conscious interest in the theatre till after middle life, she set with gusto about exploring themes, mediums and forms, always in the direction of economy and concentration :

> The success of this set me to cutting down the numbers of parts in later plays until I wrote *Grania* with only three persons in it, and *The Bogie Men* with only two. I may have gone too far, and I have, I think, given up an intention I at one time had of writing a play for a man and a scarecrow only, but one has to go on with experiment or interest in creation fades, at least so it is with me.[1]

With Lady Gregory, dramatic theory is almost entirely practice ; it is reduced, that is to say, to a few brief records of what she was prompted to try, how it worked out and what it led to in its turn. And the three are so nearly simultaneous that she never has a theory about how a thing is to be done until she comes to do it.[2] Then, a few notes, a diagram or two in different coloured pencils, the sudden synthesis of one or two reminiscences or dreams, and the play shapes, as often as not into a comedy when she meant a tragedy, or with the main figure a character she had not intended to appear. It is the experience of the workshop uncontaminated, and utterly absorbed.

But her experience is not unique ; it is only the shock of the discovery and its effect upon her way of discussing it that is peculiarly her own. The actual processes are shared with her fellow-dramatists, for they are the outcome of certain of those

[1] *O.I.T.* 90. We could wish the play ' for a man and a scarecrow only ' had been written, if but for the interesting comparison it might have offered with Scene III of Kaiser's *Von Morgens bis Mitternachts*.

[2] ' I had had from the beginning a vision of historical plays being sent by us through all the counties of Ireland. . . . I began with the daring and light-heartedness of a schoolboy to write a tragedy in three acts upon a great personality, Brian the High King. I made many bad beginnings, and if I had listened to Mr. Yeats's advice I should have given it up, but I began again and again till it was at last moulded into at least a possible shape.' (*O.I.T.* 91–2.)

' I suppose it is that " fascination of things difficult " that has tempted me to write a three-act play with only three characters. [*Grania*] . . . When I told Mr. Yeats I had but these three persons in the play, he said incredulously, " They must have a great deal to talk about." And so they have, for the talk of lovers is inexhaustible, being of themselves and one another.' (*I.F.H.* i. 195–6.)

common ideals, which demanded a basis of reality—acceptance of the facts, not only of the life they described but of the nature of their medium—supporting the apex of beauty. When we watch the ideals passing through the workshop it is necessarily this 'basis of reality', the conditions imposed by the theatre, which dramatic poetry must use and subdue, that become clearer for the moment than the poetic ideals towards which they worked.

We see in her notes and historical records the playwright in the theatre ; we watch the theatre making the drama as surely as the drama makes, in its turn, the theatre ; we follow some of the dramatist's experience frankly and simply set out ; we see the give and take between the different workers—playwrights, actors, producers, designers—and the slow emergence of certain well-tested habits, such as the use of a special dialect, which had such far-reaching consequences in the work of their immediate successors.[1] We hear, too, more of the actual process of collaboration than is to be found in conjunction with any other similar body of drama.

The influence of the theatre on the written drama is astonishing, though probably not greater than we should find it if we had similar records for the Elizabethan age. What was first intended as tragedy turns to comedy because comedy is at first the rarer kind and is needed. *Spreading the News*, perhaps the happiest of all those plays which ' Lady Gregory calls a comedy and everybody else a farce ', began with a picture much nearer the mood of *The Gaol Gate*. But there does not seem to have been any artificial violence done to the idea. Her own statement, ' I let laughter have its way ', suggests rather that the starting point was an idea, that of the ' sudden story ' rising ' out of a chance word ', that this was coloured by the mood which she allowed to illuminate it and that the central pictures from which the actual play developed grew from that :

The idea of the play came to me as a tragedy. I kept seeing as in a picture people sitting by the roadside, and a girl passing to the

[1] There is an interesting description of the development of the folk dialect in Yeats's notes (*Plays* 419–21) where he speaks of the different stages it went through in *Cathleen ni Houlihan* and *The Pot of Broth* on its way to full growth in the work of Lady Gregory and Synge.

market, gay and fearless. And then I saw her passing by the same place at evening, her head hanging, the heads of others turned from her, because of some sudden story that had risen out of a chance word, and had snatched away her good name.

But comedy and not tragedy was wanted at our theatre to put beside the high poetic work, *The King's Threshold*, *The Shadowy Waters*, *On Baile's Strand*, *The Well of the Saints*; and I let laughter have its way with the little play. I was delayed in beginning it for a while, because I could only think of Bartley Fallon as dull-witted or silly or ignorant, and the handcuffs seemed too harsh a punishment. But one day by the sea at Duras a melancholy man who was telling me of the crosses he had gone through at home said—'But I'm thinking if I went to America, it's long ago to-day I'd be dead. And it's a great expense for a poor man to be buried in America.' Bartley was born at that moment, and, far from harshness, I felt I was providing him with a happy old age in giving him the lasting glory of that great and crowning day of misfortune.[1]

Sometimes the material to be included and the very form and the order of its presentation were determined by severe practical needs, as when Synge altered his original planning of the first act of *The Playboy*, leaving out altogether ' the opening act in the ploughed field, where the quarrel between Christy and his father took place ', because ' when he thought of the actual stage, he could not see any possible side wings for that " wide, windy corner of high distant hills " '.[2] The smallness of the stage and of the company and the impossibility of even indicating a crowd in the early years made Lady Gregory pare

[1] *S.S.P.* 196–7. With this we may compare the following note on the coming together in her mind of the elements of *Aristotle's Bellows* : ' I have been looking at its first scenario, made according to my habit in rough pen and ink sketches, coloured with a pencil blue and red, and the changes from that early idea do not seem to have been very great. . . . As to the machinery of the play, the spell was first to have been worked by a harp hung up by some wandering magician, and that was to work its change according to the wind, as it blew from north to south, east or west. But that would have been troublesome in practice, and the Bellows having once entered my mind, brought there I think by some scribbling of the pencil that showed Corran protecting himself with an umbrella, seemed to have every necessary quality, economy, efficiency, convenience.' *T.W.P.* 213–15. (Compare also *I.F.H.* ii. 195–6, 205, *N.I.C.* 159–61, *S.S.P.* 201–2.)

[2] *O.I.T.* 131–2.

down the characters of *Kincora* so that in the end she ' used but servants and kings '.

Nor did it stop at this, for when the play was put into rehearsal it was still regarded, even by the playwrights themselves, as more or less plastic material, and this to a far greater degree than is usual during the testing stages of production. Yeats more than anyone else—perhaps because his material was intrinsically less theatrical and needed more adjustment—made change after change of detail and even of content. The versions of *Countess Cathleen* are well known[1] and his attitude in this case is characteristic of his readiness, all through his career, to learn his craft from the audiences and actors themselves : ' Throughout the play I have added or left out such passages as a stage experience of some years showed me encumbered the action.' ' I have written a good many plays in verse and prose, and almost all those plays I have re-written after performance, sometimes again and again, and every re-writing that has succeeded upon the stage has been an addition to the masculine element, an increase of strength in the bony structure.'[2]

In a theatre as small as this, the co-operation between the different workers was necessarily very close and, indeed, many of them filled several functions at once. This meant an almost ideal condition of give and take between them, the playwright orders or designs his own setting and prescribes or advises on the acting and speaking, while a stage designer like Fay can teach the playwright in his turn much of the significance of his own play. Yeats has described at length (in *Samhain*, 1904) the kind of acting, speaking, movement and setting that he wanted for

---

[1] *D.P.* 39 ; *P.C.* 290–1, where the original conclusion is quoted in the notes.

[2] *Samhain,* 1906. (*P.C.* 187.)

The number of plays thus altered is very considerable. *The Hour Glass* has both a prose and a verse form, *Shadowy Waters* exists both as a dramatic poem and as a play and *The Unicorn from the Stars* was a re-writing of *Where There is Nothing.* Beside these there were similar re-writings of parts of *The King's Threshold, On Baile's Strand, Deirdre, The Land of Heart's Desire* and *Diarmuid and Grania.* For notes on these see *Plays* 422–8, *Later Poems* 360 (*Shad. Wat.*), *O.I.T.* 80–1, *D.P.* 82–4 (*Unicorn*), *Autobiographies* 348 (*Land of Heart's Desire*), *D.P.* 76 (*Diarmuid*).

his own plays,[1] and, looking back upon his experience as a working dramatist, admits the effect of a design (whether setting or mask) on the mood of the play :[2] ' If some fine sculptor should create for my *Calvary*, for instance, the masks of Judas, of Lazarus, and of Christ, would not this suggest other plays now, or many generations from now, and possess one cannot tell what philosophical virility ? '[3]

With the needs and character of his theatre clearly in mind, the dramatist set about his task. What happened there is to some extent the story of all dramatic composition, in so far as that is an artistic experience and not a business proposition. Lady Gregory gives us the best descriptions (chiefly of her own experience) because she is frank and simple and without prejudice. She tells us how her skill grew by experience and experiment, speaking of ' the fascination of things difficult ' even when the difficulty was so great that ' it gave me a great deal of trouble and I wrote many versions, for I had not enough of skill to wrestle with the mass of material, and I think I kept too closely to history '.[4]

Most interesting of all are her comments on how stories and characters formed in her mind by the fusion of scattered elements and of the unaccountable changes in the plays as they wrote themselves, for here she is speaking, with utter simplicity and without aesthetic theories, of artistic processes which are seldom recorded so clearly by a practising artist without a body of accompanying theory and explanation. Three episodes came together, a story she was told, a meeting with two Galway countrywomen and a political incident, all completely disconnected, which somehow linked themselves in her mind so that *The Gaol Gate* was formed : ' These three incidents coming within a few months wove themselves into this little play, and within three days it had written itself, or been written. I like it better than any in the volume and I have never changed a

---

[1] See above, p. 71–3 cf. also Lady Gregory's descriptions of settings throughout *O.I.T.* and her directions for the setting of plays of her own in *T.W.P.* 290 and *T.L.P.* 119–20.

[2] *P.C.* 332, *Plays* VI–VII, 420, 427–8.

[3] *P.C.* 332.

[4] Notes on *Kincora*. (*I.F.H.* i. 200.)

word of it.'[1]   The result is a play which, small as it is, some of her readers also like better than anything she has done.   The same fusion of episodes, personalities and incidents gave her the story of Moses as the image of Parnell's fate in *The Deliverer*[2] and the same process is at work in *Aristotle's Bellows* and *Shanwalla*.[3]   Naturally in the history plays, where she is less free, the elements fused are less surprising, less superficially disconnected.   But in the comedies and tragedies the coming together of the major images was clearly a similar experience to that revealed in the poetic imagery of Coleridge by Livingstone Lowes's exploration of sources.[4]

In most of these cases, she seems to have accepted the process without astonishment, but some of them were more bewildering.   *Damer's Gold* was almost entirely changed by the entry of Damer himself (one of those characters who ' put out little feet of his own ' and ran on them) : ' Damer comes in, and contrary to my intention he begins to find a tongue of his own. . . .   How that play will work out I cannot be sure, or if it will ever be finished at all.   But if ever it is I am quite sure it will go as Damer wants, not as I want,' and, later, ' The idea with which I set out has not indeed quite vanished, but is as if " extinct and pale ; not darkness, but light that has become dead ".'   In the same way *The Image* is ' not what I set out to do ',[5] *Hanrahan's Oath* ' comes short of the imagining '.[6]   These seemingly irresponsible changes which the characters or the material dictated are perhaps most happy in their effect in the Wonder Plays ; *The Dragon* and *Aristotle's Bellows* both seem to have shifted unaccountably in the making, but they are fairy-tales in theme and form and the weaving together of many elements and intentions leaves their peculiar harmony undisturbed.[7]   Even with *The Canavans*, which is rather a fantastic comedy than a strict history play, this is still true : ' The play seems (to me

[1] *S.S.P.* 201–2.   In *N.I.C.* (159) she describes its ' scenario in three lines '.
[2] *I.F.H.* ii. 195–6 (cf. *O.I.T.* 95–6).
[3] *T.W.P.* 213–16, *Im.* 222–4.
[4] See J. Livingstone Lowes, *The Road to Xanadu*.
[5] *Im.* 100.
[6] *Im.* 134.
[7] *T.W.P.* 131–2, 213–16.

now) somewhat remote, inexplicable, as if written less by logical plan than in one of those moments of light-heartedness that comes, as I think, as an inheritance from my French great-grandmother . . . a moment of that " sudden Glory, the Passion which maketh those Grimaces called Laughter ". It plays merrily, and there are some who like it best of my comedies.'[1]

The influence of this poltergeist apart, Lady Gregory seems to have written most of her plays in one of three ways, the swift and certain method of *The Gaol Gate* where one would guess the artistic experience to have been complete before she began to write and where she neither hesitated nor altered ; the laboured process of *Kincora* with its many revisions, which was probably characteristic of most of the serious history plays in greater or less degree ; and the irresponsible method where the elements re-arranged themselves as she went along and made their own adjustments, which is entirely successful in fairy plays by reason of their own peculiar content and form, but is not very happy in solider material such as *Shanwalla*. Judging from these and other records that she has made, one might guess these plays, where interference occurred after she had begun work, to be the form of confusion (familiar to artists) that comes of beginning the communication before the imaginative experience is far enough advanced or has taken on a clear enough form. The result is not an integral artistic experience, but merely its elements, exposed and confused, however skilful the theatrical technique that adjusts their surface relations.

One other aspect yet of the playwright's experience is revealed by the records and practice of these dramatists and that, their habit of collaboration,[2] is intimately connected both with their experiments as individuals and with their willingness to subordinate their technique to the demands of the theatre.

Collaboration occurred in one form or another between Lady Gregory and Yeats, Lady Gregory and Hyde, Martyn and

[1] *I.F.H.* ii. 189.

[2] The broader aspects of this question of collaboration have already been suggested in Chap. 1 (pp. 9–11) in considering the relation of the Irish records to those of other bodies of drama. All that remains to do here is to describe as far as possible in the words of the dramatists themselves of what kind it was and how far it went in the early days of the Irish dramatic movement.

Moore, and Moore and Yeats, all of which has been described in some detail in *Our Irish Theatre* ; Lady Gregory's account of her gradual entry into playwriting through collaboration has already been quoted.[1] To these should be added George Russell (A.E.), whose frequent suggestions of plot and detail, though sometimes to be classed rather as inspiration, sometimes amount to actual collaboration.[2]

Of these, perhaps the most interesting results are to be found in the short plays *Cathleen ni Houlihan* and *The Pot of Broth* by Yeats and Lady Gregory and *The Workhouse Ward*, which is Lady Gregory's re-writing of *The Poorhouse* in which she collaborated with Hyde. The alteration of *Where There is Nothing* into *The Unicorn from the Stars*[3] is not collaboration in the strictest sense, in which two artists share the imaginative impulse from the beginning, and still less so is the alteration of Martyn's *Tale of a Town* into Moore's *Bending of the Bough*, for, whoever did collaborate here, it was clearly not Martyn and Moore.[4] But apart from these well-known cases, to which we must now add that of the recently recovered, though long lost, *Diarmuid and Grania*, there was continual sharing of thought and idea, rectification of plot, episode and dialogue, between one member and another of this group, and much of the finest material produced owes something to other minds than the author's. This is co-operation, which one cannot help believing to be possible at any time when a group of people work closely together under similar conditions, with sympathy in artistic intention.

Perhaps the fullest account (apart from that of Lady Gregory which has already been quoted) is Lady Gregory's description

---

[1] Above, p. 74. See also *O.I.T.* 80-3, 105 (Lady G.+W.B.Y.), 83-90 (Lady G.+Hyde), 26 and 28 (Martyn+Moore, and W.B.Y.+Moore). And compare *D.P.* 65-6.

[2] Yeats says that he gave plots or incidents (*D.P.* 78) and Lady Gregory attributes to him the story of *The Image* (*Im.* 99) and acknowledges hints from him used fruitfully in *Aristotle's Bellows* and *The Jester* (*T.W.P.* 214, 288-9).

[3] For comments upon this, see *Plays* 425-6, *O.I.T.* 80-1 and *D.P.* 82-4.

[4] It is difficult to estimate the more genuine collaboration between Moore and Martyn in *The Heather Field* and *Maeve*. For the reports of these, see, *post*, Chap. 5, *Martyn and Moore*.

of the collaboration between herself and Hyde, and Yeats's tribute to her. The aesthetic consequences of the process are, further, discussed with considerable penetration by Yeats when he describes the effects which he and Moore may have had upon each other's styles during the period of close collaboration in *Diarmuid and Grania.*

In an open letter to Lady Gregory in 1903,[1] Yeats describes their collaboration in *Cathleen ni Houlihan,* ' I thought if I could write this out as a little play I could make others see my dream as I had seen it, but I could not get down out of that high window of dramatic verse, and in spite of all you had done for me I had not the country speech. . . . We turned my dream into the little play *Cathleen ni Houlihan,* and when we gave it to the little theatre in Dublin and found that the working-people liked it, you helped me to put my other dramatic fables into speech.' And again, speaking of *The Pot of Broth,* he says, ' I hardly know how much of the play is my work, for Lady Gregory helped me as she has helped in every play of mine where there is dialect, and sometimes where there is not. In those first years of the theatre we all helped one another with plots, ideas and dialogue, but certainly I was the most indebted as I had no mastery of speech that purported to be of real life. This play may be more Lady Gregory's than mine, for I remember once urging her to include it in her own work, and her refusing to do so.'[2] This is borne out by his account of her help in non-dramatic writing, where she gave the same kind of guidance in the phrasing of certain tales, and came to use one of them, in the end, for a play herself. ' We worked together, first upon that tale, and after upon all the others, she now suggesting a new phrase or thought, and now I, till all had been put into that simple English she had learned from her Galway countrymen and the thought had come closer to the life of the people. If that style has merit now, the merit is mainly hers.'[3]

All these are records of collaborations which grew up and developed gradually and in some cases were continued willingly. Rather different, apparently, was the joint work of Yeats and

[1] Quoted *Plays* 418–19.
[2] *Plays* 421.
[3] *Early Poems and Stories,* 528.

Moore on *Diarmuid and Grania*, where two totally different processes of mind came into conflict even while in collaboration. The union was deep enough to engage both minds completely for a time but not necessarily without harm. The very fact that danger was apprehended meant, however, that the artistic experience was closely shared :

Lady Gregory thought such collaboration would injure my own art and was perhaps right. Because his mind was argumentative, abstract, diagrammatic, mine sensuous, concrete, rhythmical, we argued about words. . . . Because Moore thought all drama should be about possible people set in their appropriate surroundings, because he was fundamentally a realist . . . he required many dull, numb words. But he put them in more often than not because he had no feeling for words in themselves, none for their historical associations. . . . Our worst quarrels, however, were when he tried to be poetical, to write in what he considered my style. . . . My letters to Lady Gregory show that we made peace at last, Moore accepting my judgement upon words, I his upon construction. To that he would sacrifice what he had thought the day before not only his best scheme but ' the best scene in any modern play ' and without regret : all must receive its being from the central idea ; nothing be in itself anything.[1] He would have been a master of construction, but that his practice as a novelist made him long for descriptions and reminiscences. . . . When in later years some play after months of work grew more and more incoherent, I blamed those two years' collaboration. . . . *Deirdre* and *Baile's Strand*, unified after I had torn up many manuscripts, are more profound than the sentimental *Land of Heart's Desire*, than the tapestry-like *Countess Cathleen*, finished scene by scene, but that first manner might have found its own profundity. . . . Yet, whatever effect that collaboration had on me, it was unmixed misfortune for Moore, it set him upon a pursuit of style that made barren his later years. . . . Style was his growing obsession, he would point out all the errors of some silly experiment of mine, then copy it.[2]

The results of the collaboration, the works of art directly and indirectly affected by it, justify the process beyond dispute whatever may be the adverse psychological effects of uncon-

[1] An interesting light is thrown by this comment upon the nature of the alterations he made in Martyn's *Tale of a Town*. (For some account of these, see *post*, Chap. 5, *Martyn and Moore*.)

[2] *D.P.* 62-4 *passim.*

genial collaboration too obstinately pursued, and the sidelight given us by Yeats and Lady Gregory upon the formation of the plays we know in their final form, is not the least interesting part of what we may call the workshop records of the company.

In watching these workshop processes we have been watching the living imagination passing into the theatre and there producing living drama, that living drama whose full growth is reached in the work of Synge, which, without the existence of the workshop, would not have been possible. Because of this apprenticeship of the living imagination in the workshop of the theatre, Yeats and Synge produced poetry that is an inalienable part of the world's drama. Despite satire, then or to-day, it is their drama still that has ' the walk of a Queen '.

III

At a later date some of these ideals and of this experience resolved themselves into a partial aesthetic theory. This is perhaps of less intrinsic value than the other, more unusual records, but, scattered though it is (mostly through Yeats's later prose), it always illuminates the particular aspect of drama that it touches. Often it gathers up one of the ideals with which he and the early leaders of the movement set out ; an idea of tragedy that they reached for, the kind of character that they tried to reveal and the way of revealing it (or the inter-relations of these two) and carry it on to a theory beyond that of the early movement, a theory that then becomes peculiarly his own. The same may be said of his early desire for remoteness in treatment of poetic drama, which extends into a highly interesting theory of the functions of certain plays, like the Nō plays of Japan, where dancers, screens and masks are the medium of production. But always the theory is suggestive, not dogmatic, and it is still as much an ideal of what might be as an assessment of what is or has been. For this reason it is not particularly profitable to compare it with the main interpretations of the nature and functions of drama that have been put forward from time to time, from Aristotle downwards, for it never claims to be a complete aesthetic of its subject, only a grouping of ideas upon certain aspects. Its virtue is germinal, not judiciary.

85

The theory of tragedy and its relation to character is in some ways the most interesting of these groups.[1] To Yeats, and to some degree to Lady Gregory also, character (that is the discrimination and definition of individuality) is a hindrance to tragic ecstasy and the revelation made at the moments of lyric intensity is not individual but generic ; as the emotional experience deepens and the character explores the profundity or intensity of his own passion or thought, he ceases to be a particular man and becomes every man, sinking in from the circumference of being to its centre. This does not, I think, mean that the form of play we call a tragedy must put before us only generic humanity, offer only archetypal figures broadly differentiated, but, rather, that, as the moment of tragic ecstasy approaches, ' which is the best that art—perhaps that life— can give ' the characters will be found to resolve themselves into mediums for the expression of the underlying major realities of their being. It may be that this transition will be the more significant for following a preliminary process of relatively clear individualizing, as is, I think, the case with Yeats's own play of *Deirdre*, but whether the character is first revealed, like Orestes, in generic terms or, like Hamlet, in the subtlest possible individual detail, it is still the tragic moment, and the man's bearing in face of it, that is the essence of the play. What goes before is predetermined by this ; for Yeats himself, it means, at least in theory, the elimination of detail throughout the study of a tragic figure and the relegating of this detailed revelation to the domain of comedy.

It is a theory that wins easily upon the mind when we think of the closing scenes of some of the major Elizabethan dramatists, of Webster, of Shakespeare, of Marlowe in *Faustus* and *Edward II,* of Middleton's *Changeling* or of Ford's *Broken Heart,* and more easily still when we consider Aeschylus or Sophocles. Yeats himself has indeed called some of these to witness, and though he refers always to specific plays and never to other men's dramatic theories, his subordination of character in tragedy reminds us again and again that Aristotle too gave it only second place, putting another aspect before it :

[1] The early statements on this ideal have already been referred to (see Section I, above).

IDEALS IN THE WORKSHOP

One dogma of the printed criticism is that if a play does not contain definite character, its constitution is not strong enough for the stage, and that the dramatic moment is always the contest of character with character.

In poetical drama there is, it is held, an antithesis between character and lyric poetry, for lyric poetry—however much it can move you when read out of a book—can, as these critics think, but encumber the action. Yet when we go back a few centuries and enter the great periods of drama, character grows less and sometimes disappears, and there is much lyric feeling, and at times a lyric measure will be wrought into the dialogue, a flowing measure that had well-befitted music, or that more lumbering one of the sonnet. Suddenly it strikes us that character is continuously present in comedy alone, and that there is much tragedy, that of Corneille, that of Racine, that of Greece and Rome, where its place is taken by passions and motives, one person being jealous, another full of love or remorse or pride or anger. In writers of tragi-comedy (and Shakespeare is always a writer of tragi-comedy) there is indeed character, but we notice that it is in the moments of comedy that character is defined, in Hamlet's gaiety let us say ; while amid the great moments, when Timon orders his tomb, when Hamlet cries to Horatio ' absent thee from felicity awhile ', when Anthony names ' Of many thousand kisses the poor last,' all is lyricism, unmixed passion, ' the integrity of fire '. Nor does character ever attain to complete definition in these lamps ready for the taper, no matter how circumstantial and gradual the opening of events, as it does in Falstaff who has no passionate purpose to fulfil, or as it does in Henry the Fifth whose poetry, never touched by lyric heat, is oratorical ; nor when the tragic reverie is at its height do we say, ' How well that man is realised, I should know him were I to meet him in the street,' for it is always ourselves that we see upon the stage. . . .

. . . Tragedy must always be a drowning and breaking of the dykes that separate man from man, and it is upon these dykes comedy keeps house. . . . We call this art poetical, because we must bring more to it than our daily mood if we would take our pleasure ; and because it takes delight in the moment of exaltation, of excitement, of dreaming. . . . And there is an art that we call real, because character can only express itself perfectly in a real world, being that world's creature, and because we understand it best through a delicate discrimination of the senses which is but entire wakefulness, the daily mood grown cold and crystalline.

We may not find either mood in its purity, but in mainly tragic

art one distinguishes devices to exclude or lessen character, to dimin-
ish the power of that daily mood, to cheat or blind its too clear perception. If the real world is not altogether rejected, it is but touched
here and there, and into the places we have left empty we summon
rhythm, balance, pattern, images that remind us of vast passions, the
vagueness of past times, all the chimeras that haunt the edge of
trance. . . .

Tragic art, passionate art, the drowner of dykes, the confounder
of understanding, moves us by setting us to reverie, by alluring us
almost to the intensity of trance. The persons upon the stage, let
us say, greaten till they are humanity itself. We feel our minds
expand convulsively or spread out slowly like some moon-brightened
image-crowded sea. That which is before our eyes perpetually
vanishes and returns again in the midst of the excitement it creates,
and the more enthralling it is, the more do we forget it.[1]

This idea of the relation of tragedy and character (most fully
defined in this essay on Synge's *Deirdre*), had begun at some
earlier date and was to go on developing. In *Our Irish Theatre*,
Lady Gregory quotes a letter from Yeats in which he speaks
of a play he is then writing : ' If I can make it obey my own
definition of tragedy, passion defined by motives, I shall be
all right. I was trying for too much character.'[2] Again and
again Yeats insists on lyric passion as the essential element, for
' passion and not thought makes tragedy '[3] and tragic emotion
depends ' upon gradually deepening reverie ',[4] passion itself
being ' but the straining of man's being against some obstacle
that obstructs its unity '. As early as the *Samhain* of 1904
he had defined his tragic ideal in the very process of becoming
a theory :

The arts are at their greatest when they seek for a life growing
always more scornful of everything that is not itself and passing into
its own fullness, as it were, ever more completely as all that is created
out of the passing mode of society slips from it ; and attaining that
fullness, perfectly it may be—and from this is tragic joy and the perfectness of tragedy—when the world itself has slipped away in death.

[1] *The Tragic Theatre*, 1910. (See, *The Cutting of an Agate*, pp. 27–35 *passim*.)
[2] *O.I.T.* 106. Unfortunately Lady Gregory gives no clue to the play
or the date and I have not been able to find anyone who could.
[3] *Plays* 429.
[4] *Plays* 423.

The same kind of development may be noticed in his theory of distance in poetic drama, the necessary remoteness that must be achieved by theme, language, producing and setting.[1] The idea begins early in the *Samhain* papers, as does the theory of tragedy, is touched on at intervals after that, especially in the article on *The Noble Plays of Japan* written in 1916,[2] and forms a main part of his theory of mask plays to be found in the notes written in the same year to the *Four Plays for Dancers*. In the earlier period, especially in the *Samhain* of 1904, he is working out the terms of the necessary ' distance from naturalism' in setting, which ' will vary according to the distance the playwright has chosen, and especially in poetry, which is more remote and idealistic than prose' and already he suggests that ' every sign of deliberate order gives remoteness and ideality'. In describing, some twelve years later, the Nō plays or his own plays for dancers he finds remoteness best achieved by the absence of the mechanical means of illusion commonly used in western European theatres. ' These masked players' [in *At the Hawk's Well*] ' seem stranger when there is no mechanical means of separating them from us', and so poetic drama frees itself from scenery, footlights, a separated stage and even from the doubtful service of facial expression and naturalistic gestures and tones; for intimacy and remoteness are paradoxically akin:

My play is made possible by a Japanese dancer whom I have seen dance in a studio and in a drawing-room and on a very small stage lit by an excellent stage-light. In the studio and in the drawing-room alone, where the lighting was the light we are most accustomed to, did I see him as the tragic image that has stirred my imagination. There, where no studied lighting, no stage-picture made an artificial world, he was able . . . to recede from us into some more powerful life. Because that separation was achieved by human means alone, he receded, but to inhabit as it were the deeps of the mind. One realised anew, at every separating strangeness, that the measure of all arts' greatness can be but in their intimacy.

All imaginative art remains at a distance and this distance once chosen must be firmly held against a pushing world. Verse, ritual, music, and dance in association with action require that gesture,

[1] See also Section I, above.
[2] See *The Cutting of an Agate*, 1–24.

costume, facial expression, stage arrangement must help in keeping the door. Our unimaginative arts are content to set a piece of the world as we know it in a place by itself, to put their photographs, as it were, in a plush or plain frame, but the arts which interest me, while seeming to separate from the world and us a group of figures, images, symbols, enable us to pass for a few moments into a deep of the mind that had hitherto been too subtle for our habitation. As a deep of the mind can only be approached through what is most human, most delicate, we should distrust bodily distance, mechanism, and loud noise.[1]

My theatre must be the ancient theatre that can be made by unrolling a carpet or marking out a place with a stick, or setting a screen against the wall.[2]

These two aesthetic theories, like certain other views of art which Yeats developed, are in close union with the early ideals he held for the dramatic movement and indeed seem to have grown out of them. Certain others, like that of the relation of self and antithetical self in the artist, though of deep interest, are not specifically part of the dramatic movement nor the immediate outcome of its experience. I have not therefore spoken of them.[3] But his theory of tragedy cannot be disregarded, for, once met, it takes possession of the mind ; it compels consideration and is, within its limits, sound and enduring. The same is true also in some degree of his belief in the necessity of distancing poetic drama by every possible means when writing and presenting it, in order that intimacy and universality may be achieved. The two theories are at bottom one, for remoteness from the individual variation allows of that universality of experience which may be intimately realized by the greatest number of individual minds ; and this, in tragedy, becomes the ' tragic ecstasy ' that dissolves character and substitutes for it ' passion defined by motives '.

Such, among others, were the aesthetic theories which emerged when the ideals of the Irish Dramatic Movement had passed through the workshop of the theatre.

[1] Certain Noble Plays of Japan (1916). See *The Cutting of An Agate*, 5–7.
[2] *Note on the First Performance of ' At the Hawk's Well '*, 1916. (See *P.C.* 416.)
[3] The reader is referred to *Per Amica Silentia Lunae* (especially the section *Anima Hominis*) and *The Trembling of the Veil* (*Autobiographies*).

CHAPTER 5

W. B. YEATS

' And I would have all know that when all falls
In ruin, poetry calls out in joy
Being the scattering hand, the bursting pod,
The victim's joy among the holy flame,
God's laughter at the shattering of the world.'

I

IN W. B. YEATS the Irish drama had not only a founder, an acute business man and a courageous fighter, but something without which these would have been barren, a visionary poet. His work as critic and guide of the movement has been spoken of elsewhere.[1] Here we are concerned with his service not to a movement and an enterprise (though these too were necessary) but to dramatic poetry, to that re-marriage of drama and poetry without which poetic faith is forgotten in the very theatre, which should be one of its chief strongholds. Whether or not he was primarily a dramatist matters little ; many of the Elizabethans were not, but they produced one of the greatest surviving bodies of drama. He was, or made himself, enough of a dramatist for his purpose ; he apprenticed himself to stage technique, and his belief in the theatre as the vehicle of poetry was strong enough for him to work with endless patience at the expression of his vision in dramatic form. His plays, even the earliest, are not lyric or narrative poetry loosely attached to a dramatic form ; no more are they the drama of the library only, as were perforce those of the English poets of the nineteenth century. The union, however new to his century, was integral, not incidental.

In the early plays, *Land of Heart's Desire*, *The Countess Cathleen*

---

[1] See Chap. 2 and Chap. 3.

91

and *Shadowy Waters,* he communicated his experience of certain aspects of beauty. Neither then nor at any other time did he allow influences which were not part of his artistic experience to affect his poetry or his drama. This is not, of course, to say that he did not accept all aesthetic experience that offered itself, even to the exploration of some of the stranger territories of metaphysical speculation, as in *Where There is Nothing* at the beginning of his career or *The Words upon the Window Pane* some thirty years later. But, strict as was his discipline in such matters as theatrical technique, he never allowed even the technique of the theatre so to interfere at the moment of conception as to modify the resulting material and its inevitable choice of form. This, though it did not always make for theatrical effectiveness (it did not, clearly, in *The Shadowy Waters*), made, in the long run, for something of far deeper value, the habit of and a testimony to that artistic integrity which is at once a severe, positive discipline and the inseparable companion of great poetry. In the next phase of his dramatic writing, in *The Hour Glass, The Unicorn from the Stars* and *The King's Threshold,* thought and sensation deepened and clarified and both drew closer together, just as, in the heroic plays of the same period, *On Baile's Strand, Deirdre* and *The Green Helmet,* there was a simpler presentation, the implications lying deep beneath the surface of the words. This is still more noticeable in the five *Plays for Dancers,* where there was a plain confronting of mystery stripped of all unnecessary substance, narrative or dramatic, and most noticeable of all in the latest plays, *Resurrection, The Words upon the Window Pane* and *Purgatory.*

Meanwhile his conception of the artist's function, progressively revealed throughout his prose works and finding its fullest critical expression in *Per Amica Silentia Lunae* and *Hodos Chameliontos,* had reached high poetic expression in a play, *The King's Threshold.* There is, in a sense, no novelty in this for a poet who followed as naturally from his English predecessors of the late nineteenth century as did Yeats, upon one side ; it is rather in the fact of its expression in dramatic form, in the use of this theme—the proclamation of the absolute value of poetry—as the central action of a play, that the challenge

lies. For Seanchan's claim is Yeats's and allows of no compromise or evasion. This is no half-apologetic 'defence of
poesy', no sweet and reasonable plea for its acceptance or
deferential statement of its function. It is a flaming exaltation of that vision which is the symbol of all spiritual knowledge and the gift of the spirit beside which all other values
are disvalued. Poetry is either the root of life or it is nothing.
And so no compromise, however seemingly honourable, can be
considered, whether from kings or counsellors, lover or
disciples. Even Brand himself never proclaimed more un-
flinchingly the doctrine of 'all or nothing'. 'In principio
erat verbum. Et verbum erat apud Deum. Et Deus erat
verbum. . . . Et verbum caro factum est et habatavit in
nobis.' There, it is implied, lies the issue.

But if poetry is the root of life, its fruits are nothing less than
the undying life of man, that part of life which is heroism,
glory, joy, immortality :

> ' Cry out that none alive
> Would ride among the arrows with high heart
> Or scatter with an open hand, had not
> Our heady craft commended wasteful virtues.'

And the denial of its supreme prerogative would be the death
not only of what are commonly called the arts, but of the great
generative art of common life :

> ' If I had eaten when you bid me, sweetheart,
> The kiss of multitudes in times to come
> Had been the poorer.'

For Yeats, at this stage of his poetic experience, such defeat
was unimaginable. The poet dies, but his claim is unwith-
drawn ; he and his vision are exalted. The things that are
of the spirit are not mocked ; they are elemental and take
their own way, nor can they be broken or evaded or denied.
The voice that speaks through Seanchan is an echo of the voice
that answered Job out of the whirlwind. ' Where wast thou ? '
it asks of the principalities and policies of men, of their customary
law and habits, of the safeguards of practical life and prag-
matical wisdom, ' Where wast thou when I laid the foundations
of the earth ? . . . When the morning stars sang together

and all the sons of God shouted for joy ? ' The same challenge
of the eternal spirit to the perishable world of man's material
idolatry recurs again and again in Yeats's poetry, but in this
play, more clearly than anywhere else, it is the poet's vision
that is the symbol of the soul of the world :

> ' Cry aloud
> That when we are driven out we come again
> Like a great wind that blows out of the waste
> To lay the tables flat.'

This is the apocalyptic vision of the function of poetry ;
through poetry, something breaks in upon life, bringing with
it a terrible illumination from the world behind the world,
so that the immanent spirit passes suddenly from unseen to seen,
from hidden to manifest ; there can be no compromise between
it and the world, for what it declares is the ' Word ' and it is
' The prophet of the Most High God '.

It is, thus, at once the root of man's life and an integral part
of the invisible reality of which life is only a visible fragment ;
the poet's soul, like his intentions, draws from and returns to
an incalculable spiritual universe.

> ' Not what it leaves behind it in the light
> But what it carries with it to the dark
> Exalts the soul.'

' We perish into reality.' Nevertheless, the word *was* made
flesh and dwelt among us. Upon this issue there can be no
surrender.

This, then, is the nature of Yeats's poetic faith. It is absolute
and uncontaminated, but, being also a fighting faith, it finds
explicit expression as it did not always need to do in those that
succeeded him in drama, and had not necessarily in the great
nineteenth-century English poets, whose ways had been less
thorny. In the light of this faith the body of his poetic drama
and its function can, I think, best be approached.

II

His ideals, though he gave great honour to Ibsen and sometimes considered the movement in Scandinavia nearer to the

Irish than any other in Europe, were utterly different from those of the contemporary English playwrights who were busy developing a realistic stage technique, pre-occupied with what they called 'problems' and what Yeats called 'the surface of life'.[1] Instead he led back his age (primarily his Irish contemporaries, but ultimately many others) to a different reality, the underlying reality that reveals itself in poetic thought, in heroic and in romantic themes and that can open a world hardly explored before by English drama, a world concerned not primarily with daily life, but with things apparently remote from that actual life, 'those old stories of the folk which were made by men who believed so much in the soul, and so little in anything else, that they were never entirely certain that the earth was solid under the foot-sole'.[2] He tells us again and again that this is a deeper reality than any that can be reached by observation, for it is the reality of imagination and comes from collection, from the withdrawal of the poet's mind into itself, not from the effort to see and to record :

We lose our freedom more and more as we get away from ourselves, and not merely because our minds are overthrown by abstract phrases and generalisations, reflections in a mirror that seem living, but because we have turned the table of value upside down, and believe that the root of reality is not in the centre but somewhere in that whirling circumference.[3]

It is a truth that Englishmen are sometimes credited with perceiving less easily than the average Irishman ; but our supreme mystics, Wordsworth, Herbert, Vaughan, reach and hold it without faltering. The power to reflect this reality in art is, if I judge Yeats's view rightly, determined rather by vitality of spirit than by any specific activity of mind ; it can be reached only by believing his art to be the highest expression of the life of the spirit itself, and, for the dramatist in particular, by the possession of that living language which is spoken only by those to whom words are close to things and not abstractions, those for whom life had not 'driven the living imagination

[1] *Samhain* 5, 1905. (*P.C.* 155.) See also Chaps. 1 and 2 (above).
[2] *Samhain* 4, 1904. (*P.C.* 123.)
[3] *Samhain* 4, 1904. (*P.C.* 98.)

8

out of the world', in whom 'the imagination turned to life itself for excitement'. Such language, such poetry is filled with images and yet instinct with the spirit close behind all living sensation or speech, unconcerned with morality as such, unpurposed, except as life itself is purposed.

Blake says that a work of art must be minutely articulated by God or man, and man has too little help from that occasional collaborateur when he writes of people whose language has become abstract and dead. . . . But I never hear the vivid, picturesque, ever-varied language of Mr. Synge's persons without feeling that the great collaborateur has his finger in our business.[1]

It follows that a drama so conceived must be in some sense at a distance from life, having a quality of remoteness (not to be confused with unrealness), so that the ideal world, which alone is universal, can penetrate minds of all times, all classes, all nations equally. And this will be the most potent educative force in the world, though in a different sense from that in which Henry Arthur Jones and his English contemporaries were trying to make of their theatre an educative force :

Literature is to my mind the great teaching power of the world, the ultimate creator of all values, and it is this, not only in the sacred books whose power everybody acknowledges, but by every movement of imagination in song or story or drama that height of intensity and sincerity has made literature at all. Literature must take the responsibility of its power, and keep all its freedom : it must be like the spirit and like the wind that blows where it listeth ; it must claim its right to pierce through every crevice of human nature, and to describe the relation of the soul and the heart to the facts of life and of law, and to describe that relation as it is, not as we would have it be ; and in so far as it fails to do this it fails to give us that foundation of understanding and charity for whose lack our moral sense can be but cruelty. It must be as incapable of telling a lie as nature, and it must sometimes say before all the virtues, ' The greatest of these is charity.'[2]

In thus relating art to life he fought, as do all poets, a severe and individual fight before the chaos of life could be ordered

---

[1] *Samhain* 4, 1904. (*P.C.* 119, 120.)
[2] *Samhain* 3, 1903. (*P.C.* 57–8.)

into form. The first phase of this was, if I read it rightly, a process of selection from the material of life ; the conception of form clarified by elimination. ' I am trying to see nothing in the world but the arts,' he writes in 1906,[1] besieged by the manifold and distracting aspects, political, philosophic and aesthetic, under which life presented itself, yet seeking instinctively for that ' spiritual beauty which could alone uplift souls weighted with so many dreams ',[2] and free it from those forms that ' trouble His unity with their multitudinous feet '.[3]

At a later stage he recognizes these elements, formerly excluded, as an essential antagonist in man's spiritual drama, the antithetical self without which the poet cannot be himself, an unavoidable condition of the evolution of a great artist, that presence who comes to him, as to Dante, saying ' Ego dominus Tuus ' :

> When I think of any great poetical writer of the past . . . I comprehend, if I know the lineaments of his life, that the work is the man's flight from his entire horoscope, his blind struggle in the network of the stars. . . . We make out of the quarrel with others, rhetoric, but of the quarrel with ourselves, poetry. . . . Nor has any poet I have read of or heard of or met with been a sentimentalist. The other self, the anti-self or antithetical self, as one may choose to name it, comes but to those who are no longer deceived, whose passion is reality . . . for the revelation of reality, tradition offers us a different word—ecstasy. . . . We must not make a false faith by hiding from our thoughts the causes of doubt, for faith is the highest achievement of the human intellect, the only gift man can make to God, and therefore it must be offered in sincerity. Neither must we create, by hiding ugliness, a false beauty as our offering to the world. He only can endure the greatest imaginable beauty who has endured all imaginable pangs, for only when we have seen and foreseen what we dread shall we be rewarded by that dazzling unforeseen wing-footed wanderer . . . (this is) of all things not impossible the most difficult.[4]

It is in these passages that Yeats's vision of the spiritual

[1] *Samhain* 6, 1906. (*P.C.* 172.)
[2] *Rosa Alchemica.* (*Early Poems and Stories*, 469.)
[3] *Rosa Alchemica.* (*Ib.* 492.)
[4] *Anima Hominis* 15–24 (*passim*). cf. *Hodos Chameliontos*, Section IX : ' They have but one purpose, to bring their chosen man to the greatest obstacle he may confront without despair.'

evolution of the artist and the process by which it works becomes most sure. He knows what he is talking about and whether or not we care for the special image he uses to illustrate it, we know that this is the same in kind, if not in extent, as the experience revealed by the work of Shakespeare, of Aeschylus or of Beethoven. 'I understand why there is a deep enmity between a man and his destiny, and why a man loves nothing but his destiny.'[1] 'A hero loves the world until it breaks him, and the poet till it has broken his faith.'[2]

The conclusion of this phase is indicated in *The Hour Glass* (prose version) where the Wise Man makes the discovery that the perception of reality comes only with the annihilation of the self. Yeats is speaking in terms of universal experience, but behind it there lies, as there does behind Ibsen's similar conclusions in *Peer Gynt, The Master Builder* and *When We Dead Awaken*, the implication of the special experience of the artist :

' Go and call my pupils again. I will make them understand. I will say to them that only amid spiritual terror or only when all that laid hold on life is shaken can we see truth. . . . We sink in on God, we find him in becoming nothing—we perish into reality.'[3] 'Where there is nothing—there is God.'[4] Or, to turn back again to the prose commentary of *Per Amica Silentia Lunae*, ' I shall find the dark grow luminous, the void fruitful when I understand I have nothing, that the ringers in the tower have appointed for the hymen of the soul a passing bell.'[5]

The annihilation of the self once achieved, for the man or for the artist, the conflict of the self with the antithetical self is resolved also ; so that his interpretation of the relations between the form of art and the chaos of life is no longer, in his later thought, revealed in terms of these symbols. Manifold

---

[1] *Anima Hominis*, 31.
[2] *Anima Hominis*, 33.
[3] With this may be compared *Peer Gynt*, Act V, the second, eighth and last scenes, but especially Peer's speech in the last, ' Er der ingen, ingen i hele vrimlen ', with its climax of surrender, that is life :
　　　' de kan skrive derover : her er ingen begravet ' ;
　　　' og bagefter,—siden—! Lad det gaa, som det kan.'
[4] *Unicorn from the Stars.* (*Plays* 299.)
[5] *Per Amica Silentia*, 24.

experience, indeed, ceases now to be a potential distraction from the poet's perception of form, and becomes instead the material out of which he builds not only his art but the spirit itself which informs both art and life :

To seek God too soon is not less sinful than to seek God too late ; we must love man, woman or child, we must exhaust ambition, intellect, desire, dedicating all things as they pass, or we come to God with empty hands.[1]

It is a profound and live interpretation of the growth of the artist's mind and of his relation both to his material and to his achievement, an interpretation which holds good of more of Yeats's contemporaries and forerunners than might be supposed from a first acquaintance with the symbolism in which he offers it.

III

The plays which derive from the earliest phase of this reading of art and life are *Land of Heart's Desire*, *The Countess Cathleen* and *The Shadowy Waters*. These all went through many modifications as the author's views on stagecraft and theatrical effectiveness developed, but in no case was the fundamental quality of the play or the underlying thought sacrificed to the needs of the particular craft. They are all essentially poetic plays, the experience they denote is spiritual and they appealed to their readers' or to their audiences' innate imagination, not to the recognition of actual, everyday manners or events. They separate boldly, therefore, from the dominating influence of Ibsen's middle plays, where problems, even those that were universal in kind, were presented in terms of experience that was actual and immediate to the audience, and still more boldly from the contemporary English and French imitations of Ibsen where, if anything had to be sacrificed, it was the universality and not the immediacy that was lost.[2] The first two poetic plays of Yeats are not undramatic, except in a somewhat

[1] *Essays, 1931-6*, 129-30.
[2] With the later plays of Ibsen they have of course a closer fundamental harmony, but this is only to say that in his later plays Ibsen himself became again a poet.

arbitrary sense in which the term would be used as loosely equivalent to 'untheatrical', a sense which would rule out simultaneously certain exquisite medieval English, French or Dutch plays, a great part of the Greek drama and nearly all the English, French, Russian and American poetic drama of the twentieth century. They are, like all of these in varying degrees, made of stuff which, whether it belongs to the world of the saints or of the Sidhe is assuredly not wholly of this world. They derive, indeed, from a world of thought (in this case, Irish) 'made by men who believed so much in the soul and so little in anything else that they were never entirely certain that the earth was solid under the foot-sole' ;

> 'Do our woods
> And winds and ponds cover more quiet woods,
> More shining winds, more star-glimmering ponds ?
> Is Eden out of time and out of space ?
> And do you gather about us when pale light
> Shining on water and fallen among leaves,
> And wind blowing from flowers, and whirr of feathers
> And the green quiet, have uplifted the heart ? '[1]

It is a world known to all the early leaders of the Irish movement, to George Russell in *Homeward, Songs by the Way* and *The Earth Breath,* to Yeats himself throughout his life, to Lady Gregory when she allowed herself a holiday from the writing of comedy, to Edward Martyn, despite his sometimes unfortunate attempts to render it in dramatic form, and even to the later, realistic playwrights of the Irish movement, to Padraic Colum with his knowledge of the grip of the land upon the peasant's imagination, to T. C. Murray, with his understanding of the interplay of the seen and the unseen worlds. And there are not lacking signs that this world is returning to its own again in the most recent contemporary Irish drama.

Like most of Yeats's early plays and a large proportion of the later ones, these three are preoccupied with the theme of love ; the love of man and the love of the world that is beyond the world—sometimes the clash and sometimes the union of the two.

[1] Dedication to *The Shadowy Waters* (1900).

' By love alone
God binds us to Himself and to the hearth,
That shuts us from the waste beyond His peace,
From maddening freedom and bewildering light.'[1]

In *Land of Heart's Desire* the dramatic conflict is between this love and the deep, incalculable love of that old world of the Sidhe, where

' The wind blows out of the gates of the day,
The wind blows over the lonely of heart,
And the lonely of heart is withered away,'

and where A.E. would reincarnate the old gods in their spiritual glory, Yeats sees still an unresolved conflict, which he himself does not resolve until a later date.

In *The Countess Cathleen* the issue is far clearer, perhaps because it is founded on an old story, itself a morality play in germ,[2] and there is there already what later became one of the clearest qualities of Yeats's poetry and drama, the assurance of spiritual reality, whether in the flaming exaltation of *The King's Threshold,* the renunciation of *The Hour Glass* and *The Unicorn from the Stars* or the grim affirmation of *Purgatory.* Because of its origin in a folk tale the play defines not only the issue but the resolution of the conflict in terms of positive and simple doctrine, such as we do not find again in Yeats (though we may in Lady Gregory's Wonder Plays and moralities).[3] But it is significant that both imagery and metre have their maturest quality and their sweetest cadences in certain of the passages in which this definition is most simple and most clear, thus affirming by the surest of all indications, that it was

---

[1] *Land of Heart's Desire.* It is this same ' maddening freedom and bewildering light ' which became, in its turn, the driving force of *Where There is Nothing, The Hour Glass* and a large body of Yeats's later prose, verse and drama.

[2] For the source and circumstances of its writing, see Yeats's own note in *Plays and Controversies,* (pp. 285–91).

[3] It is odd, having so described the spiritual and ethical issues of the play (as it appears against the background of the drama of its time), to remember the violent onslaught made by certain of its contemporaries on this very play for heresy and blasphemy. (See above, Chap. 2.)

an integral part of the artistic experience from which the play results :

> CATHLEEN. Old man, old man. He never closed a door
> Unless one opened . . .
> For surely He does not forsake the world,
> But stands before it, modelling in the clay
> And moulding there His image.

> .   .   .   .

> ALEEL. [*To the Angel*]
> Look no more on the half-closed gates of Hell,
> But speak to me, whose mind is smitten of God,
> That it may be no more with mortal things,
> And tell of her who lies there. Till you speak
> You shall not drift into eternity.

> THE ANGEL. The light beats down ; the gates of pearl are wide
> And she is passing to the floor of peace,
> And Mary of the seven times wounded heart
> Has kissed her lips, and the long blessed hair
> Has fallen on her face ; The Light of Lights
> Looks always on the motive, not the deed,
> The Shadow of Shadows on the deed alone.
> [ALEEL *releases the Angel and kneels.*]

The love of Aleel and Cathleen is overruled by this universal love as is that of Seanchan and Fedelm in *The King's Threshold,* but in neither play is its glory denied ; it gives place only to a greater, ideal necessity. But in *The Shadowy Waters* the central theme is realization of ideal love in terms of, not by the superseding of, natural love ; a theme which recurs again in *Solomon and the Witch* and in the latest group of Yeats's Essays.[1] This is clearly defined in the early phase of the play :

[1] ' Maybe the bride-bed brings despair
For each an imagined image brings
And finds a real image there ;
Yet the world ends when these two things,
Though several, are a single light,
When oil and wick are burned in one.'
　　　Solomon and the Witch. (*Michael Robartes and the Dancer,* 1921.)

' An Indian devotee may recognize that he approaches the Self through a transfiguration of sexual desire ; he repeats thousands of times a day words of adoration, calls before his eyes a thousand times the divine image. He is

AIBRIC.   And yet the world
   Has beautiful women to please every man.
FORGAEL.   But he that gets their love after the fashion
   Loves in brief longing and deceiving hope
   And bodily tenderness, and finds that even
   The bed of love, that in the imagination
   Had seemed to be the giver of all peace,
   Is no more than a wine-cup in the tasting,
   And as soon finished.
AIBRIC.   All that ever loved
   Have loved that way ; there is no other way.
FORGAEL.   Yet never have two lovers kissed but they
   Believed there was some other near at hand,
   And almost wept because they could not find it.
AIBRIC.   When they have twenty years ; in middle life
   They take a kiss for what a kiss is worth,
   And let the dream go by.
FORGAEL.   It's not a dream.
   But the reality that makes our passion
   As a lamp shadow—no—no lamp, the sun.
   What the world's million lips are thirsty for,
   Must be substantial somewhere.

The end of the play is the achievement of the dream that thus
becomes substantial ' out of time and out of space ' :

   Beloved, having dragged the net about us,
   And knitted mesh to mesh, we grow immortal ;
   And that old harp awakens of itself
   To cry aloud to the grey birds, and dreams,
   That have had dreams for father, live in us.[1]

Two pairs of plays from the next period group themselves
naturally together, the early *Where There is Nothing*, with its

---

not always solitary, there is another method, that of the Tantric philosophy,
where a man and woman, when in sexual union, transfigure each other's
images into the masculine and feminine characters of God. . . .   When riding
into battle (Parsifal) prays not to God but to his wife, and she, falling into
trance, protects him.'   *Introduction to 'Mandukya Upanishad'*, Section VII.
(*Criterion, 1935*) reprinted in *Essays, 1931-6.*   (Cuala, p. 130.)
  [1] I have quoted in each case from the dramatic version, but it happens that
in each of the passages above the version of the poem is the same as that of
the play.

later form, *The Unicorn from the Stars*, and *The Hour Glass* in its prose and in its verse form. All are attempts to express in dramatic form a mystical experience which has for its culmination, in the first pair the words ' Where there is nothing there is God,' and in the second the words ' We perish into reality.' A corresponding phase in Yeats's aesthetic theory is represented by the resolution of the conflict between the self and the antithetical self.[1] The dramatic presentation in these four plays is rather concerned with the discovery of the truth to which in their different forms they lead, with the processes by which the mind feels its way to renunciation. There is considerable beauty in all of them and some at least of his readers regret the exclusion of *Where There is Nothing* from his collected works.

The difference of thought between *Where There is Nothing* and *The Unicorn from the Stars* is not great, for the best of the imagery and the great passage that leads up to the climax is substantially the same in both plays. But the accompaniments and surrounding symbolism have been altered so that while the texture of the second is undoubtedly more consistent than the first, we miss in the maturer play a certain wild, fantastic freedom of gesture that compensated all the improbabilities and extravagance of the earlier. Yet there is coherence of a kind in the original play, for it has, in the successive rebellions of Paul Ruttledge against the conventions of thought or social organiza-tion, a unity of atmosphere and purpose. It is the picture of a fanatic, an ascetic such as we might find in India or in the Arabian desert, in conflict with the stabilized thought and habits of a Western civilization. His inspiration rushes through the play ' like a great wind that blows out of the waste ' and lays all flat before it. In spite of certain weaknesses in the structure of parts of the play, the central figure has greatness, he is such a man as might, in Islam, have led a Jehad. There is in him a kind of nostalgia for primitive and essential holiness that brings back to the mind the early Celtic religious poetry

[1] See above, p. 96-8. Yeats's attempt to present the aesthetic conflict directly in dramatic form is recorded by him in his notes to *The Player Queen* (*Plays* ed. 1926, pp. 428-9), which he there describes as a farce on this subject substituted for the tragedy he had tried to write.

as does no other single play in the movement. The world
Paul longs for is the world the king's brother chooses in *King
and Hermit*.[1] But the later form, technically far less uneven
and more homogeneous, is weakened by the very things that
give it greater plausibility, by the fact that we are never quite
sure whether Martin is an inspired visionary or a bewildered
dreamer[2] and by the actuality of the surrounding figures with
their matter-of-fact criticisms and comments upon him. Lady
Gregory's influence (assuming her to be mainly responsible
for the figures of Martin's uncles and for the beggars), excellent
as it is in itself, does not succeed in making the supernatural
appear natural, but, rather, of giving a jarring discomfort
to the moods, as she does in her own *Shanwalla*, by the enforced
contact of two incompatible things.[3] Where, as in the earlier
play, this strange wind of the spirit mirrors itself in frank
improbabilities we bring to it more poetic faith and find,
I think, more poetry. There is no attempt to give greater
probability to the circumstance of the play by bringing the truth
of Paul's vision in doubt ; the author reveals it to us boldly,
leaving it to us to repudiate or to accept, *quia impossibile*.

Of the two key passages of the play, Paul's denunciation of
contemporary society in terms of and by the light of the Ser-
mon on the Mount, in Act 3, and the proclamation, in Act 4,
of the destruction of the actual to leave room for the real,
only the second was left in the later version. The first was
in any case less effective and was perhaps too blasphemous
for a generation that still rated the achievements of modern
society unduly high. But the speech to the monks in Act 4,

---

[1] See Kuno Meyer : *Ancient Irish Poetry*, for a translation of this poem.

[2] Even the highly imagined figure of Father John, which is in respect
of its beauty an unquestioned gain in the later play, does but contribute
to this doubt and so weakens the flaming paradox.

[3] I know that in holding this view I am in opposition to Yeats's own later
views, both in his annotations (*Plays* ed. 1927, pp. 425–6) and in *Dramatis
Personae* (Cuala ed. pp. 83–4). But I can at least plead a closer agreement with
his own defence of the play in its original form in *The United Irishman* (Nov.
1, 1902) where he defends it as a ' picture of the soul of man ' and explains
that we of to-day ' are interested in religion and in private morals and personal
emotion, and so it is precisely out of the rushing journey of the soul through
these things that Ibsen and Wagner get that tumult that is drama '.

that superb indictment of modern civilization which seems
to go straight back to the ideals of early Irish Christianity
and through that to a mysticism that is oriental in the elevating
of pure thought above the confusion of substantial forms,
remains for the most part intact in the later play and is a direct
link with the expression of a similar desire in *The Shadowy
Waters* and in *Anima Hominis*. I will quote from the early
(and not very easily accessible) play, rather than from the later ;
I think as much is lost as is gained by such modifications of
phrasing as were made in the second :

> PAUL. One needs a religion that is wholly supernatural, that is so
> opposed to the order of nature that the world can never
> capture it. . . . The walls are beginning to be broken up . . .
> we are going back to the joy of the green earth.[1] In the first
> days of the world when men came freshly from God they
> lived as God meant them to live. They were full of faith
> and hope and love and anger, for He had made them entirely
> living and living with every kind of life, and all life was the
> will of God. And in those days they lived in the woods and
> by the side of the woods, and they slept on the bare ground,
> and whatever they set their hands to, they had always about
> them dark and dawn and evening twilight and the green
> things. They lived always under the shelter of God's love.
> They had within them, therefore, the will of God, and His
> love was over them and about them. And as I gather these
> flowers to my heart, they gathered all His love into their
> hearts. . . .
>
> Then men ate the fruit of the tree of knowledge. And
> because when they lived according to the will of God in
> mother-wit and natural kindness they sometimes did one
> another an injury, they thought it would be better to be safe[2]
> than to be blessed, and they made the laws. The laws were
> the first sin. They were the first mouthful of the apple. We
> must put out the laws as I put out this candle.
>
> And then men began to make cities and build villages,
> because, when they lived in the midst of the love of God,
> that is the changing heavens and the many-coloured fields,

[1] Compare with this passage *The Unicorn from the Stars*, Act II. (*Plays*,
pp. 272–3.)

[2] Deirdre's discovery (in Synge's play) that ' there's no safe place on the
ridge of the world ', carries the same implication.

they were sometimes wetted by the rain, and sometimes cold
and hungry, and sometimes alone from one another. They
thought it would be better to be comfortable than to be
blessed. We must put out the cities as I put out this
candle.[1] . . .

God made everything holy because everything that is full
of life is full of His will, and everything that is beautiful is an
image of His love. But man grew timid, and called some
things holy and some things unholy, because it had been hard
to find his way among so much holiness. . . . And from these
and from like things he built up the Church. We must
destroy the Church. We must put it out as I put out this
candle. . . .

[2]The Christian . . . must so live that all things shall pass
away. He will so live that he will put out the body. (*Puts
out a candle.*) He will so live that he will put out the moon
and the stars. (*Puts out a candle.*) He will so live that he will
put out the whole world. (*Puts out a candle.*) We must
destroy the world. We must destroy everything that has
law and number, for where there is nothing there is God.[3]

Even the fifth act, which is perhaps less coherent, is shot
through with unforgettable, brief passages from Paul's preaching, which clear and emphasise all that has gone before : ' The
joyful individual life will return, everything will become
sacred, the laws will come to an end, and everyone will walk
about upon the hand of God.' ' Do you not know that death
is the last adventure, the first perfect joy ; for at death the soul
comes into possession of itself and returns to the joy that made it.'
' I have tried hard to live a good life ; give me a good death
now. . . . I go to the invisible heart of flame.'

The Hour Glass was described by its author as a morality,

[1] (A belief shared by (among others) Ghengis Khan.)

[2] Compare with this passage *The Unicorn from the Stars,* Act III. (*Plays,*
p. 299.) It will, of course, not escape modern readers that the same conception, in a different form, is to be found in the fifth part of Mr. Shaw's
Back to Methuselah, especially in the conclusion.

[3] I think the thought here is made clearer in the later re-writing : ' I thought
the battle was here, and that the joy was to be found here on earth, that all
one had to do was to bring again the old, wild earth of the stories—but no,
it is not here ; we shall not come to that joy, that battle, till we have put out
the senses, everything that can be seen and handled, as I put out this candle,'
etc. (*Unicorn from the Stars,* Act III. *Plays,* pp. 298-9.)

but it is of the modern rather than of the medieval kind. Its kinship is with the modern symbolic morality, such as the fifth act of *Peer Gynt,* with which it has interesting affiliations, and hardly at all with the strictly allegorical morality of the middle ages, (with the partial exception of the great Dutch play current in England as *Everyman*). Many themes are woven together, the enmity of reason and mysticism, the wisdom of the fool putting down that of the wise man and the reality of that other country which is masked by the actuality of this world. The conflict is symbolized by the two figures of the wise man who has put his trust in that reason that Blake abhorred[1] and the fool who, himself a nature-mystic after the kind of Wordsworth, sees in the common earth about him ' bright shoots of everlastingness '. The angel of death brings, as in *Everyman* or *Peer Gynt,* the command to the philosopher to set his house in order, and he begins, like them, to search the thought that has shaped his life for the elements which must now make his immortality. The rejection of reason (as later in *The Resurrection*[2]) is the beginning of his conversion ; utter renunciation of self, as in *Peer Gynt,* its climax. In his search for that faith which his reasoning had banished from the world he rediscovers the mood by which truth is perceived and the

[1] One of the clearest brief descriptions of the antithesis Blake perceived between imagination and reason is that written by Yeats as the Introduction to his edition of Blake's poems (Routledge, n.d.).

[2] This play lies, in point of date, far outside the scope of this book, but one closely related passage may perhaps be allowed here :

THE GREEK. Why are you laughing ?
THE SYRIAN. What is human knowledge ?
THE GREEK. The knowledge that keeps the road from here to Persia free from robbers, that has built the beautiful humane cities, that has made the modern world, that stands between us and the barbarian.
THE SYRIAN. But what if there is something it cannot explain, something more important than anything else ?
THE GREEK. You talk as if you wanted the barbarian back.
THE SYRIAN. What if there is always something that lies outside knowledge, outside order ? What if at the moment when knowledge and order seem complete that something appears ? (*He begins to laugh.*)
THE HEBREW. Stop laughing.
THE SYRIAN. What if the irrational return ?

The Resurrection. (*Wheels and Butterflies,* p. 125.)

processes by which the knowledge of it could have grown :
' Only amid spiritual terror or only when all that laid hold
on life is shaken can we see truth.' ' All creatures that have
reason doubt. Oh that the grass and the plants could speak !
Somebody has said that they would wither if they doubted.
Oh speak to me, O grass blades ! oh fingers of God's certainty,
speak to me ! '[1]

The final act of renunciation is further-reaching than Peer
Gynt's or than that of the medieval Everyman (shepherded by
the rites of the Church) : ' In manus tuas commendo spiritum
meum.' What Yeats has envisaged, it takes his contemporaries
to comprehend :[2]

All, all is plain now. We sink in on God, we find him in becoming nothing—we perish into reality. . . . We perish into reality
—strange that I never saw it until now . . . I am content to know
that God's will prevails, whatever that be. . . . May God's will
prevail, though that be my damnation. What was I born for but
that I might cry that His will be fulfilled upon the instant, though
that be my damnation. . . . I must make all plain to them, that
they may wish His will be fulfilled though that be our damnation.
There is no other truth.

A third group of plays that seem to fall naturally together
are those from the Cuchulain group of the old Irish heroic sagas.
These, though they have a considerable range in date,[3] have
certain fundamental likenesses which came not merely from the
theme but from a common reading of life not necessarily derived
from it, although *On Baile's Strand* and *Deirdre* are tragedies,
The Green Helmet a ' heroic farce ' and *At the Hawk's Well* and
The Only Jealousy of Emer among the plays for dancers written
for performance with musicians, screens and masked players.
Nor is this kinship the result of close following of the sources

---

[1] I have quoted here from the earlier prose version (*Plays,* pp. 59–60).
The verse form developes and extends the thought (*Plays,* pp. 358–9).

[2] If we go back to the seventeenth century the thought recurs more often,
especially in the poetry of Herbert. But, apart from that, it is I think, more
usual to find the experience revealed here by Yeats in certain of the English
mystical poets writing since 1918.

[3] *On Baile's Strand* 1904 and 1906, *Deirdre* 1906 (revised up to 1922),
The Green Helmet 1910, *At the Hawk's Well* 1916 and *The Only Jealousy of
Emer* at about the same date.

(few of them indeed *follow* the sources at all in any strict sense of the term) nor, as will be seen, from any uniform divergence from them. What (apart from the subject matter) makes us group them together is an essential realism in the revelation of character and motive, perfectly compatible with remoteness of theme and period (borne out as these are by setting and producing), a certain grim, penetrating knowledge of the fundamental processes of the mind and the underlying ironies and bitterness of life, which is as universal as the visionary desire of *The Shadowy Waters,* but universal now in terms of the psychologically actual instead of the poetically ideal.

This shows least fully perhaps in *On Baile's Strand,* the earliest play of the group, where the elements separate, the heroic gathering itself into the tragic story of Cuchulain's killing of his own long-desired son, and the ironic commentary lying partly in the jostle of this action against the scheming vagabondage of the blind man and the fool and partly in the tragic poetic irony that binds together the main action :

CUCH.   That's spoken as I'd have spoken it at your age. . . .
. . .   Boy, I would meet them all in arms
If I'd a son like you.

And, as Cuchulain goes forward in bewilderment, never quite recognizing, until he has killed him, in the youth from Aoife's country the son for whom he is longing, ' Life drifts between a fool and a blind man,' so that the two beggars' figures become symbols on a lower plain of the tragic confusions of the heroic theme. We find now the bitterness and the bewilderment of actual life, even if it be the high heroic life, rather than the vision of the world beyond it, which has been dominant in the other groups of plays.

There is a dry, sardonic mood in the ' heroic farce ' of *The Green Helmet* and this seems the poet's deliberate choice, for he has altered both mood and form of the old legend of the championship of Ulster,[1] transforming a bald and naïve fairy-tale into something charged with potency of quite a different kind, a grim and yet a heroic jest.. His play seems to lie closer than her narrative to the mood of the English version of the

[1] For Lady Gregory's version of this, see *Cuchulain of Muirthemne,* pp. 77-81, and, for her note on her sources, the same volume, p. 359.

generic legend in the great West Midland poem, *Sir Gawain and the Green Knight*; both, though widely different in form and tempo, are works of art, with the tautness and exhilaration of art. The closing passages of the play have the sage, if bitter knowledge of human moods and basic passions that we find in the later plays of this group, the revised *Deirdre* and *The Only Jealousy of Emer*. At the climax, which is also the close of the play, Cuchulain (like Sir Gawain) prepares to pay with his life the debt promised to the Red Man:

CUCH. Alive I have been far off in all lands under the sun,
 And been no faithful man; but when my story is done
 My fame shall spring up and laugh, and set you high above all.
EMER. [*Putting her arms about him*]
 It is you, not your fame that I love.
CUCH. [*Tries to put her from him*]
 You are young, you are wise, you can call
 Some kinder and comelier man that will sit at home in the
  house.
EMER. Live and be faithless still.
CUCH. [*Throwing her from him*]
 Would you stay the great barnacle-goose
 When its eyes are turned to the sea and its beak to the salt of
  the air.
EMER. [*Lifting her dagger to stab herself*]
 I, too, on the grey wing's path.
CUCH. [*Seizing dagger*]
 Do you dare, do you dare, do you dare?
 Bear children and sweep the house. . . .
 [*He kneels before the* RED MAN. *There is a pause*]
RED MAN. I have not come for your hurt, I'm the Rector of
 this land,
 And with my spitting cat-heads, my frenzied moon-bred band,
 Age after age I sift it, and choose for its championship
 The man who hits my fancy. And I choose the laughing lip
 That shall not turn from laughing whatever rise or fall,
 The heart that grows no bitterer although betrayed by all;
 The hand that loves to scatter; the life like a gambler's throw;
 And these things I make prosper, till a day comes that I know,
 When heart and mind shall darken that the weak may end
  the strong,
 And the long-remembering harpers have matter for their song.

In *The Only Jealousy of Emer* this interpretation of minds, bitter and yet heroic, is even clearer. In this case the original legend[1] had itself great beauty, but Yeats has so altered not only the story but its relations with the rest of the cycle that they are almost different stories. And the choice seems to be deliberate. Cuchulain's wife, Emer, and his mistress, Eithne Inguba, meet beside his seemingly bewitched body to draw back his soul from the Sidhe. It is Emer, the wife, who in the end succeeds, but to do so she has to bargain away her last hope,

> the mere chance that some day
> You'd be the apple of his eye again
> When old and ailing.

The Sidhe show her in a vision the ghost of Cuchulain, and, deep in his heart, his fidelity to her through all his faithlessness. She renounces, in order to free him from the Sidhe, the ' mere chance ' that that should some day be expressed and become the basis of their lives. He escapes thereby from the enchantment, but to call not upon Emer but upon Eithne Inguba.

The play, particularly in the speeches of the two women, is full of that tough, matter-of-fact wisdom that we recognize in all Yeats's later poetry. It does not lower the heroic mood here any more than the presence of the same quality in Shakespeare's *Troilus and Cressida* weakens verse or imagery :

> EMER. I am but his wife, but if you cry aloud
> With that sweet voice that is so dear to him
> He cannot help but listen.
> EITHNE.   He loves me best,
> Being his newest love, but in the end
> Will love the woman best who loved him first
> And loved him through the years when love seemed lost.
>
> .   .   .   .
>
> GHOST OF CUCHULAIN.   How could you know
> That man is held to those whom he has loved
> By pain they gave, or pain that he has given,
> Intricacies of pain ?
> WOMEN OF THE SIDHE. Was it from pity that you hid the truth
> That men are bound to women by the wrongs
> They do or suffer ?

[1] For Lady Gregory's version, see *Cuchulain of Muirthemne,* pp. 276–93, and, for her reference to her sources, the same volume, p. 360.

The one-act play of *Deirdre*, whether we consider it in its
original version of 1906 or with the later revisions which belong
chiefly to the year 1922[1] is a noble treatment of one of the
world's great love stories. In its final form it shows again
that hard, penetrating wisdom, that knowledge of human experience and motive which becomes increasingly characteristic
of Yeats's later work, and this without loss, but rather, indeed,
with gain, to the passion and the poetry inherent in the theme.
It does not cover the whole story as Synge's play does and the
virtues of the two are so different that there is little to be gained
by comparing them. Yeats's dramatic genius at its full maturity
turns naturally to a brief form, that chooses, with a reticence
almost Greek, the last phase of the tragedy that Synge revealed
at full length and with an extent more like the Elizabethans'.
Deirdre, Naisi, Conchubar and Fergus are isolated, upon a
background of chorus figures ; the fate that descends on them
comes swiftly, without more dramatic preparation than the
prologue-like conversation of the musicians. Within these
limits the play moves surely. The first part is rigid with suspense ; Deirdre and the musicians speak out their misgivings
of treachery ; Fergus hides and denies his with uneasy repetitions
of confidence ; Naisi calmly and unfalteringly overrides the
thought :

NAISI.   You would have known,
   Had they not bred you in that mountainous place,
   That when we give a word and take a word
   Sorrow is put away, past wrong forgiven.
DEIRDRE. Though death may come of it ?
NAISI.   Though death may come.

At the entry of Conchubar's messenger the suspense is broken
by a moment of false relief exquisitely contrived as the turning
point between the growing tension of the first part of the play
and the swift plunge to catastrophe of the second. From the

[1] See the author's own note in *Plays* (1926 ed., p. 425). For the purpose
of this study I have followed, as usually in cases of revision, unless I have given
specific reasons for not doing so, the later version, which the author himself
put forward as the form in which he wished the play to stand. For in this
chapter we are concerned less with the historical than with the permanent
value of Yeats's work.

moment at which Conchubar's treachery is revealed, the interest shifts from suspense, which had served its purpose in heightening the passions and laying bare the characters, to the contemplation of man's conduct in face of the inevitable doom :

> NAISI. What need have I, that gave up all for love,
> To die like an old king out of a fable,
> Fighting and passionate ? What need is there
> For all that ostentation at my setting ?
> I have loved truly and betrayed no man.
> I need no lighting at the end, no beating
> In a vain fury at the cage's door. . . .
> DEIRDRE. Oh, singing women, set it down in a book,
> That love is all we need, even though it is
> But the last drops we gather up like this ;
> And though the drops are all we have known of life,
> For we have been most friendless—praise us for it
> And praise the double sunset, for naught's lacking
> But a good end to the long, cloudy day. . . .
>   Bend and kiss me now,
> For it may be the last before our death.
> And when that's over, we'll be different ;
> Imperishable things, a cloud or a fire.

There is a swift recovery of the action, suspense followed by resolution, when Deirdre first tries to save Naisi's life at any cost and then upon the instant of his death sets her brains against Conchubar's and, in a superb piece of tragic acting, makes sure of her own death too. With a knife hidden in her dress she defies and beats down the old king's suspicions and goes out to look for the last time at her lover's body before giving herself to Conchubar as his queen. With her hand upon the curtain she turns and speaks to the chorus in simple yet double-edged words whose irony would befit the death-speech of an Aeschylean or a Sophoclean queen :

> DEIRDRE. Now strike the wire, and sing to it a while,
> Knowing that all is happy, and that you know
> Within what bride-bed I shall lie this night,
> And by what man, and lie close up to him
> For the bed's narrow, and there outsleep the cock-crow.

This has the authentic note of grim, tragic action, word and

deed following too swiftly for more than brief and memorable
comments. It is a universalizing of the old story, a realizing
of it again in terms of all human experience. The sources
which Synge followed with such wealth of poetic imagination
are here little more than the starting point. Yeats has travelled
far from *The Land of Heart's Desire* and *Countess Cathleen*.
There is no more remoteness from common experience, but,
instead, an immediacy as terrible as that of Middleton, severest of
Jacobean tragic poets. And it has been achieved as the Jacobean
and the Greek dramatists achieved it, not by the quenching but
by the exaltation of the poetic imagination.

The latest plays *The Cat and the Moon, Resurrection, The
Words upon the Window Pane*[1] and *Purgatory* cannot, in respect
of their date, claim to belong to the renascence of poetic drama
and the early Irish Dramatic Movement. But they are a
natural continuation of that work, and grow, equally with it,
from the inspiration by which Yeats founded the movement.
They have been referred to at intervals in this and other chapters
and they are as much a part of the later phases of the poetic side
of that renascence as are the later Irish, Scottish, English and
American poetic plays.

When we look back over the whole extent of Yeats's dramatic
work, various though it has been and continuously modified,
certain things stand clear. It is the stuff of poetry throughout.
In imagery, in the music of the verse and of the prose, there is
again and again an inevitable form, a simplicity, sincerity and
yet completeness that is poetry and that, however rich, subtle
or abstruse it may be in matter or thought, is not decoration or
ornament. In its content there is the stuff of life and of the
living imagination, whether its concern be something remote
from everyday event, yet rooted in men's hearts, or the passions
that are felt at once to be both universal and immediate. Finally,
and this I think goes nearest to the root, he is never once in
doubt that the reality of the spirit is more enduring than that
of substantial forms and of event. Was it not, after all, his
own great contemporary and collaborator who said, ' All
true poetry was written on the Mount of Transfiguration,

---

[1] See *Wheels and Butterflies,* (Macmillan, 1934).

and there is revelation in it and the mingling of heaven and earth.'[1]

Note:

The following are the dates (or approximate dates) of the completion of the main dramatic and critical works of Yeats that have been drawn upon in this chapter. For a complete list of the variant versions references should be made to Allan Wade, *A Bibliography of the Writings of W. B. Yeats* (London, 1951).

PLAYS : *Land of Heart's Desire*, 1894 ; *The Countess Cathleen*, 1899. 1911 ; *The Shadowy Waters*, 1897–1906 ; *Where There is Nothing*, 1902 ; *Cathleen ni Houlihan*, 1902 ; *The Pot of Broth*, 1902 ; *The Hour Glass*, 1903 (prose) ; *The King's Threshold*, 1903 ; *On Baile's Strand*, 1904, 1906 ; *Deirdre*, 1906 (revised up to 1922) ; *The Unicorn from the Stars*, 1907 ; *The Green Helmet*, 1908 ; *The Player Queen*, 1907–? ; *The Hour Glass*, 1912 (verse) ; *At the Hawk's Well*, 1916 ; *The Only Jealousy of Emer*, 1916 ; *The Dreaming of the Bones*, 1917 ; *Calvary*, 1917 ; *The Cat and the Moon*, 1926 ; *Resurrection*, 1931 ; *The Words upon the Window Pane*, 1934 ; *Purgatory*, 1938.

CRITICISM : *Beltaine*, 1899–1900 ; articles and speeches reported in *The United Irishman, Contemporary Review, Irish Statesman*, etc., c. 1899–1920 ; *Samhain*, 1901–8 ; *The Arrow*, 1906–9 ; *Anima Hominis*, 1917 ; *Anima Mundi*, 1917 ; *The Cutting of an Agate*, 1919 (Essays 1902–16, chiefly 1905–11) ; *The Trembling of the Veil*, 1922 (especially Books II, III, IV) ; *The Irish Dramatic Movement*, 1923 (Articles and Speeches reprinted from *Samhain, The Arrow*, etc.) ; *Dramatis Personae*, 1935.

[1] A.E. *Imaginations and Reveries* (' Ulster ').

CHAPTER 6

MARTYN AND MOORE

'Form is my beauty and my love.'

EDWARD MARTYN is a hard man to understand, perhaps impossible to an Englishman. He inherited on the one side the tradition of the West of Ireland gentry and peasant and on the other ' the grand aesthetic distinction of Catholicism ' and the citizenship of Europe. As man or as artist he leaves an impression strong beyond all proportion to any one achievement, and those who have written of him have made penetrating interpretations— which differ fundamentally. His attachments and his capacities were strong and incompatible ; the result less an organism than a state in conflict, bound together by a mastering will. Nature-mystic and satirist, devout pietist and ambitious dramatist, affectionate in friendship and a hater of women, ascetic in habit of life and cosmopolitan in culture, a Greek scholar, a lover of Palestrina and an acrimonious politician—no sooner do we settle upon one quality than its opposite comes to confound it. Various in interests and parochial in mood, a subtle and acute critic of Ibsen and as naïve as a child in his own estimates of men, it is easy to draw a series of portraits, but hard, to the verge of impossibility, to see the man.[1]

Moore has left picture after picture, unforgettably vivid, re-vealing through the medium of habits, clothes and mannerisms, the obfuscation of intellect and the immovable massivity of soul. ' One comes very often to the end of a mind that thinks clearly, but one never comes to the end of Edward.'[2] His other great contemporary, Yeats, briefer and more analytical, looks rather for the underlying structure of the mind. It was,

[1] Mr. Denis Gwynn's full length study *Edward Martyn and the Irish Revival* (1930), to which all students of this subject are indebted, achieves a synthesis which cannot be attempted here.

[2] George Moore : *Ave*. 134.

he says, ' As though fate had deliberately prepared for an abstract mind that would see nothing in life but its vulgarity and temptations. In the tower room, in a light filtered through small stained glass windows, without any quality of design . . . he had read Saint Chrysostom, Ibsen, Swift, because they made abstinence easy by making life hateful in his eyes.'[1] Even his admiration of ' the saturnine genius of Beardsley ' served to feed his ' hatred of life ' and ' I was certain, even then, I think, that he would never learn to write ; his mind was a fleshless skeleton.' ' What drove him to those long prayers, those long meditations, that stern Church music ? What secret torture ? '[2]

He was one of those men whose minds have been divided deeply and early by strong influences in conflict with each other and with the proper nature of the man, and whose lives, by consequence, are not a growth but a succession of actions, who survive rather by the sum than by the height of their achievements and whose vast energy passes into the stream of events without making for itself any one memorial commensurate with its force.

And the artist was like the man, a mass of conflicting tendencies and of inconsistent levels of thought. To study his eight plays is a baffling and in some ways a thankless task, for not many of them have great intrinsic merit and nearly all of them are contorted and spoiled by unevenness of intention and execution. Yet, hard to understand, he is also hard to turn away from, for his success and his failure alike lead directly to some major problems of dramatic aesthetics. Moreover the mind, and its record of deep and incoherent suffering, becomes dear to us. ' There is always the original pain,' a pain which Martyn, by reason of his tradition and discipline, never falsified nor weakly condoned.

He began his career in the Irish Literary Theatre with his best work—*The Heather Field* and *Maeve*, in successive years. In both these plays he seems to have owed something to Moore's advice

---

[1] *D.P.* 2.

[2] *D.P.* 3, 4, 5. There are other portraits of Martyn, but Yeats's close-cut agates are worth more than the others—as much, perhaps, as Moore's, in the final summation of the man.

in the structure and to Symons's in the style.[1] This complicates
the position but does not confuse it. For the later plays, that
Martyn wrote alone, show a consistent lack of dramatic and
theatrical tact and a consistent likeness of idea and theme. So
that much of the adroit stage-handling of *The Heather Field*, the
combination of speed and probability, the neat gradations to
the climax, even the relatively sympathetic treatment of Tyrrell's
wife and the balance that results, should, perhaps be credited
to Moore. As Yeats remembers it, ' He had constructed *The
Heather Field*, he said, telling Martyn what was to go into
every speech but writing nothing, had partly constructed
Maeve.'[2]

Martyn himself was never a dramatist, for all his love of the
theatre, and this by reason of one fundamental disability that
showed directly Moore's guidance went ; a lack of sympathy
with common human nature. Already in the early plays there
is a sharp distinction between two sets of characters, the few with
whom Martyn sympathizes—and the rest. In *The Heather
Field* there is some attempt to comprehend all the characters
and sympathize with each in turn, even, as has been said, a brief
and partly successful struggle to look through the eyes of
Tyrrell's wife. But, in view of the transformation worked by
Moore's hand in the one known case—that of *Tale of a Town*
into *Bending of the Bough*—it is more than probable that Moore
has here dictated the content if not the words of the play. But
the passionate sympathy with one group of figures, Carden
Tyrrell, Kit and Barry Ussher, is all Martyn's own and it appears
more strongly in the sharp cleavage between Maeve and Peg
Inerny and the other characters in the second play. These
people, and the central figures again in *An Enchanted Sea* (1902)
are all illuminated by Martyn's own nature love, which in his
earlier years was almost nature mysticism ; they are all symbols
of poetic idealism frustrated at the hands of coarser selfishness
and materialism. Increasingly, in these three plays, such characters call up the sympathy of the audience, and, increasingly,
Martyn's own sympathy is withdrawn from all the other
groups. In the latest plays, therefore, where there are few or

[1] See *D.P.* 50 and Gwynn, 122.
[2] *D.P.* 50.

no figures that live by this idea, the author seems to have no relation to his characters but indifference or hatred. The lack of sympathy that showed at intervals in the early plays has extended and engulfed them all.

We may say, then, that whatever were Martyn's powers (and they were strong) they were not those of a dramatist. He never lived in all his characters, each in turn. In all the plays there is more or less of Martyn himself ; they are composite of opinions, prejudices and passions. Even a theatrically neat presentation of character is often fundamentally undramatic because the speeches, however faithful to probability, are the work of objective observation, not of sympathy. Even the delicate psychological perception he shows in certain spheres is too limited ; it omits too much of common life. And the things he omitted lay at the root of common experience ; the relations of everyday men to each other and everything into which women entered intimately. As he grew older and the poetry of his youth died down, these became his only themes and *The Place-hunters, Grangecolman, The Dream Physician* and *The Privilege of Place* live mainly by his ' hatred of life '.

But in the earlier plays there were passages not unworthy of the poetic inspiration of Yeats, Hyde and A.E. Intimately related to the ideals of the national revival, it was yet individual, sharp-flavoured and distinct from that of any of the other members of the group. So distinctive is it, and yet so fundamental, that *Maeve* (which was interpreted by the public as a nationalist play[1]) seems, to this day, to illuminate one side of the Celtic revival more fully than any single play. The love of nature, of Martyn's native landscape of bog and mountain and sea, the sense of a spirit transfused from it into the man born into it, the love of an ideal beauty imaged by it and realized at the full in the past glory of Ireland or the kindred past of Greece, these things, in varying tones, are the original and the living parts of *The Heather Field, Maeve* and the *Enchanted Sea* :

TYRELL. Barry, would you believe it, often in moments of darkest anxiety I am arrested by the sight of some flower or leaf or some tiny nook in the garden out there. And oh—I become

[1] See Lady Gregory's report *O.I.T.* 27-8.

then at once so peaceful that I care not what may happen to me. I think it is only when we turn to them in our misery that we can really see the exquisite beauty of these things. . . . Oh, to feel that despite all suffering one has the firmament, the earth, the sea ! What more can one really require from the world . . . Have you ever seen on earth something beautiful beyond earth—that great beauty which appears in divers ways ? And then have you known what it is to go back to the world again ?

USSHER. I know, I know—the pain of loss——

TYR. Is it not misery ? But you have seen the great beauty, have you not ? Oh, that immortal beauty—so far away—always so far away——[1]

This is the tragedy of Carden Tyrrell until the mercy of God in the form of madness guides him back again to the ideal beauty from which his marriage has led him ' out into a lonely world ' :

TYR. Yes, it seems as if it would always be morning now for me.
USS. Always morning——?
TYR. Yes—its genius somehow is always about me.
USS. And what do you call this genius of the morning ?
TYR. [*With a strange ecstasy*] Joy ! Joy !
USS. Yet—great beauty—is it not for ever far away ?
TYR. No—it is for ever by me. . . . I dreamed that my lot was to wander through common luxurious life—seeing now and then in glimpses that beauty—but so far away ! And when the vision left me—ah, you do not know the anguish I felt in looking again at my lot in life.
USS. And this was only a dream ?
TYR. [*Fervently*] Thank heaven only a dream ![2]

That this is Martyn speaking there can be no doubt, but, innate as it is, it is a part of his mind that never seems to have found expression except in these groups of characters in the plays. If this or something deriving from it could have grown by natural degrees and held its own against the crabbed, the satirical, the dogmatic, his mind might not, after all, have been ' a fleshless skeleton '. And the quotation from *Maeve* at the

[1] *The Heather Field*, Act III. This seems to me to bear, in several phrases, the unmistakable mark of a genuine mystical experience.
[2] *The Heather Field*, Act III.

head of this chapter might have been not the paradox it is, but plain truth.

In *Maeve*, this love of nature is linked with a love, equally passionate, for the past civilization of Ireland, that civilization from which have come down the great legends re-told by Standish O'Grady, and the lyrics translated by Kuno Meyer. It is not one of the least astonishing paradoxes of this divided and agonized mind that he, of all the group of poets and dramatists of the early revival, should seem sometimes to come nearest to that fresh, clear beauty. The voice is the voice of the late nineteenth century, Martyn's overlaid by Arthur Symons's, but the instinct is for the uncontaminated wisdom of the Celtic nature poet. For Carden Tyrrell, 'The world is such a great lonely place,' but Maeve sees in it a double beauty, nature's and the 'beautiful dead people' who were in their day so near a part of nature. 'I am dying because I am exiled from such beauty.' To her, 'this moonlit night—this Irish night comes like a fawn' :

> PEG. Come, then, to the mountains, Princess.... See how bright it is. The night is lit for your visit. . . .
> MAEVE. How white the moon rays dance upon the mountains !
> PEG. It is the mountains, Princess, that are white with the dancing feet of the fairies ! . . .
> MAEVE. Oh, beauty of my day-dreams come forth from the mountains.
> PEG. Princess, what is it that you see ?
> MAEVE. My love, like an exhalation from the earth to the stars ![1]

The scene is set where ' great leafless ash trees grow upon the pale green grass '; behind them, ' stony mountain ranges ' under the bright moon. The idea in this play is clearer focussed than in *The Heather Field*. For Maeve, as for Carden Tyrrell, the conflict is between ' common luxurious life ' and the worship of beauty, but for her it brings a sharper claim. ' Thou hast killed him by deserting thy chosen way of life ; for there are no more who live for beauty.' And in the vision of Queen Maeve the thoughts are woven together bright and clear :

---

[1] *Maeve*, Act I.

MAEVE. Yes, there, far away—coming on the wings of the March
wind—don't you hear ? . . . The fairy March wind which
races at twilight over our fields, turning them to that strange
pale beauty, like the beauty of a fairy's face. . . . Oh, the
beautiful frosty night ! I cannot keep it from me. The
greatest beauty, like the old Greek sculpture, is always cold ! . . .

. . . .

QUEEN MAEVE. He is coming over the mountains. He is coming
over the mountains.
MAEVE. Yes, I knew he was coming on the fairy March wind. . . .
QUEEN MAEVE. I will take you to the land of joy.
MAEVE. To Tir-nan-ogue—O Queen, do you rule in Tir-nan-
ogue ?
QUEEN MAEVE. The empire of the Gael is in Tir-nan-ogue.
There during life he is at peace in the building of beauty from
the past. . . . Each man who comes to his ideal has come to
Tir-nan-ogue.[1]

Already in *Maeve* this is linked also with the beauty of Greece,
of that Greek thought and art which had so possessed Martyn's
mind in youth and where, but for the harsher claims and
conflicts, he too might have found peace. In *The Enchanted
Sea*, the worship of this threefold beauty—of the western Irish
sea-coast, of the Irish past and of the Greek are closely interwoven, till each becomes intimately a part of the others. Parts
of this play have still the ecstasy of *Maeve*, but the enchanted
sea is at war not only with the ' common luxurious life ' that
Martyn hated, but with the satirical bitterness that was held back
in the other two plays, to find fierce outlet here in the portrait
of Mrs. Font, jarring and unbalancing the delicate poetry of
this myth in which Hellas and Mananaan mingle. Yet even
here the dreams are immortal. ' They have not ended. They
have gone forth to live.'

That such a poet should be hidden in such a satirist would be
unbelievable if the evidence were not there to show that not only
was Martyn in both minds at once—for *The Tale of a Town*
was written between *Maeve* and *The Enchanted Sea*—but that
he had an equal, perhaps a fiercer, interest in the second. *The
Tale of a Town* is so melancholy a failure that one would pass it

[1] *Maeve*, Act II.

over without comment but for two things, that it is a subject of his own creating and of his own unaided handling and that Moore's alteration, the highly successful *Bending of the Bough*, contrasts the technical weaknesses of Martyn's work with the skill of Moore's and indicates through some of its specific alterations what may have been the direction of Moore's influence in *The Heather Field*.

In *The Tale of a Town*, his third play, Martyn deliberately chose a subject that offered no poetry or very little : the bitter, domestic politics of a small Irish sea-port. The choice was original and he knew his subject from direct experience, as he had known the lives of the Irish country gentry that he used in *The Heather Field*. He was opening a field which, as it happened, the other writers of the early Irish Dramatic Movement did not explore ; it was middle-class material, not ' folk '.[1] He was probably led to it also by his great veneration for Ibsen, though it is clear from the first that here is no slavish imitation of the small-town society of, say, *An Enemy of the People*. His choice of middle-class material and of Ibsen's method would not necessarily have separated him from the movement if he had been able to use the possibilities that he was so well able to perceive. But neither here nor in the later social plays, could he ever convert his material wholly to theatrical or dramatic form, and in *The Tale of a Town* the originality and the graceless inflexibility of Martyn's mind are more hopelessly at odds than in any other play. No wonder Moore's heart sank. It reads like a self-conscious translation by Bulwer Lytton of a bastard that Ibsen had refused to acknowledge.

It is best to let Moore tell the tale :

The first half dozen pages pleased me, and then Edward's mind, which can never think clearly, revealed itself in an entanglement ; which will be easily removed, I said, picking up the second act. But the second act did not please me as much as the first, and I laid it down, saying : Muddle, muddle, muddle. In the third act Edward seemed to fall into gross farcical situations, and I took up the fourth act sadly. It and the fifth dissipated every hope, and I lay back in my chair in a state of coma, unable to drag myself to the

---

[1] He anticipates in intention, though not in achievement, the work of the realistic dramatists from Padraic Colum and Lennox Robinson onward.

writing-table.[1]   All the same it would have to be put right, and this
Edward could not do.   It was more a matter for a cunning literary
hand than for a fellow like Edward with a streak of original genius
in him, and very little literary tact.[2]

After some painful, gloomy and tumultuous discussions the
cunning literary hand got to work in freedom and undisturbed :

I give you the play, Edward said, starting to his feet.   Do with
it as you like ;   turn it inside out, upside down.   I'll make you a
present of it. . . .   Do with my play what you like ;   and he rushed
away.

I am afraid, Yeats, his feelings are very much hurt.[3]

Moore indeed did with it pretty much what he liked, making
of it one of the most successful plays of the movement.   The
process is interesting to trace and is, I think, worth tracing,
because the peculiar weaknesses in dramatic and theatrical tact
which were the despair of the other directors of the theatre
appear, in greater or less degree in the plays Martyn wrote
afterwards and nothing exposes them more clearly than Moore's
way of setting about amending them in the specimen he was
allowed to handle.

Martyn attacks his subject with a kind of raw immediacy that
jars us into attention until ill-proportioning and confusion lose
that attention again.   He finds his material for himself, asking
no man leave or guidance, and he sees with his own eyes.
The local politics of a small Irish sea-port and the mixture of
graft, self-seeking and jealous aggressiveness that wreck the
policy of the borough councillors and make them an easy prey
to English business men and lawyers, all this is new and
rich in possibilities.   There was passion enough in the interests,
public and private ;   there were implications of tragedy, of
contrasts in national character and conflict of ideals, true for
its own and all time.   This, and more, Martyn saw and knew

----

[1] *Ave.* 127.
[2] *Ave.* 215–16.
[3] *Ave.* 219.   When Martyn published his original play in 1902 he added
a note which indicates his point of view : ' There was an adaptation of *The
Tale of a Town* called *The Bending of the Bough* made by Mr. George Moore,
with my consent, for the Irish Literary Theatre performances in 1900.
Edward Martyn.'

he saw. Yet, as so often in his plays, when he came to dramatic presentation he could not reproduce coherently what he saw. He would have been happier, with this subject, in the roomy ease of prose satire, in another *Morgante the Lesser* ; the pitiless, disciplined rapidity of dramatic technique here leaves him fumbling, slow and out of temper with the conditions of his medium. And yet the material is as full of dramatic possibility as the material of *An Enemy of the People.*

' Muddle, muddle, muddle,' said Moore. Now the muddle of parochial policy was part of what Martyn wanted to convey, and he knew it. But here as so often he could not distinguish between giving a picture of a thing and immersing the reader in the thing itself. Gossip, conflict, confusion and parochialism are main factors in his theme, as they had been in *An Enemy of the People,* but Martyn, having grasped this, cannot select, as Ibsen does, so that, while the characters see only the confusion, the audience watches a shape emerge. Long stretches of his dialogue read like short-hand minutes of an acrimonious council meeting ; they lead nowhere and reveal nothing, not even (as does at least happen in actual experience) the distinctions between the characters. Martyn might have pleaded—did indeed so plead to Moore—that this is what happens and that, being actual, it must be true. Moore, as far as we know, contented himself with showing what was wrong by putting it right. His English contemporary, Henry Arthur Jones, would probably have told him also what was wrong with his theory:

Perhaps you will think, ' Then we have only to go down into the streets, into the hotels, into the stores, and write down what we see and hear, and make it up into a play.' No, you will not get any very worthy play in that way. You will merely get a more or less interesting catalogue of facts and speeches—at best something akin to a photograph or a phonograph.[1] And all attempts to put upon the stage a veritable slice of real life are generally as dull as real life ; they only succeed in portraying the inorganic, disconnected, uninteresting series of humdrum occurrences that is constantly passing before our eyes. In the drama, as in the other arts, art is art because it is *not* Nature.[2] I have been watching real life very carefully

[1] Henry Arthur Jones : *Literature and the Modern Drama* (1906). (*The Foundations of a National Drama,* p. 59.)

[2] H. A. J. *The Drama and Real Life* (1897). (*Foundations,* 151.)

for more than thirty years, and it has never offered to me any one single scene that could be put on the stage.[1]

At first glance it might seem that Martyn could have learnt this : it was a principle within the grasp of a far less original imagination than his. And yet, when we look on to, say, *Grangecolman*, there is the same inability to combine the transmitting of necessary information with dialogue that reveals manners and characters. He insists in both plays upon taking up the legacy of Ibsen's social drama, the naturalistic drama that, in the hands of Ibsen's ablest descendants, brings to exquisite finish the technical pretence that a play is not a work of art at all, but an immediate experience. But the more he fumbles for naturalism the less he is able to insinuate the necessary facts and the more his scenes separate into two layers : pure character without action and pure information, like an interpolated chorus, with the temporary abandonment of character. Sometimes one feels, at the back of Martyn's theories on how drama should be written, the shadow of Aristotle side by side with that of Ibsen. But neither Aristotle nor Ibsen had much share in the following dialogue, and one hears instead the voice of Moore, ' Edward is a beginner, and he isn't progressing, I said, and may remain a beginner,'[2] which, in point of fact, he did.

FOLEY. Good morning, good morning—I hope you are all very well. I hope you are beginning to feel disposed to act in concert at last.

KIRWAN. Certainly—if only someone would come with an uncontentious proposal.

FOLEY. In honour and conscience, I feel bound to take some action at the meeting to-day.

CASSIDY. Whether you obtain general support or not, Alderman Foley, will largely depend upon the nature of your action.

FOLEY. You have read my article in the ' Weekly Denouncer ' ?

KIRWAN. It was full of fury, as usual, against the enemies of our town.

FOLEY. The sense of our wrongs fills me with uncontrollable indignation. It is nothing but the sense of our wrongs that keeps me before the public at all.

[1] Ib., p. 147.
[2] *Ave.* 159.

CLORAN. Indeed, Alderman Foley, the people do say that you have a mission among them.

FOLEY. I am naturally austere. I could never appreciate what people call the comforts and good things of this world.

KIRWAN. Bosh——

FOLEY. What ' bosh '——? I tell you I am austere, and have a mission to guard the public interests. You're not going to stultify yourself by advocating carelessness of public interests. . . .[1]

Now the play is full of this kind of thing, and when it is extended over whole scenes not only are the main lines of action and the significant events entangled in superabundant and irrelevant material, but the characters lose distinctness in vociferation, and the tempo of the play and of individual scenes becomes formless ; acceleration and retardation of emotion and action appear to have had no value for Martyn. Always he seems on the verge of a good picture of the manners of a raw and vital society and always, before he can fairly achieve it, the dialogue runs him into a bog of prattle and gossip in which his pithy and often memorable satiric comments are so far lost that not even Moore can salvage them.[2]

But what Moore does accomplish is the more remarkable : (' Edward. . . . If you don't feel the scene, perhaps it would be as well if you allowed me to sketch it out for you. It's all quite clear. . . .')[3] And it is not the least part of Moore's achievement that, from a play whose contents appear to have been shaken out of Teufelsdröckh's ' six considerable paper bags ', he did indeed make something lucid in form and detail, as lucid as the English into which he converted the too intimately overheard vulgarity of the souls of Martyn's people.

In the passage already quoted from the opening of the council meeting in Act I, Moore, having cut three and a half pages of Martyn's preliminary six, takes Foley straight into a brief,

---

[1] *T. of a T.*, I. i. (There is no reason why the quotation should end here, except that there is, equally, no reason why it should go on.)

[2] An instructive contrast may be found in Jones's treatment of rather similar material in parts of *Saints and Sinners* (1884). There what is original, the picture of non-conformist society, is handled with some theatrical skill and becomes easily the most interesting part of the play.

[3] *Ave.* 180.

clear explanation of the political situation, an abstract from an article he has just written, and then, with ease and clarity works back to Martyn's dialogue, or his own substitute for it :

FOLEY.   Oh for a little more unanimity, for some kindly feeling, avoidance of personal attack even when we disagree.

KIRWAN.   But the last number of your paper, Foley, contained an attack against everyone.

FOLEY.   You read my articles in ' The Denouncer ' : they were all mine, the whole of the back page was mine.   What did you think of it ?

KIRWAN.   I thought you were an advocate of union.

FOLEY.   So I am, but not of union with traitors.   The sense of our wrongs fills me with indignation, but to right them all I would not hold out my hand to anyone with whom I could not entirely agree.

CLORAN.   The last number of ' The Denouncer ' was a glorious one, full of fury against the enemies of our Town.   The people say that you have a mission.

FOLEY.   Do they ?   [Pause.]   I always felt I had a mission.

POLLOCK.   What is your mission ?

FOLEY.   No man can define his mission, you must feel your mission.   [*Looking round*] ; it must be a terrible thing not to feel that you have a mission.

KIRWAN.   You are a journalist, Foley, to your finger-tips, which are inky.   You exist in the day, in the very hour.

FOLEY.   And what is life but an accumulation of days and hours ?[1]

If the two passages are examined line by line most of us will probably admit that we have heard more boards and councils talk like Martyn's—or at least more like Martyn's—than like Moore's.   But if we look at the two dialogues as wholes and as parts of many other dialogues it is Moore who, with his cool distance, his humour and his grace, gives the impression of reality.

And so it is throughout the unfortunate play.   Moore hacks out irrevelant episodes and pedantic naturalism, changing them again and again into something more generalized and far less immediate, but, unreal though the result probably is, producing an effect of reality.   There is enough photography to be

[1] *B. of B.* I, i (ed. 1900, pp. 9–10).

graphic, but it is no longer automatic ; it is selected, even faked, but it makes its intended effect. Characters are deepened and balanced against each other, their relations at strategic points revealed. The main lines of the ideas and of the action are lifted clear, and character, plot and tempo have grace and proportion, knit together by little touches of anticipation or repetition. The lighting of the play is entirely altered by the wit, the humour of the phrasing, the charm and apparent beauty of some of the speeches. In his hands a part of Martyn became far greater than the whole.

Yet it is more than mere clearing away that Moore does, and as the later acts come on (which he liked, we remember, even less than the first) his additions become bolder and firmer, while argument, character and emotional content become firmer and stronger too.

This is clearest in his rescuing and re-vitalizing of the characters of Kirwan and of Millicent ; Kirwan, from an abortive study of incoherent honesty, becomes an Irishman guided by that almost mystical faith in the innate wisdom of the peasant which some of the leaders of the national movement shared, while Millicent, from a disjointed puppet, the caricature of the ' educated ' woman that Martyn hated, becomes a sensible, practical, unimaginative, every-day creature.

With the character of Kirwan, Moore brings back the symbolism that Martyn had let slip from the play. He and through him Jasper Dean see as their objective ' the spiritual destiny of the Celt ' and in the policy of the English town its ' spiritual death ', and though this is a little obvious and serves perhaps unduly to remind us of Augustus Moon who heard a voice in Brixton calling him to Ireland,[1] it deepens the implications of the play, freeing it from mere gossip, spite and peevish satire and giving it some imaginative beauty :

KIRWAN. That is public life. How does it strike you ?
DEAN. The first thing that strikes me is a sense of unreality ; my real self is not here. Macnee, who has only just gone out, seems to me like something I have dreamed.

---

[1] See Martyn's later play *The Dream Physician*, Act III, for this notorious portrait of Moore.

KIRWAN. I love their simple minds and their mysterious, sub-conscious life—the only real life. To be with them is to be united to the essential again. To hear them is as refreshing as the breathing of the earth on a calm spring morning.

DEAN. But they understand nothing of our ideals—that man, for instance.

KIRWAN. The earth underfoot does not understand our words, but it understands as we may not. So it is with the people.

DEAN. I envy you your deep sympathies and their sudden simplifications of the world.[1]

By this treatment of Kirwan, Moore brings out, as by a sharp reagent, the rivalry between him and Millicent for the mind of Jasper Dean and so invests Dean's final collapse with some-thing near tragedy. By treating Millicent with sympathy instead of with Martyn's contemptuous, shallow objectiveness he makes the personal side of the story a straight fight between a sensible, practical woman who loves but misunderstands Dean, instinctively mistrusting the idealist in him, and Kirwan who, himself a nature mystic, stimulates the idealist. That done, he can let the lovers separate in a kind of dream, which also contains a vision, where Martyn can only part them in a petty quarrel.

DEAN. The difficulty in life is the choice, and all the wonder of life is in the choice.

MILL. Between what ?

DEAN. The world within us and the world without us. You are the world that is outside of me, I am the world that is outside of you. Do you understand ?

MILL. . . . . Your feet have begun to travel the way which it would be a life-long regret to turn back from. You would feel at the end of the journey that you had not walked in life, but alongside of life.

Again, at the end of the play, it is Moore's wide knowledge and his sympathy with subtle and intimate conflict that creates something Martyn could not attempt :

DEAN. Happy ! Ah ! I have chosen the delight of the passing hour ; I've not known how to do the one needful thing.

[1] B. of B. III, i (ed. 1900, pp. 55–6). Reference may be made to W. B. Yeats's comment on Moore's ' celticism '. (D.P. 51–2.)

ARABELLA.   What is that ?

DEAN.   To sacrifice the passing hour to the idea.

Martyn's crabbed and spiteful picture had no chance beside this. We feel that if Moore had gone on writing plays at this stage of his career they must have been successful and they might have become distinguished.[1]

And yet, when all is said, it was Martyn who found the subject, and Moore's success might have been impossible without him.[2]   There is, in all his plays, a choked and impeded passion that makes them noticeable even in their frustration. Like many pioneers, he opens up new country only to lose his way in it. He cannot see the significance of his own discoveries and, though he worships Ibsen, is parochial only, where Ibsen is simultaneously parochial and universal. Yet Moore's clarification is no solution. In effect he refuses the challenge, substituting for the raw, fierce indignation of Martyn a mellifluous charm that takes the pith out while it universalizes. Martyn was on the track of an idea, but blundering ; Moore's ' cunning literary hand ' was concerned to make a shapely composition from already known elements. Martyn, too close to his model always, drew out of proportion, but he drew what he thought he saw ; Moore drew rather what his audience would like to think they had seen. ' One comes very often to the end of a mind that thinks clearly, but one never comes to the end of Edward.' True, perhaps, in a sense that Moore did not intend.

Neither man contributed again to the plays of the Irish Literary Theatre or of the Abbey Company. Moore's other plays have no connection with the movement[3] and Martyn's, produced by other companies of Irish players that he supported in the years just before the European war, are mainly interesting

[1] On Moore's constructive ability and possibilities as a dramatist, W. B. Yeats has some interesting comments. (D.P. 61–2.)

[2] "He can find subjects," Moore said, "and I cannot, but he will never write a play alone." (D.P. 50.)

[3] With the exception, of course, of Diarmuid and Grania (which he and Yeats wrote in collaboration) produced on Oct. 21, 1901. The earlier play, The Strike at Arlingford was produced in London by the Independent Theatre in 1893. The Passing of the Essenes was not produced until 1930 (Arts Theatre) and The Apostle has not, so far as I know, been attempted in the professional theatre.

in showing a curious lack of development and in justifying by results Moore's acute foreboding that he would remain a beginner always.

Martyn was apparently held to his task by two things, his indomitable obstinacy and a reverence for the genius of Ibsen which was more independent and imaginative than that of many of his contemporaries. This was not part of the cult which spread over England and was satirized in Shaw's *Philanderers*, for Martyn was one of the last men in Ireland likely to draw his opinions from England. It was in closer sympathy with the continental, perhaps particularly the German, view of Ibsen and it arose directly from his own intellectual appraisal. Moreover it was a costly devotion, for it cut him off from the other promoters of the Irish Dramatic Movement, who were at that time limiting their work to Irish themes while he sought always for a theatre which should be international as well as national. That he stumbled in practice and even sank out of sight of Ibsen's meanest achievement is undeniable, yet he was an acute and imaginative critic, especially of Ibsen's later work. It is no mean discernment that chooses the later plays, from *The Wild Duck* onwards, rather than the more popular and less representative social dramas of Ibsen's middle period, for the double service of criticism and of reproduction. The symbolism which is the finest part of *The Heather Field*, *Maeve* and *The Enchanted Sea*, grows out of a loving study of those later plays and his criticism, always acute, becomes penetrating and illuminating when he touches *The Master Builder*, *Little Eyolf* and *The Lady from the Sea* :

For the way with these wonderful plays, where subtle mental poetry finds expression in the most direct realism of speech, as here (*Little Eyolf*) and in *Rosmersholm* and above all in *The Master Builder*, is to give the sensation of rare harmonies, to produce with their triumphant construction the effect of a symphony where idea grows naturally from idea, where dramatic effects are but the natural outcome of logical combinations of circumstances, where profound knowledge of the human heart and character is set down with such certainty of intellect as may be seen in the lines of a drawing by some great master.[1]

[1] Martyn papers, quoted Denis Gwynn : *Edward Martyn*, p. 142.

Little Eyolf at least has this in common with its predecessor : in those scenes between the husband and wife, especially in the third Act, there is the same symphonic beauty, with an exaltation of beauty that lingers haunting our souls. When, out of the psychological subtleties of the characters of Alfred and Rita Allwers, the respective mental tragedies of husband and wife rise to a climax of conflict, there is brought home to an audience with tremendous impressiveness how greater far is the dramatic situation of psychology than that of the mere exteriority expressed only in bodily action.[1]

Martyn, speaking thus, is independent alike of the Irish men of letters and of the English dramatic critics, yet his discernment brings him to the same position as Ellis, Gosse, Archer and Wicksteed in England, as Passarge, Brandes, Gran and Reich on the continent, seeing in Ibsen not primarily a social reformer nor the man who re-shaped the dramatic technique of his age, but one of the profoundest poetic psychologists of all time.

His deepest reverence was, then, for the poetic psychologist in Ibsen, ' which finds expression in the most direct realism of speech '. It was a union which he could understand but could not reproduce, for he had only satire to bring to the service of realism, where Ibsen brought pity and indignation. The satirist in Martyn helps him to break new ground, after Ibsen's own fashion, in *The Tale of a Town, The Enchanted Sea, Grange-colman* and *The Dream Physician*, but it ' feeds his hatred of life ' till there is little left in the plays but a hatred of the characters. The satiric mood prompts him to his attacks, but there is no wide humanity to carry him beyond, not even Strindberg's reiterated ' Men are to be pitied.' His satire was happiest in the shapeless ease of prose fantasy where, as in the seventh book of *Morgante the Lesser*,[2] he may tumble together the elements of subtle, savage or gloomy social satire till he recalls now Thomson's *City of Dreadful Night*, now Swift's *Laputa*, now Beckford's Eblis, now *Erewhon*, always *Gargantua*, and often the last lines of the *Dunciad*. His idealism is happiest when it escapes to Tir n'an ogue, to the past splendours of the Gael or the irredeemable grace of the Greek, to ' choristers singing of youth in

---

[1] *Ibid.*, p. 143.
[2] *Morgante the Lesser. His Notorious Life and Wonderful Deeds, arranged and narrated for the first time.* By Sirius. London, 1890.

an eternal sunrise', to the happiness and joy that come in awakening from the dream of life. It was an ill conjunction to attempt, and for Martyn to attempt it in drama, however nearly the balance might seem akin to Ibsen's, whom he worshipped, was fatal. It resulted only in an interesting and individual form of artistic failure, where in spite of promising material, intelligence and patience, the synthesizing power of artistic experience seems to have been withheld. He declared in *Maeve*, and it would seem to be his own voice speaking, ' Form is my beauty and my love '; yet the man who loved Greek art and thought, who loved the music of Palestrina and devoted a fortune to its preservation, who loved and was no mean interpreter of the form of Ibsen's poetic thought, owed, it would seem, to Moore and Yeats and Symons what technical form there is in the two successful plays he has left. It is a bitter paradox; the most searching and least comprehensible of many in a man whose writings are compact of contradictions.

Perhaps only when he was most devotedly following Ibsen, in *The Heather Field* and in *Maeve* did he come near to warranting the hopes of his fellow-dramatists who saw in him for a time the most effective writer of the early years of the movement. In the presence of that mighty shade, whether as dramatist or critic, his energy became disciplined for a moment to a *virtù ordinata,* his imagination became humanized, his symbolism spiritualized and form indeed his beauty and his love.

CHAPTER 7

LADY GREGORY

" Born to see the glory of the world in a peasant mirror."

LADY GREGORY was a woman of middle age when the Irish Dramatic Movement began. She had had wide experience of men and affairs in many countries ; she was a great landowner, the widow of a distinguished Colonial Governor, occupied chiefly in nursing the property for her son, still in his minority, and in looking after the tenants of her Galway estate in the grand old feudal style. She had done a little polite writing, editing her husband's life and letters as many another lady of the late nineteenth century might have done. But her experience had, so far, largely omitted the theatre.

In four years she had begun to write plays, in a few more she was the most popular comedy writer of the movement. In 1909 she conducted a skilful and successful fight against the attempts of Dublin Castle to put down the production of *Blanco Posnet*. In 1911 she took the company to America and conducted it triumphantly through fight after fight with the Irish-American nationalists, including its arrest and trial in Philadelphia. From then onwards she was the grand old lady of the Abbey Theatre, an ' old lady ', moreover, who could still say ' no '. In 1928 she published her last volume of plays[1] and withdrew from active work in the movement she had vitalized for thirty years, a decision ' made without advice save from the almanac, and rather from pride than modesty ',[2] her brilliance, whether as playwright or theatrical adviser, unimpaired. In 1932 she died at Coole in Galway. Few men or women have had so rich a flowering so late in life and fewer still have kept, unsuspected by themselves or others, so fine a genius unused and yet unsoured. Truly she could have said with Hans Andersen, ' My life itself has been a wonderful fairy-tale.'

[1] *Three Last Plays* (1928).
[2] *Three Last Plays*, p. 271.

Yeats, her most intimate friend and worthiest biographer, has commented acutely on the odd coming together of the psychological factors that made possible this liberation of her genius. The native dramatic power must always have been there ; the spontaneity and luxuriance of the plays themselves reveal it[1] and no less do her own often naïve comments on how she found her way to writing them. But the directing of that genius into the happy channel that it found seems to have turned upon two things, upon her life-long affection for the Galway peasant and his mode of speech and upon the contrast offered by her very different experience in the sophisticated society of her day. ' Lady Gregory, in her life much artifice, in her nature much pride, was born to see the glory of the world in a peasant mirror.'[2] ' She does not know why she has created that world where no one is ever judged, a high celebration of indulgence, but to me it seems that her ideal of beauty is the compensating dream of a nature wearied out by over-much judgment.'[3] And so it would seem that, at Coole she began ' a transformation of her whole mind into the mind of the people '[4] and when she began to write in earnest, her earliest attempts, the translations, were ' in the dialect of the neighbourhood, where one discovers the unemphatic cadence, the occasional poignancy of Tudor English '.[5] All this had been made possible by that mingled past, ' semi-feudal Roxborough, her inherited sense of caste, her knowledge of that top of the world where men and women are valued for their manhood and their charm, not for their opinions '.[6] ' She knew Ireland always in its permanent relationships, associations

---

[1] She has, as Yeats indicates, the fundamental quality of sympathy with all—not with some alone—of her characters. ' Lady Gregory alone writes out of a spirit of pure comedy, and laughs without bitterness and with no thought but to laugh. She has a perfect sympathy with her characters, even with the worst of them, and when the curtain goes down we are so far from the mood of judgement that we do not even know that we have condoned many sins.' (*Samhain*, 1905.)

[2] *D.P.* 87.
[3] *Per Amica*, 12.
[4] *D.P.* 67.
[5] *D.P.* 86.
[6] *D.P.* 86.

—violence but a brief interruption—never lost her sense of feudal responsibility, not of duty as the word is generally understood, but of burdens laid upon her by her station and her character, a choice constantly renewed in solitude. " She has been," said an old man to me, " like a serving maid among us. She is plain and simple, like the Mother of God, and that was the greatest lady that ever lived." '¹   It was a good heritage ; its privileges and its demands, its normal balance and its imaginative food.

But, for all this, neither she nor those about her foresaw the development of powers which these conditions had been fostering. 'During these first years (of the Irish Dramatic Movement) Lady Gregory was friend and hostess, a centre of peace, an adviser who never overestimated or underestimated trouble, but neither she nor we thought her a possible creator. And now all in a moment, as it seemed, she became the founder of modern Irish dialect literature.'²   'I no more foresaw her genius than I foresaw that of John Synge, nor had she herself foreseen it.'³   Her task at the beginning was as Yeats defines it, to make conditions in which men of genius could work and to distract them ' as little as may be with the common business of the day ', and, as he admits, ' often we can do no more for the man of genius ' than this.   With his customary generosity of acknowledgement he says, ' I doubt if I should have done much with my life but for her firmness and her care.'⁴

Even her first experiments in playwriting grew out of this self-created function, for it was while acting as secretary to Yeats and other poets of the movement that she began now to suggest a word or two, then a speech and then to help unravel a situation, until suddenly she was in the thick of collaboration and, from that, of independent work.   Even then the others were sceptical, so hard was it to believe that a woman with her lack of training could possibly make anything for herself of their craft, and she says humorously, when describing her first adventure into history with *Kincora*, ' If I had listened to Mr.

¹ *D.P.* 13.
² *D.P.* 85.
³ *Autobiog.* 467–8.
⁴ *Autobiog.* 464.

Yeats's advice I should have given it up.'[1]   But Lady Gregory
was not in the habit of giving up, as the nationalists, Dublin
Castle and the Clan na Gael in America were to discover, each
in turn.   And the early scepticism of her colleagues was royally
amended in the generosity of their applause.

And indeed when we consider her as an artist it is hard not
to believe that, after the fostering conditions which Yeats has
analysed, it was her lack of training that was her greatest asset.
The game was new to her.   It was a succession of delightful
shocks.   ' Desire for experiment,' she wrote later, ' is like
fire in the blood,'[2] and after the clearly defined ideals of Yeats
and Martyn and the theories of Moore there are few things more
surprising than to find in the fourth member of the movement
a playwright whose dramatic theory is, so to speak, almost
entirely practice.   From the descriptions she gives in *Our Irish
Theatre* and in the illuminating but scanty notes to her plays, it
would seem as if she never had a theory about how a thing
should be done until she came to do it.   Even a scenario that
she had sketched briefly would change in her hands—to her
delighted surprise.   It often sounds as though her artistic experience was very near that advocated by the modern surrealist
school of poets ; she seems to listen to dictation from within
and to obey it.   It is hard to believe that her freedom from
notions and prejudices, the long years of indifference to the
theatre, had not served her well.

But if from the artlessness of her own comments we allowed
ourselves to assume that there was little or no art in the plays
they describe we should be equally astray.   There is a wide distinction between conscious theory and formative power and
Lady Gregory offers us the plainest and pleasantest illustration
of this, for she has as little as would seem possible of the one and
all that her art requires of the other.   Martyn was as full of
theories of drama, its nature and functions, as an egg is of meat,
but it did not save him from writing *The Tale of a Town* or
The Dream Physician.   Lady Gregory, with none of this prepara-
tory meditation, knocks off a fantasy like *Spreading the News*, in
which it is impossible to cut out as much as two or three

[1] *O.I.T.* 92.
[2] *O.I.T.* 91.

sentences without losing some essential fragment of the logic of the plot's dementia. The case seems rather to be that her innate dramatic capacity grew through long years of close association with simple and vigorous people and that, her interest in play-making having been strongly stimulated, her technique was formed rapidly and surely by what may perhaps be the best process of all, the constant discussion of *their* work as they went about it in the workshop, with poets who were already major artists in this or some other form. But formed it was, however unconscious the process or surprising to herself the results ; and whatever may be at fault in a play of hers, of whatever scope or size, it is, I think, never the sense of the theatre that fails.

Lady Gregory is probably most widely known by those comedies of Irish character which rest upon what she herself calls ' our incorrigible genius for myth-making ', by *Spreading the News, The Jackdaw, Hyacinth Halvey, The Image, The Bogie Men, Hanrahan's Oath, The Full Moon* and her share of *The Pot of Broth*, while near to them in the affections of her public are those short arabesques of dialogue in which the play is nothing but an episode that arises out of and resolves itself into talk, that is in the last analysis mainly rich comic imagery ; *The Workhouse Ward, Coats, The Wrens* and that play that she so regrettably decided not to write ' between a man and a scarecrow '.

But there were other potentialities in Lady Gregory's genius, as we see in short plays such as *The Rising of the Moon* or her share of *Cathleen ni Houlihan*, where patriotic passion mingles with the humour and carries the play to a climax of exultation that is almost like religious fervour. And there is one unforgettable brief peasant tragedy, *The Gaol Gate*, where she shows a sudden surprising kinship with the tragic side of Synge. So that when she touched imaginative and poetic themes a mingling of mirth and pathos stood her in good stead : *The Travelling Man, The Dragon, Aristotle's Bellows, The Jester, Sancho's Master, Dave* and such virtue as there is in *Shanwalla* all depend for their quality upon this.

In the history plays she grappled with something tougher yet. Those that she calls ' the tragic-comedies ', *The Canavans, The White Cockade* and *The Deliverer* show, though the first is almost pure comedy, a progressive strengthening into something which, if it is comedy, is comedy of a grim order, and those that she calls ' tragedies ', *Grania, Kincora, Dervorgilla,* have a moving power that is often painful, though less beautiful than the tragedies of her great contemporaries or than much of her own fairy or ' wonder ' plays.

It is a wide range in mood, in treatment and in theme ; wider, perhaps, than that of any one other writer of the movement.

The group by which she was first and best known is, as I have suggested, the comic fantasies spun out of the confusions arising from half-heard or misapprehended statements, which rise to a climax of emotional excitement or even of vigorous action, like a house of cards, upon no foundation but that of the nice adjustment of successive misconceptions. Universal as is the enchantment in these plays, it is hard to see how they could be written in terms of any other race, for such misunderstandings depend for their favourable growth upon the eager, exuberant fancy of the hearers, the rapidity and agility of their inferences and upon the fact that they seldom give each other time to explain anything. Indeed the detailed technique of the intrigue depends very largely upon Lady Gregory's adroit use of this last habit. Moreover, these habits of mind, the amazing fertility of inventive argument and the rich comic imagery, are a source of keen delight in themselves, though Lady Gregory is, in all but a very few cases, too fine an artist to exploit this independently and divorce it from its dramatic function, as many a playwright, having discovered it, might have been tempted to do. Sometimes the action seems to drag a little as in parts of *Hyacinth Halvey, The Jackdaw* or *The Image,* but only because, in portraying the humours of garrulity she has momentarily immersed us and herself in garrulousness, giving, instead of the dramatic illusion of the experience, the experience itself. But even in *The Workhouse Ward* the comic dialogue is not, in the last analysis, merely a conversation piece, it is at once an image of the character out of which the eventual action comes and an essential part of the emotional process that leads to the action. These habits of thought and speech, once she had converted them to dialogue and subdued that dialogue to dramatic function, became an inseparable part of all her later technique, and led on to the interesting development of this form in the hands of Synge.

Technically the most skilful of all these is the earliest of the kind, *Spreading the News,* where the idiosyncrasies of the pompous new magistrate, the deaf, gossiping Mrs. Tarpey at her apple-stall, the melancholy Bartley Fallon and the casually impetuous Jack Smith raise between them a rapidly widening whirlwind of rumour that sweeps half the characters into court on a murder charge without anyone having been murdered. It is a tribute to the close texture of this apparently diaphanous play that it is impossible to reproduce the story without loss in less space than Lady Gregory needed for dramatic presentation. But some of the main points of the dialogue can stand alone to illustrate the quality of the speech, and of the peculiar features of this technique, if not of the full scope of its dramatic function.

The opening is promising. The newly-appointed Removable Magistrate, investigating the town with a view to sweeping it clean, happens upon the apple-stall of the deaf Mrs. Tarpey.

POLICEMAN. [*Shouting*] The gentleman is asking do you know the town ! . . .
MAGISTRATE. [*Shouting*] What is its chief business ?
MRS. TARPEY. Business, is it ? What business would the people here have but to be minding one another's business ?
MAGISTRATE. I mean what trade have they ?
MRS. TARPEY. Not a trade. No trade at all but to be talking.
MAGISTRATE. I shall learn nothing here.

The audience, on the contrary, has learnt a good deal. It is an unerring dramatic judgement that has chosen Mrs. Tarpey as the clearing-house for village gossip ; she hears in her better moments about two-thirds of what is said to her, but this in no way ' puts her behind ' ; what she passes on loses nothing : ' if it was not altogether the same, anyway it was no less than the first story '.

It is a few minutes later that Bartley Fallon and Mrs. Fallon are talking by the apple-stall, preparing to go home from the fair. Mrs. Tarpey has her back to them arranging her apples. Jack Smith comes on carrying a hayfork. From that point the action begins to move.

MRS. FALLON. Where's herself, Jack Smith ?

JACK SMITH. She was delayed with her washing ; bleaching the clothes on the hedge she is, and she daren't leave them, with all the tinkers that do be passing to the fair. It isn't to the fair I came myself, but up to the Five Acre Meadow I'm going, where I have a contract for the hay. We'll get a share of it into tramps to-day. [*He lays down hayfork and lights his pipe.*]

BARTLEY. You will not get it into tramps to-day. The rain will be down on it by evening, and on myself too. It's seldom I ever started on a journey but the rain would come down on me before I'd find any place of shelter.

JACK SMITH. If it didn't itself, Bartley, it is my belief you would carry a leaky pail on your head in place of a hat, the way you'd not be without some cause of complaining.

[*A voice heard, ' Go on, now, go on out o' that. Go on I say.'*]

JACK SMITH. Look at that young mare of Pat Ryan's that is backing into Shaughnessy's bullocks with the dint of the crowd. Don't be daunted, Pat, I'll give you a hand with her. [*He goes out, leaving his hayfork.*]

MRS. FALLON. It is time for ourselves to be going home. I have all I bought put in the basket. Look at there, Jack Smith's hayfork he left after him ! He'll be wanting it. (*Calls.*) Jack Smith ! Jack Smith ! He's gone through the crowd— hurry after him Bartley, he'll be wanting it.

BARTLEY. I'll do that. This is no safe place to be leaving it. [*He takes up fork awkwardly and upsets the basket.*] Look at that now ! If there is any basket in the fair upset, it must be our own basket ! [*He goes out.*]

MRS. FALLON. Get out of that ! It is your own fault, it is. Talk of misfortunes and misfortunes will come. Glory be ! Look at my new egg-cups rolling in every part—and my two pound of sugar with the paper broke——

MRS TARPEY. [*Turning from stall*] God help us, Mrs. Fallon, what happened your basket ?

MRS. FALLON. It's himself that knocked it down, bad manners to him. [*Putting things up.*] My grand sugar that's destroyed, and he'll not drink his tea without it. I had best go back to the shop for more, much good may it do him !

[*Enter Tim Casey.*]

TIM CASEY. Where is Bartley Fallon, Mrs. Fallon ? I want a word with him before he'll leave the fair. I was afraid he might have gone home by this, for he's a temperate man.

MRS. FALLON. I wish he did go home ! It'd be best for me if he went straight home from the fair green, or if he never came near one at all ! Where is he, is it ? He's gone up the road [*Jerks elbow.*] following Jack Smith with a hayfork. [*She goes out to left.*]

TIM CASEY. Following Jack Smith with a hayfork ! Did ever anyone hear the like of that. [*Shouts.*] Did you hear that news, Mrs. Tarpey ?

MRS. TARPEY. I heard no news at all.

TIM CASEY. Some dispute, I suppose it was that rose between Jack Smith and Bartley Fallon, and it seems Jack made off, and Bartley is following him with a hayfork !

MRS. TARPEY. Is he now ? Well, that was quick work ! It's not ten minutes since the two of them were here, Bartley going home and Jack going to the Five Acre Meadow ; and I had my apples to settle up . . . and when I looked round again Jack Smith was gone, and Bartley Fallon was gone, and Mrs. Fallon's basket upset, and all in it strewed upon the ground—the tea here—the two pound of sugar there—the egg-cups there—— Look now, what a great hardship the deafness puts upon me, that I didn't hear the commincement of the fight ! Wait till I tell James Ryan that I see below ; he is a neighbour of Bartley's, it would be a pity if he wouldn't hear the news !

[*She goes out. Enter Shawn Early and Mrs. Tully.*]

TIM CASEY. Listen, Shawn Early ! Listen, Mrs. Tully, to the news ! Jack Smith and Bartley Fallon had a falling out, and Jack knocked Mrs. Fallon's basket into the road, and Bartley made an attack on him with a hayfork, and away with Jack, and Bartley after him. Look at the sugar here yet on the road ! . . .

[*Enter James Ryan and Mrs. Tarpey.*]

JAMES RYAN. That is great news Mrs. Tarpey was telling me ! I suppose that's what brought the police and the magistrate up this way. I was wondering to see them in it a while ago.

SHAWN EARLY. The police after them ? Bartley must have injured Jack so. They wouldn't meddle in a fight that was only for show !

MRS. TULLY. Why wouldn't he injure him ? There was many a man killed with no more of a weapon than a hayfork.

JAMES RYAN. Wait till I run north as far as Kelly's bar to spread the news ! . . .

LADY GREGORY

MRS. TARPEY. Stop a minute, Shawn Early, and tell me did you see red Jack Smith's wife, Kitty Keary, in any place ?

SHAWN EARLY. I did. At her own house she was, drying clothes on the hedge as I passed.

MRS. TARPEY. What did you say she was doing ?

SHAWN EARLY. [*Breaking away*] Laying out a sheet on the hedge. [*He goes.*]

MRS. TARPEY. Laying out a sheet for the dead ! The Lord have mercy on us ! Jack Smith dead, and his wife laying out a sheet for his burying ! [*Calls out.*] Why didn't you tell me that before, Shawn Early ? Isn't the deafness the great hardship ! Half the world might be dead without me knowing of it or getting word of it at all.

I have quoted this passage at some length and with only two brief cuts of a sentence or two so that the skill and rapidity of its development might be plain. The sureness with which the pace is maintained is, I think, unsurpassed by any comedy of the kind that I can recall. Every fresh reading (and more still every fresh attempt to cut it) shows the firm delicacy of its articulation, the technique peculiar to this kind at its best.

In this and other plays of the same group, Lady Gregory has used adroitly the ' incorrigible genius for myth-making ' which raises these sudden fantasias like soap bubbles blown from a child's clay pipe. Near as it seems to farce, it is not a kind that can easily be imitated, for it needs delicate aesthetic tact and it has its own strict limitations. In the first place, there is a limitation in length, for the single, rounded episode which is its natural scope demands a single act and cannot easily be extended. It is difficult to construct a sequence of linked or derived episodes to fill out a longer play, for they fall into a succession of separate plays, and the single episode extended to a full length play, as in *The Image*, wears dangerously thin before the end. The form of myth-making which works up to a climax in situation through a succession of fictitious events is Lady Gregory's discovery and she herself brings it to its perfection in the one-act plays. It remained for Synge to make a rather different application of the habit to the construction of mythical character, which, with its greater psychological scope and depth, at once made him free of the full length play.

145

The graver side of Lady Gregory's imagination is seen at its best in three brief plays, *The Rising of the Moon, Cathleen ni Houlihan*[1] and *The Gaol Gate*, though it adds substance to some of the history plays and significance to the fairy-tales and miracles. Of these three, the first two are filled with the exultation of patriotic or nationalistic passion, while the third, which is also touched with these, has the same sense of implacable fate as lies behind *Riders to the Sea*. The interesting thing about this small group—among the few plays of tragic intensity which she wrote or had a part in—is that the passion revealed is stirred by causes or ideals. They are not vehicles of narrow, political fervour, but of the underlying ideas of patriotism, dedication, sacrifice, which are universal and common to all specific forms of nationalism. We find again, as so often in this movement, a creative nationalism whose appeal is international.

Already, in *The Rising of the Moon* there is a mixture, and in *Cathleen ni Houlihan* a subtler blending, of humour with exaltation ; the second play is written strictly in terms of Irish peasant character, the thrifty hardness that Colum, Robinson and Murray later described so minutely, is as essential a part in the older people as the sudden poetic glory which sweeps through Michael and Cathleen. This perception, whether Lady Gregory discovered it alone or learnt it by co-operation with Yeats, remains in much of her later work. The fairy plays, those that she includes in the volume of *Wonder Plays* and one or two others that may be classed with them have a beauty which deserves to be better known than it is in England. The same dialogue is there, the same blending of poetic and comic imagery in living language that reveals swiftly the twists and corners of character. But now it is used not for realistic comedy of Irish country life, but for plays that are sometimes pure fairy-tales, sometimes miracles or moralities and sometimes a blend of the three like the fairy-tales of Hans Andersen, or, rather, like a combination of the moods of *The Tin Soldier, The Marsh King's Daughter, The Wild Swans* and *The Ugly Duckling*,

---

[1] I include this among Lady Gregory's works as well as among Yeats's because, according to his statement, it was impossible even for the authors to know who wrote the greater part.

with the sentimental pathos of the Danish writer replaced by the clear and literal faith of the pious Galway peasant. The interplay of idealism with peasant craft or caution, of religious and poetic beauty with humour and shrewd characterization produces a jostle of elements that seems at once actual and fantastic ; a world in which the men and women are real and the spirits, ogres, witches and dragons—or merely, it may be, the events themselves—of the Other World, but neither are for long, or very successfully, evil. It is not precisely the pagan world of *Gods and Fighting Men* or of Cuchulain and the heroic cycles, that she herself used in the sterner folk-history plays, but a fairyland sweetened by centuries of matter-of-fact faith in miracles and in goodness, whose men and women believed ' so much in the soul and so little in anything else, that they were never entirely certain that the earth was solid under the foot-sole '. It matters little whether she uses a magical element, as in *The Dragon, Aristotle's Bellows, The Jester* and *The Golden Apple*, or whether the magic is replaced by a Christian miracle, as in *The Travelling Man*, or a mystical experience which would be accepted by a modern psychologist, as in *Dave*. For the quality that marks these plays as individual lies in the sure and sane mingling of two worlds, every-day Irishmen such as we might find in her comedies and supernatural figures or events, each accepted by the other as plain matter of fact. This habit of crossing the borderline between the two worlds a dozen times in one dialogue, is part of the essence of all genuine fairy-tales, but it seems also, in these plays, to be a result of Lady Gregory's observation of a certain kind of mind. The same habit of mind interested Yeats, and perhaps puzzled him a little in his early days, leading him to make a profound and careful study of it in *Where There is Nothing*. A.E., that distinguished mystic, himself familiar with the experience, takes it for granted, as mystics do, in all that he writes. But Lady Gregory's treatment of it is different from either ; she too takes it for granted, but she sees it objectively and reproduces it and, being the genuine dramatist that she is, leaves us in doubt whether she does indeed see it entirely from outside or whether she partly shares the experience of Yeats or that of A.E.

This matter-of-fact blending of elements, which distinguishes

Lady Gregory's picture of this territory from the interpretations of the other two, is seen at its best in *The Golden Apple* or *The Dragon*, both ' wonder ' plays. *The Dragon* is a fairy-tale in which the princess is threatened like Andromeda with destruction by a sea-monster, though the mingling of the comic, romantic, pathetic, farcical, heroic and supernatural dissociates the play in all but its bare elements from the classical tale. The climax of the play brings the medley of characters and emotions to a delightful seeming confusion, over which Lady Gregory, nevertheless, is in serene control. The unfortunate princess is waiting while the dragon foretold by Fintan makes its way up from the sea. She is surrounded by the king her father, her managing English stepmother, Dall Glic and the other palace servants, and her three wooers, Taig, the tailor disguised as the King of Sorcha, Manus the real King of Sorcha disguised as a cook and the King of the Marshes, who has visited her with two of his seven maiden aunts.

Fintan, having seen his prophecy of disaster proved correct, withdraws, like many a prophet, gloomily satisfied ; but the emotions of the others range from comic apprehension to poignant, romantic devotion. No more damage is done by one mood to another than there would be in the hands of Shakespeare :

FINTAN. Well, good-bye to ye ! Ye'll maybe believe me to have foreknowledge another time, and I proved to be right. I have knocked great comfort out of that ! [*Goes.*]

KING. Oh, my poor child ! My poor little Nu ! I thought it never would come to pass, I to be sending you to the slaughter. And I too bulky to go and face him, having led an easy life !

PRINCESS. Do not be fretting.

KING. The world is gone to and fro ! I'll never ask satisfaction again either in bed or board, but to be wasting away with watercresses and rising up of a morning before the sun rises in Babylon. . . .

DALL GLIC. . . . I have meddled enough at your bidding. I am done with living under dread. Let you blind me entirely ! I am free of you. It might be best for me the two eyes to be withered, and I seeing nothing but the ever-living laws !

PRINCE OF THE MARSHES. [*Coming to Princess*] It is my grief that with all the teachers I had there was not one to learn me the handling of weapons or of arms. But for all that I will not run away, but will strike one blow in your defence against that wicked beast.

PRINCESS. It is a good friend that should rid me of him. But it grieves me that you should go into such danger.

PRINCE OF MARSHES. [*To Dall Glic*] Give me some sword or casting spears.

PRINCESS. I am sorry I made fun of you a while ago. I think you are a good, kind man. . . .

GATEMAN. [*He rushes in*] The Dragon ! The Dragon ! I seen it coming and its mouth open and a fiery flame from it ! And nine miles of the sea is dry with all it drank of it ! The whole country is gathering the same as of a fair day for to see him devour the Princess. . . .

[*King, Queen and Dall Glic look from window.*]

QUEEN. I see him ! I see him ! He would seem to have seven heads !

DALL GLIC. I see but one.

QUEEN. You would see more if you had your two eyes ! He has six heads at the least !

KING. He has but one. He is twisting and turning it around.

DALL GLIC. He is coming up towards the flaggy shore !

KING. I hear him ! He is snoring like a flock of pigs !

QUEEN. He is rearing his head in the air ! He has teeth as long as a tongs !

DALL GLIC. No, but his tail he is rearing up ! It would take a ladder forty feet long to get to the tip of it ![1] . . .

QUEEN. There is the Prince of the Marshes going out now, and his coach after him ! And his two aunts sitting in it and screeching to him not to run into danger ! . . .

DALL GLIC. Stop a minute . . . there is another champion going out. . . .

GATEMAN. Great news and wonderful news and a great story !

FIRST AUNT. The fight is ended.

[1] To the present-day reader this is disconcertingly like a description of a hunting accident by Somerville and Ross. The capacity for pure aesthetic enjoyment shown by the spectators of the horrible advent might not, of course, be readily paralleled among adult Englishmen. But my Irish readers will not need reminding that hypocrisy about this is not one of their weaknesses—a fact not overlooked by such modern writers as Sean O'Casey and Denis Johnston.

SECOND AUNT. The Dragon is brought to his last goal !

GATEMAN. That young fighting man that has him flogged ! Made at him like a wave breaking on the strand ! They crashed at one another like two days of judgment.

FIRST AUNT. You'd say he was going through dragons all his life ! . . .

PRINCESS. And the stranger that mastered it—is he safe ?

FIRST AUNT. What signifies if he is or is not, so long as we have our own young prince to bring home !

GATEMAN. He is not safe. No sooner had he the beast killed and conquered than he fell dead, and the life went out of him.

PRINCESS. Oh, that is not right ! He to be dead and I living after him ! . . . There is a man that gave his life for me, and he young and all his days before him, and shut his eyes on the white world for my sake ! . . . I never will wed with any man so long as my life will last, that was bought for me with a life was more worthy by far than my own ! . . . The man that died for me, whether he is of the noble or of the simple of the world, it is to him I have given the love of my soul.

But the end of the play is happier, for the heroic Manus returns unharmed after all and the Princess who had died of a broken heart is brought back to life by the Prince of the Marshes who gives her (despite the protests of his aunts) his own ' three leaves from the Tree of Power that grows by the well of Healing ' :

PRINCE OF MARSHES. [*To Manus*] And if I have given her my love that it is likely I will give to no other woman for ever, indeed and indeed, I would not ask her or wish her to wed with a very frightened man, and that is what I was a while ago. But you yourself have won her, being brave.

MANUS. [*Taking leaves*] I never will forget it to you. You will be a brave man yet.

PRINCE OF MARSHES. Give me in place of it your sword ; for I am going my lone through the world for a twelve-month and a day, till I will learn to fight with my own hand. . . .

DRAGON. [*Putting his head in at window*] Manus, King of Sorcha, I am starved with the want of food. Give me a bit to eat.

FINTAN. He is not put down ! He will devour the whole of us ! I'd sooner face a bullet and ten guns !

DRAGON. It is not mannerly to eat without being invited. Is it any harm to ask where will I find a meal will suit me ? . . . It is not bullocks I am craving, since the time you changed the heart within me for the heart of a little squirrel of the wood.

MANUS. [*Taking a cocoa-nut from table*] Here is a nut from the island of Lanka, that is called Adam's Paradise. Milk there is in it, and a kernel as white as snow. [*He throws it out. Dragon is heard crunching.*]

The writer of these scenes can, it is true, feel ' like the common people ', but, for all that it is a mere fairy-tale, we see something also of ' that top of the world where men and women are valued for their manhood and their charm, not for their opinions '. In this and the plays like it, whether they are fairy-tales in which the moral and the humorous mix as in *The Dragon, Aristotle's Bellows* and *The Golden Apple* or modern blends of the morality and the miracle play, as *The Travelling Man* or *Dave*, the elements are the same, though they may be differently proportioned and mingled. Her graver writing appears in passages of *Dave*, especially in the description of Dave's vision at the end, which, though it is reached by a series of rather too rapid psychological progressions, is sound enough in itself and seems to be what she intended from the first to reveal :

DAVE. It was as if all the herbs of summer were in blossom— I think no one could be sick or sorry there. I would nearly say it had what should be the sound and feeling of home.

KATE. It was maybe not in this world you saw that good harbour. . . .

DAVE. I want to be in it now.

KATE. Any place that has the love of God in it is a part of that garden. You have maybe brothers under trouble to reach a hand to, and to beckon them to it, as there was a hand reached out to you.

DAVE. What way could I do that, being as I am all badness, without goodness or grace ?

KATE. Poor child, it is because they were always putting a bad name on you that you don't know you are good.

DAVE. Good—— You are the first ever said that to me.

KATE. It is certain the Man Above never sent you here without some little flame of His own nature being within you.

DAVE. That is a great thought if it is true.

KATE. It is true, surely.

The Irish folk-history plays[1] are Lady Gregory's most ambitious work. Those that she calls ' tragedies ', *Grania*, *Kincora* and *Dervorgilla*, have not the ease or characteristic grace of the early comedies or of the fairy-tale plays, but they have a gravity and power which entitles them to attention even if they do not charm. The ' tragic-comedies' of this group, *The Canavans*, *The White Cockade* and *The Deliverer* are artistically happier, for her bold originality seems to return to her and she interprets easily and imaginatively in terms of modern thought and feeling characters drawn from Irish or ancient history.

The three tragedies from early Irish history or legend have a statuesque dignity ; *Grania* and *Kincora* impress by cumulative effectiveness, though for many readers they fail to stir passion or emotion as Yeats and Synge can stir them with similar themes or as Lady Gregory herself could do when she wrote of more immediate things. For all their careful shaping, and for all her knowledge of her material, they remain too far distant ; the men and women in them are beings of a different world and though their stature may be greater than ours their voices are remote. She seems oppressed with the weight of her material, with the responsibility of touching these heroic figures, and not until she throws off responsibility and, in the tragic-comedies, transposes the minds and habits of her own contemporaries into the times and persons of the drama does she give life and reality to them again. In this second group, she does indeed use all her powers fully ; the comedy of *The Canavans* is as immediate in a sixteenth-century setting as that of *Hyacinth Halvey* in the world of her own day ; the mingled tragedy and farce of *The White Cockade* stirs us, as very little of *Grania* or *Kincora* does, and the figure of Sarsfield suffers no contamination from this rich infusion of actuality into the world about him. And the Mosaic play, *The Deliverer*, whether or not we recognize

[1] First Series : The Tragedies : *Grania, Kincora, Dervorgilla* (1912).
Second Series : The Tragic-Comedies : *The Canavans, The White Cockade, The Deliverer*.

the story of Parnell that is shadowed in it, is a potent and a moving piece of work. In all of these, but especially in the last, Lady Gregory again found her way to a new kind of playwriting,[1] one which had a fruitful succession in English drama. She solved here at one blow the problem that from time to time troubles historical novelists and dramatists—that of portraying not only the customs and conditions but the minds of another age—by frankly abandoning the reconstruction of remoter psychological processes and substituting those of her own day. In *Grania* and *Kincora* she had done what many a novelist has done, she had tried to work in terms, if not of the mental processes, at least of the mental furniture of another period, a method which, if followed to its logical conclusion, can only produce an imitation of what has been written, or might have been written, in that period itself. (Thus an eighteenth-century novel which tried to give a picture not only of the external world but also of the minds that looked out on that world and had been formed by it would soon resolve itself into an attempt to imitate *Tom Jones* or *Clarissa Harlowe*.) Lady Gregory seems to have realized consciously or unconsciously that an historical novel or play must either try to reproduce thought as well as setting and so be a lifeless imitation of what only that age could have written, or must risk the reproach of not letting the characters live in terms of their own world. She is safest, I think, when she abandons the first alternative, which she tries for in *Kincora* and *Grania*, and goes to the opposite extreme, transposing modern minds back into the earlier age, thus opening up a wide field which has been fruitfully occupied by English and French dramatists ever since. We are familiar now with this treatment of history, which is, in effect, a return to the free treatment of historical sources that we find in Marlowe, Greene, Shakespeare and Ford ; Shaw's *Saint Joan* is, in modern times, substantially of this kind, so is Drinkwater's *A Man's House* and Mr. Bridie's *Tobias and the Angel* and *Jonah and the Whale*. But in Lady Gregory's time, certainly in 1905 when she finished *The White Cockade* (and even in 1911 when she wrote *The Deliverer*), historical fact and local colour had

[1] Or, as Synge put it, she ' made the writing of historical drama again possible '. *I.F.H.* ii. 194.

become sacred presences—and there was a larger proportion of stillborn historical novels and plays than in Shakespeare's day or in ours. She made this innovation as she made all her discoveries, lightheartedly and apparently unconsciously. As in the early comedies with which she began her career, she seems to have happened upon a dramatic form or modification of a form in sheer artistic exuberance and, once it was discovered, to have handled it with as much tact and sureness as if it had been in use for years.

Yet there are readers of Lady Gregory who place the serious work of the first group above the bolder and more original treatment of history that is to be found in the second series and it is possible to regard *Grania* as a notable achievement and her finest work.[1] For this reason it is worth while to look at *Grania* in some detail, for it will serve as representative of this part of Lady Gregory's work and of her method of using historical sources. It is, moreover, like enough in theme to the *Deirdre* plays to define some of the differences between Lady Gregory and the two greatest poets of the movement, Yeats and Synge. It is her most ambitious attempt to dramatize a great tragic myth ; and it shows at once the reverence and the strength with which she—and all these writers—treated legendary material. Yet it seems to fall short of its original sources as a reading of life, and of the two chief *Deirdre* plays in concentration ; it is seldom poetry and not often drama. But there is keen penetration into the motives of Grania and this study of motive was, as Lady Gregory tells us, her main interest.[2]

The material was hard to shape, one of those long narratives of wanderings and successive adventures that seem at first sight

---

[1] Mr. Malone (*The Irish Drama*, pp. 160–1) is one of the strongest advocates of this play and finds dramatic virtue in many places where I find the opposite. But I readily agree with him that the test of production, not yet applied, will be the decisive one.

[2] ' I think I turned to Grania because so many have written about sad, lovely Deirdre, who when overtaken by sorrow made no good battle at the last. Grania had more power of will, and for good or evil twice took the shaping of her life into her own hands. The riddle she asks us through the ages is, " Why did I, having left great, grey-haired Finn for comely Diarmuid, turn back to Finn in the end, when he had consented to Diarmuid's death ? " ' (*I.F.H.* i. 195.)

the most unready for dramatic form. But this is not the cause of the play's weakness ; Lady Gregory is no slavish follower of a source in her conduct of event and hacks out her material with a free hand into shapes quite unlike those of the original story.[1] Moreover, that original was one that she had already shaped into narrative form by selection from many sources in her *Gods and Fighting Men*. She was familiar enough with it,[2] and the altering of its events, motives and moods was her choice and her delight.

It is interesting, therefore, to discover that, in altering this formally undramatic legend into dramatic form, she, the experienced playwright, has lost much of the potentially dramatic power of the narrative which she herself had already written, and this to a greater extent than did either Yeats or Synge or A.E. in handling the Deirdre legend.[3] It is true, the story of Deirdre is high romance, standing, as one of the world's undying legends, beside that of Tristram and Iseult, while Grania's tale mingles beauty and ugliness of motive and act in a way more like the grim matter-of-factness of Icelandic saga. But this does not of itself explain away Lady Gregory's loss of dramatic tension as compared with Yeats and Synge in their transformation of the corresponding legend.

The legend of Diarmuid and Grania separates out from the body of the Finn Cycle to stand by itself as a moving tale of bitter and beautiful experience. It is a love-story no more romantically handled than that of many a twentieth-century novel and yet it is filled with that kind of experience (which, if we must not call it romance, I do not know by what name we can call it) that is terrible when close at hand and comely to look back upon :

Then Diarmuid said : ' It is a bad journey you come on, Grania.

[1] ' For the present play I have taken but enough of the fable on which to set, as on a sod of grass, the three lovers, one of whom had to die.' *I.F.H.* i. 195.

[2] See *I.F.H.* p. 195, for her reminder of this, *Gods and Fighting Men* (ed. 1905) pp. 315–99 for the story and p. 470 for the list of her sources for the Diarmuid and Grania legend.

[3] For Lady Gregory's prose version of the Deirdre legend, see *Cuchulain of Muirthemne* (ed. 1902) pp. 104-42 and, for the list of sources she used, pp. 359–60.

For it would be better for you to have Finn, son of Cumhal, as a lover than myself, for I do not know any part or any western corner of Ireland that will hide you. And if I do bring you with me,' he said, ' it is not as a wife I will bring you, but I will keep my faith to Finn. And turn back now to the town,' he said, ' and Finn will never get news of what you are after doing.' ' It is certain I will not turn back,' said Grania, ' and I will never part with you till death parts us.' ' If that is so, let us go on, Grania,' said Diarmuid.

But in Lady Gregory's play the grudging reluctance of the man and the masterful urgency of the woman have both gone, to give place to something more superficially appealing, a bewildered girl overpowered by love and a chivalrous and protecting man ; the keystone of the story has been sacrificed, the curve of the action broken. The old legend gives us a Grania who might have walked straight out of *Man and Superman*, and gives it, like the great legends, without apology, without analysis, without comment. We touch something that is as real and hard as life itself. There is no puzzling over motives ; they may be mixed and confused together, like the smells of a hot, summer day, but there is no doubting their strength and nature. The tale, like the characters is tough and has sinew in it.

To feel the full effect of that story it must be read in its place in the Finn legend, for it is the character of Finn that supports the story and gives significance to what is actually only one episode in a heroic tale. For Finn passes, in the course of the saga, from a young man, beautiful, the bravest among men and the most irresistible to women, to become, in this episode, an old, grey-haired king, obstinate and vengeful, defeated in love by the younger Diarmuid. The slow narrative reveals Finn, for all his treatment of Diarmuid, as one of the greatest kings that epic or narrative have described and yet shows, with matter-of-fact faithfulness, the warping and wearing away of his nobility at the end. It is such a story as, being radically true to human experience, seems to speak to each successive generation in its own terms. There emerges clearly from the simple and apparently inconsequential narrative just such a picture of a king as might have been chosen by Shakespeare ; a man overstrained by a lifetime of high enterprise and the vigilance asked by a succession of emergencies, who has never allowed himself the compensation of animal indulgence that is so often an effective balance to these demands. Finn was never brutal and never base ; he was a poet, a druid, a musician, a warrior, a law-giver and a leader, keeping to the end the devotion of his men, even of Diarmuid and of Goll whom he treated worst. The break-up of Finn himself is only a part of the tragic but inevitable break-up of the great company of the Fianna and both are chronicled without lamentation or comment. Either the tales were shaped by actual experience or by men with clear if unconscious knowledge of the nature of idealism and its fate. Yeats called the story childish ; the details of the telling, the absence of philosophic comment, may be naïve, but they shadow a tale that is epically conceived and its reading of life is profound, if bitter.

Much of this must necessarily be lost when a part of the saga is shaped into a play. We cannot ask that a play should reproduce the epic quality of the original, for this was leisured and non-dramatic in method. But when we consider Synge's reshaping of the similar legend we feel that, in altering the balances, he has lost nothing of the tension and emotional power of his original : he has given us an illumination or re-expression of it in dramatic form, dramatic concentration compensating the loss of epic scope. Lady Gregory, on the other hand, has lost much of the poetic power inherent in the story and has lost it, it seems, by a too nice attention to dramatic technique and a disregard for those more fundamental elements of drama, passion, tension of situation and absolute harmony between character and conduct. She has hampered herself needlessly at the beginning by limiting her character list to the three main people, and in doing so, has shorn away the great heroic background from which they all sprang.[1] They cease to be kings

[1] This means, further, that technical gymnastics take too much of her attention—and ours. Necessary information, such as the marriage of the lovers and all else that has happened in the interval, has to be conveyed in dialogues between the chief people themselves. In parts, such as the opening of Act II, this becomes tiresomely improbable. We feel constantly that the Lady Gregory who could write *The Gaol Gate* would have been better employed in imagining the passions of her characters than in theatrical virtuosity. She, who talked less about technique than any of her fellow dramatists, comes nearer than any of them to spoiling a play by an unseemly

and queens and heroes when there is nothing but their own statements to tell us that they are ; the crown that Grania throws away is less real and of less worth, and so, by comparison, is the love she prizes above it ; Diarmuid suffers in the same way, becoming less a man torn between conflicting obligations than a Tennysonian knight-errant, a figure that it is hard to bring down to terms of real passion ; and Finn suffers most of all, for it is only in the third act that he rises above a vindictive oriental tyrant—and then it is too late for him to win our sympathy and so give dramatic intensity to the play. Moreover, no light can be thrown on the characters obliquely, from outside their own immediate circle ; no other aspects of their minds shown but those they show to each other ; none of their comments, even, upon each other, unless to the third person of the conflicting triangle. So that we not only lose the rich suggestions of their relations to the society they live in, which would give them distinction and roundness, but find grave limitations imposed on the aspects of their own characters which can be revealed. Paradoxically, by never seeing any but these three people we see less of them than if they were supported, as in the old story, by a warrior or two, an attendant, a messenger, or, it might be, a travelling beggar, a hermit, a bard.

It is this, I think, which is primarily responsible for the slackening of dramatic tension in spite of the theatrical virtuosity of the play. Since all that we know of the characters must come from themselves they are driven to explain the contents of their minds, and that rather improbably, to the people immediately concerned. The analysis that Grania makes of her own motives when she is arguing with Diarmuid in Act II is penetrating and sure, but it is the method of the psychological novel, not the way of passion or poetry ; it is not dramatic, or, at least, not in that situation and in that story. The characters of a psychological play such as M. Lenormand writes to-day, can analyse themselves as though they were bringing their case before a psychotherapist (as, indeed, they frequently are). But not

---

attachment to it. She is not the first case in which an initiation into play writing through the strict discipline of farce has led to the tendency to over estimate pure technique in the profounder business of tragedy.

LADY GREGORY

Grania, who has fled from the vengeance of Finn through seven years of danger and dread, talking to Diarmuid the morning after their marriage night, while they hide in a cave from Finn's pursuing soldiers.

And yet what Grania says is, as analysis, sound and sure :

GRANIA. . . . I would wish to bring you back now to some busy peopled place.

DIARMUID. You never asked to be brought to such a place in all our time upon the road. Are you not better pleased now than when we dragged lonely-hearted and sore-footed through the days ?

GRANIA. I am better pleased, surely—and it is by reason of that I would wish my happiness to be seen, and not to be hidden under the branches and twigs of trees. . . . It is not my mind that changes, it is life that changes about me. If I was content to be in hiding a while ago, now I am proud and have a right to be proud. And it is hard to nourish pride in a house having two in it only.

DIARMUID. I take pride in you here, the same as I would in any other place.

GRANIA. . . . It is to thronged places I will go, where it is not through the eyes of wild startled beasts you will be looking at me, but through the eyes of kings' sons that will be saying : ' It is no wonder Diarmuid to have gone through his crosses for such a wife ! ' And I will overhear their sweethearts saying : ' I would give the riches of the world, Diarmuid to be my own comrade.' And our love will be kept kindled for ever, like the rushlight in a cabin by the bog. For it is certain it is by the respect of others we partly judge even those we know through and through.

This is an unerring and penetrating analysis of motive and process of mind ; it has the same ring of truth as the words in which she accuses Finn in the last scene. There is nothing soft, remote or shadowy in either, but hard knowledge gleaned from hard life :

GRANIA. . . . It is little I would have thought of hardships and we two being lovers and alone. . . . We to have a settled home and children to be fondling, that would not have been the way with us, and the day would have been short, and we showing them off to one another, and laying down there was no one worthy to have called them into the world but only our two selves.

FINN. You are saying what is not true, and what you have no right to say. For you know well and you cannot deny it, you are man and wife to one another this day.

GRANIA. And if we are, it is not the same as a marriage on that day we left Almhuin would have been. It was you put him under a promise and a bond that was against nature, and he was a fool to make it, and a worse fool to keep it. And what are any words at all put against the love of a young woman and a young man ? It was you turned my life to weariness, and my heart to bitterness, and put me under the laughter and the scorn of all. For there was not a poor man's house where we lodged, but I could see wonder and mockery and pity in the eyes of the woman of the house, where she saw that poor as she was, and ugly maybe and ragged, a king's daughter was thought less of than herself. Because if Diarmuid never left his watch upon the threshold he never came across it, or never gave me the joy and pride of a wife !

It is a penetrating analysis, but the reader cannot keep back the thought that we should do better if we could see part of this through the eyes of some bystanders, as we do in Shakespeare's plays or in Synge's. Both Shakespeare and Synge knew how impressive, how satisfying are these brief comments thrown out by onlookers, how quickly they give the revelation that must be made slowly, as self-discovery, if it is to come convincingly from the people themselves. Lavarcham and the old woman tell us what Deirdre could not tell without losing the swiftness of action and brevity of speech that is native to her and that gives the sense of headlong motion to the play. Now, in Lady Gregory's play, the characters again and again explain themselves, instead of revealing themselves and leaving the explanation to others, and this cripples the pace not so much of the action as of the emotion. They reach perhaps the strength of a sentiment (seldom, until the third act, of passion), but that sentiment is not integral to, and inevitable in the action of the play nor is it consistent with the aspects of their characters which are revealed in action. For the first two acts we find ourselves listening to descriptions distributed among three speakers with different points of view : it is on the emotional level of the medieval dramatic debate, and however excellent are some of the things they say, there is a fundamental improbability about these passages when we are asked to accept them as the conversation of people at the pausing places of a life of violent action and passionate experience. It is for this reason chiefly that the characters do not win upon us nor their feelings become our feelings—Diarmuid never, Finn only in the third act and Grania in these and kindred passages in the last two acts. Yeats had indeed put his finger unerringly on the dangers when he said doubtfully, on hearing the plan for a three-act play with three characters, 'They must have a great deal to talk about.' They have. But they ought not to have, if action and speech are to be in harmony, revealing in different ways the same personality. Repeated readings of these plays seem only to convince us that Lady Gregory's quality was at its height in brief comic, tragic or romantic episodes or in those longer plays where fairy-tale or history more light-heartedly treated allowed some part at least of her genius for comic interpretation to have its way.

Lady Gregory's contribution to the drama of the Irish movement is marked by no one outstanding play which can be ranked beside the finest of Yeats or of Synge, but rather by fertile innovation and discovery in form, subject and details of technique. From her derives the characteristic dialogue which often appears, variously modified by her successors, in one form or another to the present day. The imagery, syntax and vocabulary that she drew from her experience of the Irish speaking peasants of Galway passed on into the hands of Synge, and became for a time the familiar dialect of the folk plays of the Abbey Theatre. That there were later reactions against this was, of course, inevitable, but the language which she discovered made a deep impression upon the early playwrights and audiences and some, at least, upon their descendants. From her derives the one-act comedy of errors which grew into a subtler form with Synge, and from her also a new way of approaching history, a return to something more like the attitude of the Elizabethans to their sources. She is at her best in prospecting, exploring and discovering, and perhaps because her achievement is never in any one instance among the highest, her indirect service to the theatre and to later drama is liable to be underestimated. We would do well perhaps, in looking back upon her work, to remember Yeats's own comment. ' I have written these words . . . that young men to whom recent events are often more obscure than those long past, may learn what debts they owe and to what creditor.'[1] For her contribution to the movement was, even as a writer, still characteristically feminine ; it provided the means or the medium by which men of genius could realize themselves.

[1] *Autobiog.* 468–9.

CHAPTER 8

JOHN MILLINGTON SYNGE

'. . . he had come
Towards nightfall upon certain set apart
In a most desolate stony place,
Towards nightfall upon a race
Passionate and simple like his heart.'
W. B. Yeats. (Lines on Synge in *Major Robert Gregory*.)

SYNGE IS THE only great poetic dramatist of the movement ;
the only one, that is, for whom poetry and drama were inseparable, in whose work dramatic intensity invariably finds
poetic expression and the poetic mood its only full expression
in dramatic form. All the other playwrights of the movement
seem, in the last analysis, to have been either dramatists in whom
the instinct for dramatic expression sometimes brought with it
the poetry of diction, imagery or cadence, or poets who turned
for a time to the dramatic form, returning, sooner or later, again
to other forms. But it is hard to imagine this separation in
Synge ; poetic and dramatic expression in him are one and
simultaneous, as they appear to have been with Shakespeare
and with Webster, in whom the presence of a high degree
of one mood meant the presence of a high degree of the other,
whether the form were prose or verse, the matter comedy or
tragedy.

Yet there is a paradox in Synge's genius, a dualism of a
different and a rarer kind. For while he is essentially a dramatic
poet, one of the roots of his poetry is mysticism, such as he
recognized in the mountain and sea-faring Irish peasants living
far enough out of reach of civilization to respond to and reflect
the nature about them. And mystical experience, particularly
the extreme form of nature-mysticism that we find in Synge,
is in itself as nearly as possible incompatible with dramatic
expression. Yet the presence of nature is as strongly felt in the
plays as in *The Aran Islands* and *In Wicklow and West Kerry*

163

and it is not there as a digression, irrelevant or undramatic. Nature is a protagonist in *The Shadow of the Glen* and *Riders to the Sea,* so filling the minds of the characters as to shape their actions, moods and fates ; it is the ever-present setting, genially familiar, of *The Well of the Saints* and *The Tinker's Wedding* ; it remains as a continual and surprising source of imagery and incidental reference throughout *The Playboy* and becomes again a poetic protagonist in *Deirdre.* When Synge began to draw his material from the Aran Islands he had found, by one of those accidents of fortune which sometimes save genius from extinction, the people who alone could stimulate his imagination and offer him something on which this strange combination of dramatist and nature-mystic could work. They were the human theme which drama must have and yet they were in part at least nature itself.

Moreover, Synge, who thinks less than any of his predecessors about Nationalism[1] or the Gaelic League or the past civilizations of Ireland, is one of the few followers of the movement who, through affinity of spirit, seem to carry on unbroken the tradition of ancient Irish nature poetry. In that poetry a distinctive quality is the sense of intimacy between man and nature about him ; animals, birds, trees and flowers are not only a source of delight but almost a part of man himself.[2] And it is, paradoxically, in the descriptive imagery of Synge, whose comedies are never wholly free from tragedy or tragic irony, that the happy, gay and friendly relations with nature are to be found (as in the ancient poets) as clearly revealed as those fiercer or sterner moods which his contemporaries converted more often to pathetic or romantic poetic symbolism. For Synge, who perceives the intermittent savagery of human nature, and yet believes that, ' Of all the things that nourish

---

[1] W. B. Yeats could only remember one remark of Synge's that could be interpreted as even partly political. (*Cutting of an Agate,* p. 142 and *Autobiographies,* p. 424.)

[2] The comparison with the early poetry of A.E. inevitably suggests itself at this point. The distinction I am trying to draw is between Synge's direct communion with physical nature and A.E.'s spiritualizing of natural forces, which begins as early as *Homeward, Songs by the Way* and *The Earth Breath.* Synge's most explicit statement is perhaps that in the description of the seagulls in *The Aran Islands* (Vol. i, Allen and Unwin, 1921, p. 43).

the imagination, humour is one of the most needful ', finds little
that is sad or wistful in the Celtic twilight. That twilight,
against which Lady Gregory expostulated humorously in her
turn, throws a curious mist over Irish scenery for those who view
it from a distance. But Synge, who knew Ireland rather than
what was written about Ireland, who understood profoundly
the despondency and melancholy common in the Wicklow
Hills,[1] reveals also, even in that earliest play, the brilliance and
the strength of nature. For he, like the ancient poets his
ancestors and like his own tinkers and beggars, the direct
descendants of the ancient peasants, saw, as well as the mists
of the Wicklows and the thunders of the sea upon the Aran
Islands, a glad, bright, positive illumination. It is when we
study his imagery that we recollect that *Maeve* is not the whole
nor necessarily the truest picture of that ancient Ireland which,
after all, contained also Saint Patrick, the king's brother who
was a hermit and the monk who had a white cat. Synge does
not dwell in the Celtic twilight because he belongs, not by
sentiment and wistful longing, but by the roots of his nature
to the Celtic noonday which had been sweet and sane. Any
reader who goes back from the nature imagery of Synge to
Kuno Meyer's translations of the old poetry, echoes again
that great scholar's inspired comment, ' the true history of
Ireland has never yet been written '[2] and it then seems as though
Martyn's backward gaze upon the ancient glories through a mist
of regret not only sentimentalizes the hard genius of the race
but dims the clear radiance that he would honour.

Synge stood alone, then, in this distinctive balance of nature-
mystic and dramatic poet, a balance rare before him, though
soon after to be found in one or two English writers. It is,
I think, something different from the combination, found from
the Greeks to the Elizabethans, of dramatic poetry with an
awareness and love of outdoor nature. Even when the love
of nature is strong, as it is in poets as far apart otherwise as
Aeschylus, Sophocles, Seneca, Shakespeare and many later

[1] Descriptions and references to this run through *The Shadow of the Glen*
and *In Wicklow and West Kerry*. Sometimes they are almost identical in
substance and in phrasing in the play and in the prose writings.
[2] Introduction to *Ancient Irish Poetry*, p. xii.

dramatic poets, the sense of nature as a background, however close that background comes, is still distinct from the fusion that we find in Synge.[1] For in Synge natural beauty is not merely one of many forms of beauty that he loves or reveres, and nature is not merely a background in harmony with the play, a kind of setting kept before our eyes by allusions coming naturally out of the poet's own affection. It is an actor recognized by the other human actors, sometimes (as in the *Well of the Saints*) as a constant, familiar companion, sometimes (as in the *Shadow of the Glen* and *Riders to the Sea*) as a presence or even an agent who forms their moods or draws down their fates. Very few Irish cities are big enough, even now, to breed men ignorant of country life, and most Irishmen, to this day, are at heart countrymen, responsive to the familiar miracle of their own mountains, rivers, islands and seas. But in Synge himself, as in A.E. and in the peasants with whom Synge was in natural sympathy, there is a reach of experience beyond this, and animals and birds, even the stranger powers of hills, mists, storms and seas are accepted as part of the same creation as man himself, experiencing the same moods as he does and drawing him into their spirit. 'In Inishmaan one is forced to believe in a sympathy between man and nature.' He may consent or resist, but it is still himself.

There are many varieties of this relationship and nowhere does Synge show more clearly the extent of his own experience of nature than in the variety of portraits he gives of men's differing responses to what they all accept as a main part of their lives. There is an easy, comfortable friendliness in nature as it is known to the blind beggars of the *Well of the Saints*; it is their familiar companion and when, after having their sight for a while, they recover the blessed state of blindness, it is the warmth of the sun and the scent of the broom that gives them their greatest joy.

MARY DOUL. There's the sound of one of them twittering yellow birds do be coming in the spring-time from beyond the sea,

---

[1] I can only call to mind one play, the *Oedipus Coloneus*, in which the function of nature is as intimate as in the plays of Synge; in the Elizabethans it appears to be, so far as I can judge, at most a significant setting, though often (as in *Lear*) in the closest harmony with the central idea of the play.

and there'll be a fine warmth now in the sun, and a sweetness
in the air, the way it'll be a grand thing to be sitting here quiet
and easy, smelling the things growing up, and budding from
the earth.

MARTIN DOUL. I'm smelling the furze a while back sprouting
on the hill, and if you'd hold your tongue you'd hear the
lambs of Grianan, though it's near drowned their crying is
with the full river making noises in the glen.

MARY DOUL. [Listens] The lambs is bleating, surely, and there's
cocks and laying hens making a fine stir a mile off on the face
of the hill.

In comparison with the outdoor world that they apprehend
through their four senses nothing else seems to afford them
delight, and even the fantasies of vision that they create are not
of palaces or cities, celestial or earthly :

It's ourselves had finer sights than the like of them, I'm telling
you, when we were sitting a while back hearing the birds and bees
humming in every weed of the ditch, or when we'd be smelling
the sweet, beautiful smell does be rising in the warm nights, when you
do hear the swift, flying things racing in the air, till we'd be looking
up in our own minds into a grand sky, and seeing lakes, and big
rivers, and fine hills for taking the plough.

It is the stuff of their every-day life, their only continuous
possession and they take it for granted with no suggestion,
on their part or the poet's, that there is anything unusual in this.
The saint who temporarily heals them seems for a moment
to be more conventional when he adjures them to look upon
God's creation and give thanks for the wonder of sight restored.
But in him too the native Irish nature-worship breaks through,
and if it is the glory of God that the mountains serve to reveal,
God very soon in turn becomes indistinguishable from the
mountains : ' It isn't on your two selves you'll be looking . . .
but on the splendour of the Spirit of God, you'll see an odd
time shining out through the big hills, and steep streams falling
to the sea.' It is a more exalted strain than Martin and Mary
Doul's but it grows out of the same habit ; the exact
nature of the relationship varies according to the man's capacity
and temperament, but it is as natural and inevitable that he
should have it as that he should have relations with his fellow-

men, and what he makes of the one is as clear a revelation
of his character as what he makes of the other.

The peasants of the Wicklow Hills look on nature with
more awe. Those empty, misty mountains offer no easy
relationship, but the people in *The Shadow of the Glen* never lose
sight of that presence and betray a constant preoccupation with
it, telling the time of day by the shadow moving up the glen
and the sun sinking in the bog, and admitting as frankly their
fear of the melancholy of the mountains that draws the imagination. No one is such a fool as to call that fancy in a country
where men run mad and rush out in the mist to die alone in the
mountains. And yet, even here, there are two different
attitudes which reveal distinct experiences. Nora, who has
lived in her cottage at the end of the glen, as in a garrison
against the mountain's power, is terrified of the loneliness and
the gloom ; but the tramp who, like Wordsworth's shepherd,
has been alone among the hearts of many hundred mists, has
reached some kind of union, where, though there is still awe,
there is also knowledge and love. Indeed the most interesting
theme in the play is perhaps the study of her conversion from
the terrified repudiation of nature by the power of the man who
can at times at least identify himself with it.

NORA. For what good is a bit of a farm with cows on it, and
sheep on the back hills when you do be sitting looking out
from a door the like of that door, and seeing nothing but the
mists rolling down the bog, and the mists again and they
rolling up the bog, and hearing nothing but the wind crying out in the bits of broken trees were left from the great
storm, and the streams roaring with the rain.

TRAMP. We'll be going now, lady of the house ; the rain is falling, but the air is kind, and maybe it'll be a grand morning,
by the grace of God. . . . We'll be going now, I'm telling
you, and the time you'll be feeling the cold and the frost,
and the great rain, and the sun again, and the south wind
blowing in the glens, you'll not be sitting up on a wet ditch,
the way you are after sitting in this place, making yourself
old with looking on each day and it passing you by. You'll
be saying one time, ' It's a grand evening, by the grace
of God,' and another time, ' It's a wild night, God help us ;
but it'll pass, surely '. . . . You'll be hearing the herons

crying out over the black lakes, and you'll be hearing the grouse and the owls with them, and the larks and the big thrushes when the days are warm. . . .

Nature in *Riders to the Sea* is yet more terrible to man, and it is beyond the power of any but the young men, who still have some of its own fierce hardness, to accept it. 'It is the life of a young man to be going on the sea,' and Bartley is filled with a hard fierce glory like that of the storm that devours him almost with his own consent. But the others are broken by it; Maurya's resignation is not that of love, hardly perhaps of understanding, but of relief that the end has come to a heroic contest, even if in defeat: 'There isn't anything more the sea can do to me.' In this play nature is the protagonist, the main actor and inevitably victorious. Yet it is not an alien thing responsible only for event, but something to which they have grown so akin that their familiarity with its ways takes all astonishment, all horror from their fate. It is the sea that is the real theme of the play and sometimes the human characters seem there only to reveal by their responses what its nature is, like a painting in which grass and trees and clouds serve by their colour and line to reveal the movement of the else invisible wind.

This nature is before us from the beginning of the play and there is no serious moment that is not touched with references to it or images drawn from it. Everyone in the play, young and old, women as well as men, know the state of the sea, the signs of the weather, the strength and direction of the tides, the set of the wind. The phrase 'when the tide turns' runs through the first five minutes of the dialogue like a prophecy: 'It's worse it'll be getting when the tide's turned to the wind.' 'He won't go this day with the wind rising from the south and west.' 'The tide's turned at the green head, and the hooker's tacking from the east.' 'That wind is raising the sea, and there was a star up against the moon, and it rising in the night.' It is the same unconscious acceptance of the intimate presence of nature as in the other plays; seas and winds and tides and storms are their book here, as the shadows were in the Wicklow Glen and the warmth of the sun to the blinded beggars in *The Well of the Saints*. They are one and all in the direct descent from that older nature-worship where men swore ' by the sun and moon and the whole earth ' and called upon the air to bless them ' and water and the wind, the sea, and all the hours of the sun and moon '.

In *The Playboy* the direct part played by nature is far less. It is by no means a main actor, hardly even an actor at all. Indeed, in such a play as this, a wild comedy, set, not in a lonely mountain-hut, but in a public house which is the social centre of its district, there would seem no place for the presence of nature. But Synge and his Mayo peasants know better than that, and their references, though sparser than those of a comedy of outdoor life like *The Well of the Saints,* are significant, perhaps because of their apparent detachment from the main subject. Men come in from the outdoor world into the lighted inn still mindful of the darkness and the silence broken by the breathing of sleeping cows, and they bring in that dark, enveloping outside world with them until we know that even there we are among people to whom being within doors is a temporary, almost an accidental, condition. We could draw the district round Flaherty's inn, simply from these constant, unobtrusive references, the shore and the wide shallow sands, the river and the stepping stones and the widow Quinn's cottage on the little hill, the only house within four miles by the road. They are delicate, natural, accurate observers and every man and woman in the play has familiar knowledge of nature's moods and habits. But it is Christy Mahon, the natural poet, who in this play has the fuller experience that belongs to Synge and to the peasants of the Aran Islands or of *Riders to the Sea.* For in his memory of the crisis of his life the picture of the place where it happened, the high windy corner of the distant hills, is more real for him and for us than the deed itself. He alters and expands the deed ; it is subject to fantasy. But not the setting. The ' cold, sloping, stony, divil's patch of a field ' and the sun that ' came out between the cloud and the hill and it shining green in my face ', are not forgotten. This is a man for whom nature is not a background to life but an inseparable part of his keenest experience :

PEGEEN. And it's that you'd call sport, is it, to be abroad in the darkness with yourself alone.

CHRISTY. I'd be as happy as the sunshine of St. Martin's Day, watching the light passing in the north or the patches of fog, till I'd hear a rabbit starting to screech and I'd go running in the furze. Then, when I'd my full share, I'd come walking down where you'd see the ducks and geese stretched sleeping on the highway of the road.

Nature, no longer an actor in the play, has become an undertone, but one of a rather curious interest ; for the brilliance of the colours, standing sharp and clear against each other and giving radiance each to each, convey, no less than the rich and glorious images and rhythms of the talk, the vitality and fertility which are the essence of the play. The ' rich joy found only in what is superb and wild in reality ' is revealed as much by the imagery as by the actions of the people.

In *Deirdre of the Sorrows* nature is as intimate a part of the people's life and speech as ever, but there is perhaps more definition, almost more consciousness in Synge's perception. For in the ancient Irish legends from which he drew for this play—and which he followed sometimes as faithfully as Shakespeare did the phrasing of Holinshed—he found an experience like his own. Just as his knowledge of the Aran Islanders helped him to understand the primitive yet aristocratic civilization of ancient Ulster, so his understanding of their relation to nature made him one, instantly, with the tradition of ancient Irish nature poetry ; in this last play the nature experience of his life-time seems to meet and join hands with that undying tradition of Irish thought and poetry. It is no ornament. It is woven deep. And in the moments of intensest passion it seems more essential than the passion itself.

LAVARCHAM. She's little cause to call to mind an old woman when she has the birds to school her, and the pools in the rivers where she goes bathing in the sun. . . . I'd do as well speaking to a lamb of ten weeks and it racing the hills. . . . It's not the dread of death or troubles that would tame her like. . . .

DEIRDRE. Since that, Naisi, I have been one time the like of a ewe looking for a lamb that had been taken away from her, and one time seeing new gold on the stars, and a new face on the moon. . . .

AINNLE. By the sun and the moon and the whole earth I wed
Deirdre to Naisi. May the air bless you, and water and the
wind, the sea, and all the hours of the sun and moon.

Thus far, as has been suggested, the nature poetry of Synge's
plays reveals experiences which, in their range and kind,
are curiously like those of the ancient poetry of his own race.
The allusions and descriptions in the comedies, a clear, gay,
noonday poetry of nature, as sane as it is happy, can be matched
in the poems translated by Kuno Meyer,[1] *King and Hermit,
Summer has Come, Songs of Summer, Arran, The Blackbird,
Columcille's Greeting to Ireland, The Scribe* and several others ;
the fiercer side, the glory and terror of storm and the violence
of nature in such lines as the *Song of the Sea* ; its remorseless
bleakness in *A Song of Winter* or *Summer is Gone* and the familiar
intimacy with nature, particularly that phase which sees animals
and men as creatures separated by no barrier, sharing their
experiences and sympathy, in *The Deserted Home* or *The Monk
and his Pet Cat*. In the ancient poets, as in Synge, there is
nothing sentimental or wistful ; there is nothing to remind us
of the Celtic twilight, probably because we are so often
irradiated with the Celtic noonday. Perhaps in the ancient
poetry there is less of the majesty and implacableness of nature
by which man is so often accidentally destroyed, and more
of that rare, robust quality of gladness. But the vividness
of the experience, its depth and intimacy are the same in both :

GUARE. Why, hermit Marvan, sleepest thou not
Upon a feather quilt ?
Why rather sleepest thou abroad.
Upon a pitchpine floor ?

MARVAN. I have a shieling in the wood
None knows it save my God

[1] I have referred chiefly to the volume of translations *Ancient Irish Poetry,*
published by Kuno Meyer in 1911, as being perhaps on the whole the most
easily accessible to English readers. But all the translations of the Irish
literature written between the eighth and the tenth centuries that I have read
are full of such allusions and images, notably Dr. Hyde's two famous volumes
and the recently published translations by Dr. Robin Flower (1931) and
Mr. Frank O'Connor (1939).

JOHN MILLINGTON SYNGE

An ash-tree on the hither side, a hazel bush beyond,
A huge old tree encompasses it.

A choice pure spring and princely water
To drink :
There spring watercresses, yew-berries,
Ivy bushes thick as a man.

Fairest princes come to my house,
A ready gathering :
Pure water, perennial bushes,
Salmon, trout.

A bush of rowan, black sloes,
Dusky blackthorns,
Plenty of food, acorns, pure berries,
Bare flags.

When brilliant summer-time spreads its coloured mantle
Sweet-tasting fragrance !
Pignuts, wild marjoram, green leeks,
Verdant pureness.

Swarms of bees and chafers, the little musicians of the
    world,
A gentle chorus :
Wild geese and ducks, shortly before summer's end,
The music of the dark torrent.

Fair white birds come, herons, seagulls,
The cuckoo sings between—
No mournful music ! dun heathpoults
Out of the russet heather.

The voice of the wind against the branchy wood
Upon the deep-blue sky ;
Falls of the river, the note of the swan,
Delicious music.

Without an hour of fighting, without the din of strife
In my house,
Grateful to the Prince who giveth every good
To me in my shieling.

GUARE. I would give my glorious kingship
With the share of my father's heritage—
To the hour of my death I would forfeit it
To be in thy company, my Marvan.

Synge's kinship in this experience is not limited to his fellow
countrymen of the great period of Irish civilization and poetry ;
it is shared at different points by nature poets of all times.
It is an essential part of Synge's objective and dramatic nature
that he makes no philosophic inferences from it.[1] Indeed it is,
as we saw at the outset, the peculiar characteristic of Synge
that he is at once a nature-mystic and a dramatist, that the two
things are one in him, as perhaps in no other poet before him,
that each, that is, is revealed in terms of the other, nature in
terms of man's character, thought and fate, and man himself
in great part in terms of his relations with nature.

That he was able to do this depended almost entirely upon
Synge's discovering in the world of his own day people whose
experience was like his and who could become the stuff of
drama.   That is why Yeats's lines quoted at the head of this
chapter seem to me the fittest summary of the processes and the
materials out of which Synge's drama was made. No one
who has considered his record of nature and man's relations to it
can doubt that side of his experience, no one who has felt the
power and ease of movement through action, character and
speech can doubt that the instinct of the dramatist was as strong
in him as in the major Jacobeans. Yet it was a paradoxical
combination and it was no less than a miracle that he found—
perhaps by his own, perhaps through Yeats's perception of his
need—the race of people who were themselves the inheritors
of the original Irish worship of nature.

What Synge made of this material is known throughout the
English-speaking world. *Riders to the Sea* and *The Playboy of
the Western World* are played wherever Irish drama is known,
and *Deirdre*, especially the last act, which is the only part he left

[1] Nor does he, in the plays, make any explicit statement on the relationship
which he continually indicates.   In the two prose volumes, on the other hand,
he shows that his awareness was also conscious and critical, describing the
experience and interpreting the characters of the islanders in the light of it.

in finished form, is read wherever tragic poetry is honoured. His development as a dramatist is swift. Scope and humour broaden and deepen successively from play to play ; structural subtlety and irony define more and more clearly the grim, the paradoxical and the tragic implications of life. Yet at no time was he uncertain, and if *The Shadow of the Glen* is slighter, as I think it is, than any part of the last two he wrote, it is already clear and complete as a play. His tragedies are untouched by comedy ; relief, in them, comes, as with the Greeks, in poetry, and the relief of poetic thought grows more comprehensive as we go from the hard condensation of the early *Riders to the Sea* to the wide and sunny beauty of *Deirdre*. But his comedies are either a frank mixture of the two elements or such laughter as trembles always on the verge of tragedy, and the intimacy of the blending becomes subtler, more bewildering, as we go from the simple contrasts and balances of *The Shadow of the Glen* through *The Well of the Saints* and *The Tinker's Wedding* to *The Playboy of the Western World*. There is at work a watchful mind, slowly observant, grave and capacious. It is never didactic, never abstract, never philosophical, yet full of that intent vigilance which science and tragedy share. It is concrete and dramatic ; it works through the human individuals of its creating whose experience is yet universal, and values above all else the inwardness and individuality of that experience.

Because of this steady progression through the six years of Synge's career, it is probably *The Playboy* that shows his dramatic power at its ripest ; for *Deirdre,* left unfinished at his death, lacks the final shaping. But the earlier play is a triumphant consummation of the form, perhaps essentially Irish in its material and so in its shape, which subsidiarizes event and takes for its main theme the growth of fantasy in a mind or a group of minds. It is often described by English audiences as ' nothing but talk ', and this (which they do not necessarily mean as depreciation) seems true if we compare it with much English comedy, in which character, event and situation interlock and react upon each other ; for here character is sometimes no more than the necessary foundation upon which situation can be built and dialogue as much occupied with the service of event and situation as with the revelation of character. If we compare *The Playboy* with a fair, representative comedy by Lyly, Chapman, Ben Jonson, Middleton, Marston, Fletcher, Congreve, Sheridan, Pinero, or Galsworthy, this becomes clear. For the new Irish comedy of the early twentieth century does something which might else seem only possible to a certain kind of psychological tragedy (such as Ibsen's *John Gabriel Borkman*) ; it dispenses with all but the minimum of outward event and takes for its theme a mind's exploration and discovery of itself. This, which can carry weight and even passion when the events are tragic, is by no means easy in comedy and except in the comedy of Irish life, where the ' incorrigible genius for myth-making ' provides its material, it is liable to relapse into revelation by event. Continuous self-revelation is only possible in comedy where the characters all have a natural tendency to find the processes of their own and other people's minds of absorbing interest, an astounding succession of shocks— ' What business would the people here have but to be minding one another's business ? ' Mrs. Tarpey is right ; this is the essential pre-supposition. From this characteristic of the dramatist's originals comes not only that comic, poetic imagery and description which is the main substance of Lady Gregory's shorter plays, but that delighted exploration of his own unfolding personality which Christy Mahon pursues breathlessly through *The Playboy*. Moreover, the central figure can rely upon the equally delighted co-operation of a society of fantasy-builders as expert and as fruitful as himself, whether in the construction of the tale of catastrophic conflicts between Bartley Fallon and Red Jack Smith or in the creation of a hitherto non-existent Christopher Mahon. And here Synge, both in *The Well of the Saints* and in *The Playboy*, advances upon Lady Gregory, who was the originator of this kind of comedy ; he sees that the genius for myth-making finds its supreme expression in creating the most satisfying myth of all, that of personality. The substance and scope of his comedies at once becomes greater than hers and he can create a full length play out of that very habit which, when used to create only a myth of event, runs to no more than one act.

The form of *The Playboy*, then, its succession of conversations and narrations (slenderly interspersed with episodes) which leads up to the double reversal of the climax, comes directly from its main theme, the growth, like a Japanese paper flower dropped into a bowl of water, of Christopher Mahon's new self.

His evolution from what his father brutally but succinctly describes as a dribbling idiot, not merely into ' a likely man ', but into a poet-hero, ' the only playboy of the western world ', is rapid but sure.   So sure that when the reversal comes the new Christy is capable of ousting the original and perpetuating itself. It is the favouring atmosphere of a world of fantasy-builders that starts the process, a world in which whatever is unknown is presumed to be magical and where no talker is without honour, provided he has the luck or sense not to carry on his craft in his own country.   Christy creeps into Flaherty's inn and the fostering warmth is enough.   The ' polis ' never come there ; ' it is a safe house, so ', and the crime for which he had fled in terror on the roads of Ireland since ' Tuesday was a week ', becomes ' maybe something big '.   The mystery quickens the blood of his audience, they ' draw nearer with delighted curiosity ' and, looking into his own mind for the first time by the illumination of this tribute to his art, he perceives that there is not ' any person, gentle, simple, judge or jury, did the like of me '.   From that moment a glorious and brilliant magnification of his deed and his situation sets in, he has ' prison behind him, and hanging before, and hell's gap gaping below '. Once the confession is out his audience contributes royally. They perceive that he is no ' common, week-day kind of a murderer ', but a man ' should be a great terror when his temper's roused ' and ' a close man ' into the bargain.   (In fact, a complete Machiavellian, lion and fox together.)   As the legend expands at the hands of his audience he accepts the additions, assimilating them so rapidly that they soon become part of his own memory of the event.   With becoming modesty he gives the glory to God, but soon realizes that, ' up to the day I killed my father there wasn't a person in Ireland knew the kind I was, and I there drinking, waking, eating, sleeping, a quiet, simple poor fellow with no man giving me heed '.   Before the evening is out the widow Quinn has completed the first stage of his development ; ' It's great luck and company I've won me in the end of time—two fine women fighting for the likes of me—till I'm thinking this night wasn't I a foolish fellow not to kill my father in the years gone by.'

In the second act the blossoming begins, to pass rapidly on to the fruits of confidence in Christy's victory at the sports at the beginning of the third act : ' Didn't I know rightly I was handsome, though it was the divil's own mirror we had beyond, would twist a squint across an angel's brow.' Christy enters upon a romantic career of bardic self-glorification. Each time he tells his story (' and if it was not altogether the same, anyway it was no less than the first story ') he gathers in adroitly whatever had been contributed to the saga by each preceding audience. It is ' a grand story ', and ' he tells it lovely '. Honor's comment is true ; whichever of his two antithetical selves Christy is at bottom, he is always a fine dramatic raconteur ; herein lies his power of convincing himself and giving conviction, of sinking utterly into the myth that he is acting. In the love scenes with Pegeen he sorts the somewhat conflicting elements in his memory, rationalizing and explaining away the old Christy until finally, after the victory at the sports has given him incontestable proof, he grasps the new self so powerfully that it cannot be shaken even by the father he has dreaded all his life. ' I'm master of all fights from now.' He acknowledges the part his admiring audience has played, and whether it has contributed to self-realization, as he thinks, or to the expansion of a superb fantasy, as we half suppose, matters little, ' for you've turned me a likely gaffer in the end of all, the way I'll go romancing through a romping life-time from this hour to the dawning of the judgment day '.

The audience, led by Pegeen, with a reaction common to most romancers when romance presents itself on their doorstep, draw back in horror from the killing which they had glorified so long as it happened in ' a windy corner of high, distant hills '. They have learnt, for the moment, ' that there's a great gap between a gallows story and a dirty deed '. But Pegeen at least is won round at the last, for, after all, what she (and indeed all of them) has loved has been not so much the deed but the man ' that has such poet's talking, and such bravery of heart '. Beside this gift, with its power to bring glory and stir into a world of bog and stone, dirty shebeens and drunken wakes, little else matters. Any other man, beside Christy, is but ' a middling kind of a scarecrow with no savagery or fine words in him at all '. It is Synge's supreme skill in mixing the elements of comedy and tragic irony that leaves us at the end understanding not only how the hero-myth has been created but why. It is not Christy only, but the whole population of the small community he lights upon that has gone ' romancing through a romping life-time ', at least for the space of two days. The starved imaginations have made themselves drunk on fantasy as an alternative (or accompaniment) to the ' flows of drink ' at Kate Cassidy's wake, and when the curtain falls on the dreary public bar and the dishevelled, half-drunk men, we see what Pegeen and they have lost in the man ' who'd capsize the stars '. The life, aspirations and frustration of a whole country-side is in the play.

The richness of indwelling imagination, revealed in *The Playboy* in comic and in poetic imagery and description, in character and in the ironic interplay of fact and fantasy, gives to that tragi-comedy both its bewildering breadth and its penetration. In *Deirdre* the relations are less complex ; theme, character, even imagery are clear and distilled. Though there is always tragedy or potential tragedy mingled with Synge's comedy, there is no comedy nor even humour in either of his tragedies. The richness of this last play lies not in breadth or manifold implications, but in the brilliance of its colouring, in its nature imagery and description which carries a light like that he describes in *The Aran Islands,* bringing familiar things to an apotheosis of radiance :

It has cleared, and the sun is shining with a luminous warmth that makes the whole island glisten with the splendour of a gem, and fills the sea and sky with a radiance of blue light.
I have come out to lie on the rocks, where I have the black edge of the north island in front of me ; Galway Bay, too blue almost to look at, on my right, the Atlantic on my left, a perpendicular cliff under my ankles, and over me innumerable gulls that chase each other in a white circus of wings.[1]

[1] *The Aran Islands,* I, 42.

About sunset the clouds broke and the storm turned to a hurricane. Bars of purple cloud stretched across the sound where immense waves were rolling from the west, wreathed with snow phantasies of spray. Then there was the bay full of green delirium, and the Twelve Pins touched with mauve and scarlet in the east.

The suggestion from this world of inarticulate power was immense, and now at midnight, when the wind is abating, I am still trembling and flushed with exultation.[1]

The power of the play lies in the sharp, penetrating sweetness of its poetic utterance, the words of people who have won, like Synge himself, the knowledge that there is no safe place on the ridge of the world. Beside the riotous and wealthy *Playboy* the play is simple ; it has only two themes but they are the greatest in the world, love and death. And from the beginning they are fatally interwoven ; the love of Naisi and Deirdre is begun, consummated and cut short under the shadow of death whose imminence sharpens it to an almost unbearable brilliance, like mid-May trees and flowers seen against thunder clouds gathering behind them. In this last play, comedy, humour, irony, savagery, even the preoccupation with character itself fell from Synge and he saw nothing in life but beauty— the beauty of Deirdre, of that nature of which she is inseparably a part, of her passion and of her worship of life. Though it is unfinished, the design is for a great poetic tragedy and the fifth act wholly and the rest in part fulfils that design.

> DEIRDRE. Do many know what is foretold, that Deirdre will be the ruin of the Sons of Usna, and have a little grave by herself, and a story will be told for ever ? . . . I was in the woods at the full moon and I heard a voice singing . . . and I saw you pass by underneath, in your crimson cloak, singing a song, and you standing out beyond your brothers are called the Flower of Ireland. . . . Since that, Naisi, I have been one time the like of a ewe looking for a lamb that had been taken away from her, and one time seeing new gold on the stars, and a new face on the moon, and all times dreading Emain. . . .
>
> I will not live to be shut up in Emain, and wouldn't we do well paying, Naisi, with silence and a near death. I'm

[1] *The Aran Islands*, I, 98.

a long while in the woods with my own self, and I'm in little dread of death, and it earned with riches would make the sun red with envy, and he going up the heavens ; and the moon pale and lonesome, and she wasting away. Isn't it a small thing is foretold about the ruin of ourselves, Naisi, when all men have age coming and great ruin in the end ?[1]

The proportioning is true. There is just appreciation here of both the protagonists, love and death ; the lovers enter upon a heritage that is as clearly of the spirit as that of A.E.'s play. And sharp pangs force the spirit out from safety, comfort and ease. Deirdre knows well enough that she will be ' lonesome, and I thinking on the little hill beyond, and the apple-trees do be budding in the spring-time by the post of the door ', that it's ' a heartbreak to the wise that it's for a short space we have the same things only ' and that ' death should be a poor, untidy thing, though it's a queen that dies '.

But Synge's wisdom is now the wisdom of a man who sees death so near that the world becomes transparent, letting through the radiance of another world of light ; he sees it with the simultaneous detachment and tenderness possible only to the man who also sees more. A.E., in his *Deirdre*, speaks of ' the shining life beyond this ', he makes us aware of the world to which the beauty of this is but the garment we see it by. But Synge, who worked always by direct presentation and never by reflection, does but concentrate that sharpness of colour, light and line beside the imminent tragedy, the deathless courage of love, until the spiritual beauty declares itself the essence and these other images its garments.

DEIRDRE. It's a long time we've had, pressing the lips together, going up and down, resting in our arms, Naisi, waking with the smell of June in the tops of the grasses, and listening to the birds in the branches that are highest. . . . It's a long time we've had, but the end has come, surely.

NAISI. Would you have us go to Emain, though if any ask the reason we do not know it, and we journeying as the thrushes come from the north, or young birds fly out on a dark sea ?

DEIRDRE. There's a reason all times for an end that's come. . . . We're seven years without roughness or growing weary ;

[1] Act I.

seven years so sweet and shining, the gods would be hard
set to give us seven days the like of them. . . . It may be
we do well putting a sharp end to the day is brave and glorious,
as our fathers put a sharp end to the days of the kings of Ireland.

Deirdre is a simply constructed play ; it has a single theme
with so little complication that the end is foreseen from the
beginning. By this means, of continually anticipating the end,
Synge puts it (even for the English reader) into the category
of plays whose stories are already well known to the audience,
as did the Greek dramatists. Such hold as it has upon the
audience will depend, therefore, upon certain virtues found also
in theirs, on power and sincerity of passion and thought, on the
poetic reality of the experience presented, on the unforgettable
expression of the emotions of the people who meet it, and on
the implication, through all these, of the poet's reading of some
aspect of life. This, as I have tried to suggest, Synge does by
revealing the spirit and passion of his people so closely in terms
of that beauty of nature which is a part of them that the two
become an inner and an outer aspect of the same spiritual reality.
In this, the play is the consummation of his dual power, that of
dramatist and of nature-mystic. What had been in *The
Playboy* two deliberately separated themes running in counter-
point, the nature-imagery appearing superficially unrelated to
the theme of the play, are here inseparably one.

This does not mean that, even in its unfinished condition,
the play is naïvely constructed. The simplicity of form and
content are those of a master, not of a novice. The society
Synge has imagined is clearly defined because he has not sought
to reconstruct an ancient civilization but has realized the kinship
of the world of the old legends and its modern descendant.
Yet again, but in a different way, the people of the Aran Islands
have been his source, for they have given him a primitive
society in which the individuals have the qualities of aris-
tocracy :

Their way of life has never been acted on by anything much more
artificial than the nests and burrows of the creatures that live round
them, and they seem, in a certain sense, to approach more nearly

to the finer types of our aristocracies—who are bred artificially to
a natural ideal—than to the labourer or citizen, as the wild horse
resembles the thoroughbred rather than the hack or cart-horse.[1]

There is no need for shadowy personages or remote language ;
Lavarcham is no longer the druidess of A.E.'s play, but 'Deirdre's
nurse' ; Conchubor need have no lofty, chivalric ideals ;
he is the head-man of a tribe, with real burdens and real needs :
'The like of me has a store of knowledge that's a weight and
terror. It's for that we do choose out the like of yourself that
are young and glad only. . . . I'm a ripe man and in great love,
and yet, Deirdre, I'm the King of Ulster.'

There is simplicity, too, in the fewness of the characters.
In a play which is a passionate tragedy of love and a conflict
between two groups of great warriors, no little skill is needed
to keep them so few. But Synge avoids the over-virtuosity
of Lady Gregory who reduced the similar theme of *Grania*
to three characters. He has thus certain powers and facilities
which she unnecessarily denied herself, for he has always people
standing by—old women, servants, friends—who can make the
brief comments on the events and characters that go so far
to make a play seem three-dimensional and leave those who are
vehicles of passion, and who make or are made by event, free
for action and brevity of speech. Both commentary and
passionate utterance thus become charged and imagistic, not
meditative and expository :

LAVARCHAM. She's as good right as another, maybe, having her
    pleasure, though she'd spoil the world.
OLD WOMAN. Be quick before she'll come back. . . . Who'd
    have thought we'd run before her, and she so quiet till to-
    night. Will the High King get the better of her, Lavarcham ?
    If I was Conchubor, I wouldn't marry with her like at all.
LAVARCHAM. Hang that by the window. That should please
    her, surely. When all's said, it's her like will be the master
    till the end of time.

The events of the story are, as we have said, foreseen ; but
the bearing of the people who meet them is not foreseen,
and it is this that in each of the three plays on this story makes

---

[1] *The Aran Islands,* I, 29.

a different climax in the last act, each different again from the old story. Synge's climax is a paean of triumph, where love and immortality break through the grave and death, as in the fourth movement of Brahm's first symphony. Deirdre's keen over Naisi before she kills herself is a song of life, not of death, but it springs from that close knowledge of death which alone can measure life :

DEIRDRE. I see the flames of Emain starting upwards in the dark night ; and because of me there will be weasels and wild cats crying out on a lonely wall where there were queens and armies and red gold, the way there will be a story told of a ruined city and a raving king and a woman will be young for ever. I see the trees naked and bare, and the moon shining. Little moon, little moon of Alban, it's lonesome you'll be this night, and to-morrow night, and long nights after, and you pacing the woods beyond Glen Laoi, looking every place for Deirdre and Naisi, the two lovers who slept so sweetly with each other. . . .

I have put away sorrow like a shoe that is worn out and muddy, for it is I have had a life that will be envied by great companies. . . . It was not a low thing to be chosen by Conchubor, who was wise, and Naisi had no match for bravery. It is not a small thing to be rid of grey hairs, and the loosening of the teeth. It was the choice of lives we had in the clear woods, and in the grave we're safe, surely. . . . I have a little key to unlock the prison of Naisi you'd shut upon his youth for ever. Keep back, Conchubor ; for the High King who is your master has put his hands between us. It was sorrows were foretold, but great joys were my share always ; yet it is a cold place I must go to be with you, Naisi ; and it's cold your arms will be this night that were warm about my neck so often. . . . It's a pitiful thing to be talking out when your ears are shut to me. It's a pitiful thing, Conchubor, you have done this night in Emain ; yet a things will be a joy and triumph to the ends of life and time.

The drama of Synge is severely, almost deliberately limited. In comedy he writes only of one kind of man, the peasant of the east or the west of Ireland. Yet he chooses so unerringly what is fundamental in the manners and motives of his people that his comedies, though local, are universal, though national, international. In tragedy, the limitation is even more austere, for complexity of mood and theme are alike foregone ; there is no mingling of comedy to give breadth to his suggestion and no complication of plot to bring a corresponding sense of the multifariousness of event. There is, moreover, a curious absence of metaphysical or religious implication in the tragedies, which shows the more clearly beside Yeats's and A.E.'s. This gives to Synge's two tragedies something hard, abrupt, pagan. He shapes a fragment of life, man's and nature's intermingled, a fragment charged with passions that beat against fate, and, giving it clear form, leaves it isolated. Except for the insuperable and undying power of love in *Deirdre,* whose immortality even there is rather implied by its own strength than defined by comment or suggestion, there is no relating of the world of men with any wider, less tangible metaphysical universe. This puts his two tragedies in a peculiar position, for though their potency is unquestionable they have not, what great tragedy almost invariably carries with it, the implication of resolution. They are splendid, isolated fragments of human experience, but the human spirit in them, though itself of a high poetic or imaginative quality, is unrelated to any other spiritual value. Even nature, a sympathetic half-human power, is not a divine power, and the plays leave in the mind a sense of unresolved pain that is hard to parallel except in so totally different a play as Marlowe's *Faustus.* It may be that the synthesis of Synge's mind is not so complete as we at first supposed, that the seemingly impossible reconciliation of nature-mysticism and dramatic form was not as yet accomplished to the full and that the core of that undramatic and almost inexpressible faith did indeed remain unexpressed.

Synge often leads us back in thought to the Jacobeans and even those of us who most often recognize this kinship, wonder at times precisely where it lies. Yet we need hardly do so. For he has something of their knowledge of the inevitable, though hidden, movements of the spirit in the supreme moments of tragic experience. He, who knew so much of the fundamental loneliness of human life, who lived so constantly with death at his elbow, shared their knowledge of the searching interplay of death and life. 'I am in the way to study a long silence. To prate were idle.' The same power to condense thought and passion into all but silent and inarticulate vision that gave them their mastery over tragic event is his also. And he too can show, in these brief sentences spoken at the height of tragic revelation, depth below depth of knowledge. There are few words in twentieth-century drama that bring the same shock of conviction as Deirdre's or Maurya's in the face of death. Synge's is a profound knowledge, the knowledge of the freedom that comes from the parting of the last of the bonds of life : 'They're all gone now. *And there isn't anything more the sea can do to me.*' This is the grief ' that cuts the heart-strings ', freeing the spirit from the claims of the world ; Cleopatra, Imogen, Cornelia, the Duchess of Malfi and Calantha are among those who share it.

Perhaps the most satisfying interpretations of Synge have been made by his own great contemporary and fellow-poet, Yeats.[1] They are not long or elaborate but they mark, sometimes almost in indignant protest, the power and the penetration of Synge's poetic thought to which the world during his lifetime was blind. But Yeats, who was not blind, who recognized him instantly—indeed, almost foresaw him—spoke his fitting epitaph :

' Our Daimon is as dumb as was that of Socrates, when they brought in the hemlock ; and if we speak among ourselves, it is of the thoughts that have no savour because we cannot hear his laughter, of the work more difficult because of the strength he has taken with him, of the astringent joy and hardness that was in all he did, and of his fame in the world.'[2]

[1] See *Samhain*, 1903, 1904, 1905, *A People's Theatre* (P.C. 211), *Per Amica Silentia Lunae* (14–15), *Autobiographies* (423–6) and, especially, the four articles in *The Cutting of an Agate*—*The Tragic Theatre, Preface to the First Edition of ' The Well of the Saints', Preface to the . . . Poems and Translations* and *J. M. Synge and the Ireland of his Time.*

[2] *Preface to the First Edition of John M. Synge's Poems and Translations.* (C. of A., p. 124.)

CHAPTER 9

CONCLUSION AND PROSPECT

Our dramatists, and I am not speaking of your work or Synge's but of those to whom you and Synge and I gave opportunity, have been excellent just in so far as they have become all eye and ear, their minds not smoking lamps, as at times they would have wished, but clear mirrors. . . . We have been the first to create a true ' People's Theatre ', and we have succeeded because it is not an exploitation of local colour, or of a limited form of drama possessing a temporary novelty, but the first doing of something for which the world is ripe, something that will be done all over the world and done more and more perfectly : the making articulate of all the dumb classes each with its own knowledge of the world, its own dignity, but all objective with the objectivity of the office and the workshop, of the newspaper and the street, of mechanism and of politics. Yet we did not set out to create this sort of theatre.[1]

IN THESE WORDS, Yeats, looking back in 1919 upon the achievement of the movement in the first twenty years of its life summed up the change which had come over it since those early years with which our study is mainly concerned. It had been a change from poetic to realistic drama, from the imaginative interpretation of theories which were often remote in time or mood to the objective study of what was immediately at hand. The shift of interest and attitude is, though not sudden, so clear that the early phase separates from the later ones as naturally as does the drama of the late from that of the early Jacobean period, forming another demanding its own separate treatment. It is at once the conclusion of the early phase and a fresh beginning.

But the beginnings of the later Irish drama were already there in the early years of the movement, and the naturalism that we associate with the names of Colum, Robinson, Murray and a long line of writers down to our own day was already a part of Synge's own mastery, while the main work of Colum and

[1] W. B. Yeats to Lady Gregory. (P.C. 204–6.)

187

the early work of Robinson and Murray itself fell before the pausing place of 1912. Already, from 1903 onwards there was much that pointed forward to the post-war and present-day Irish drama, which forms, from that point onward, a web that, though of varying colours, is seamless.

When we look at the records of the theatre we find that, while the work of Yeats, Lady Gregory and Synge was still at its height, new names were beginning to come in, some of them names that are known wherever the movement is known ; and these new writers, though as distinct and highly individual as the original leaders, all shared in some degree the quality of objectivity, just as the earliest writers had shared that of poetic imagination. Colum's plays were produced in 1903, 1905, 1907 and 1910 ; Boyle's earliest in 1905, 1906 and 1912 ; Robinson's earliest in 1908, 1909, 1910 and 1912 ; Murray's earliest in 1910 and 1912. Besides these are the names of George Fitzmaurice, Conol O'Riordan, Lord Dunsany, St. John Ervine and Rutherford Mayne, while there are ten or a dozen names of others[1] all of whom wrote drama which, whether bitter or light-hearted, was naturalistic in its choice of theme and sometimes satirical in its treatment of humanity.

Within this large group there is, as we should expect, great individual variety, both in mood and material. The interpretation of life ranges from tragedy in Colum's *The Land*,[2] Robinson's *The Clancy Name* and Murray's *Maurice Harte* to the satirical comedies of Boyle. The material interpreted may be the world of the peasant, the small farmer, the small-town man or the people of the Dublin suburbs. But it is all immediate, in time and place, and in the hands of the most powerful of these writers, Colum, Robinson and Murray, it has a clear-sighted strength that is not easily forgotten. It is perhaps in the work of these three that the change may be most clearly

---

[1] Among them should be mentioned W. M. Letts, W. F. Casey, D. L. Kelleher, R. J. Ray, Seumas O'Kelly, E. H. Moore.

[2] *The Land* is described by its author as ' An agrarian comedy ' ; technically it belongs to that class, inasmuch as, in Fletcher's words, ' It wants deaths, which is enough to make it no tragedy.' But the sum of suffering in the play makes it just such a ' comedy ' as Ibsen's *An Enemy of the People* and, in considering mood rather than form, I have ventured to call it tragedy.

traced; the rest, except Boyle, fell out of the movement or developed along other lines or in other countries, and Boyle, for all his great popularity, his excellent stage-craft and his one good play (*The Building Fund*), never arrives at the strength or the distinction of these three.

Padraic Colum's *The Land*, Robinson's *The Clancy Name* and Murray's *Maurice Harte* may perhaps stand as representative of what was developing in the Irish realistic drama between 1905 and 1912. Other plays by the same authors or other authors might be chosen—Fitzmaurice's *Pie-dish*, Colum's *Thomas Muskerry*, Robinson's *Harvest*, Murray's *Birthright*, Ervine's *Mixed Marriage*[1]—but few other groupings would perhaps comprehend among them so many different aspects of the power and originality of this new reading of Irish life.

The Land has its roots, as its name implies, in the peasant farmer's love of the land which so many playwrights have since recognized.[2] The play opens on 'the day of redemption' at the crisis of the agrarian settlement. All the men have, in their different ways, that love of the land, and some of them, through it, a love of Ireland which is the land, or of 'the Irish nation that is waiting all this time to be born'. In Murtagh Cosgar it is the love of the hard-working, hard-bargaining, self-made man (like Bat Morrissey in Murray's *Birthright*) who is slave himself to the land he has mastered and would make his children serve it with the same fanatic ardour as his own. This passion is set against the rebellion of the young who will live their own lives and make their own service, who escape, when too hard-driven, into emigration, and denude the land. The two driving forces wrestle together throughout the play; Murtagh's will against his own children, till ten of them have emigrated and only the last two are left; the pull of the land against the pull of America, the cities and the street, 'To be doing other work, and to be meeting strange people. And instead of bare roads and market-towns, to be seeing streets, and crowds, and theatres.'[3] The conflict is joined again in the mind of Matt Cosgar who rebels against his father's dominance and yet has

[1] All produced between 1908 and 1911.
[2] The most interesting of these, for purposes of comparison, is perhaps Rutherford Mayne's *Red Turf* produced at the Abbey Theatre in 1911.
[3] Act II.

his own deeper and more imaginative love of the land, ' I've put my work into the land, and I'm beginning to know the land. I won't lose it, Ellen . . . the land is better than that when you come to know it, Ellen.' [1]

But the play is no thesis ; it is a cross section of a living society with men and women who are individual through their like-nesses, a society in which men do the right thing the wrong way and there is no plain, cut-and-dried issue. Murtagh Cosgar, the fanatic, Martin Douras the scholar-farmer, the patriot who has been imprisoned for the national cause, are blessed (or cursed) with children part like, part unlike themselves ; to Murtagh belong Matt, who has his father's virility, and so rebels, crushing down his own love of the land which left to itself would have held him, and Sally, the simple, industrious, unintelligent slave ; to Martin, Ellen with book-learning and intelligence like his own, but without his love of the land to hold her to it, and Cornelius, who has something of the willing industry of his betrothed, Sally, but whose stupidity takes the form of garrulity, a half-developed imitation of his father's and sister's lively intelligence. All these are distinct with indi-vidual variations ; the play is three-dimensional :

MARTIN DOURAS. You're right to take it that way, Ellen. School doesn't mean scholarship now. Many's the time I'm telling Cornelius that a man farming the land, with a few books on his shelf and a few books in his head, has more of the scholar's life about him than the young fellows who do be teaching in schools and teaching in colleges.

CORNELIUS. That's all very well, father. School and scholar-ship isn't the one. But think of the word ' Constantinople ! ' I could leave off herding and digging every time I think on that word !

MARTIN DOURAS. Ah, it's a great word. A word like that would make you think for days. And there are many words like that.[2]

It has the mood of tragedy all through, not the tragedy that leads to or is symbolized in violence and sudden death, but the tragedy of wasted effort, broken dreams and divided lives. Matt stifles the love of his land and emigrates with Ellen ;

[1] Act I.
[2] Act I.

Martin is left without Ellen, the only child who understood him, and Murtagh without a son to inherit the land he had won. The fight is tough and sinewy, like the men who work on the land ; the break-up of the stoutest fighter, Murtagh, comes too late to save what half that compliance earlier would have kept.

MURTAGH COSGAR. The men will be in soon, and we'll drink to new ownership.

MATT. Oh, what's the good in talking about that now ? If Ellen was here we might be talking about it.

MURTAGH COSGAR. To-morrow you and me might go together. Ay, the bog behind the meadow is well drained by this, and we might put the plough over it. There will be a fine, deep soil in it, I'm thinking. Don't look that way, Matt, my son.

MATT. When I meet Ellen Duras again, it's not a farmer's house I'll be offering her, nor life in a country place.

MURTAGH COSGAR. No one could care for you as I care for you. I know the blood between us, and I know the thoughts I had as I saw each of you grow up.

It is much the same world that we find in Colum's other plays, except *Thomas Muskerry,* which is the small-town society that Lennox Robinson has treated since, the world of shop-keepers and bank-managers, of competition and intrigue, where the poorest of the paupers and the simple-minded Muskerry himself are the only decent characters in a world of hard or shiftless sharpers. In Colum's plays, country-men, faithfully and without prejudice as they are revealed, are a finer and more vital growth than the people of the small towns : here, as elsewhere, apparently, if God made the country and man made the town, the devil made the country-town.

Lennox Robinson's world, though ultimately it became a rather different one, is at first the same as Colum's ; the early plays, *The Clancy Name, Harvest,* are of the country-side, and its people. *The Clancy Name,* a brief but memorable play, is yet another picture of the hard-working, thrifty, dominating Irish peasant. Mrs. Clancy has fought to keep the farm together for her son John and to keep the family name clear of dishonour, only to find at the end that he has committed murder. The struggle between her passion, not so much

14   191

for the land as for the good name of the family that belongs to it, and his desire for the solace of confession and retribution ends in his heroic but self-chosen death ; he carries the secret of his crime to the grave unspoken and her fight is won at the expense of his life. The play ends with that irony of which Robinson has so often since shown himself a master and the adroitness of its structure, the compactness given by the growing tension, suspense and tragic relief, foreshadows his later, exquisite skill as a structural artist. But his technical gift does not lead him into virtuosity and the play remains a stern record of hard fact and hard character :

FATHER MAHONY. I'm afraid there's no hope ; he's quite dead.

MRS. CLANCY. Quite dead ?

FATHER MAHONY. Yes, quite dead, poor woman.

MRS. CLANCY. He'll never speak again ?

FATHER MAHONY. Never again.

MRS. CLANCY. [*To herself*] Never again.

FATHER MAHONY. Ah, Mrs. Clancy, 'tis you should be the proud woman this day. I know well how proud you are of the Clancy name—you're a Clancy yourself—and how sorry you are to think your son has left no one to carry it on. But of all the Clancys, and they're a great family and a respected family, I venture to say that in years to come the greatest and most respected member of them will be your son, John Clancy, who gave his life to save a little child.

MRS. CLANCY. [*In a low voice, kneeling at John's side*] I'm sure it's very good of your reverence to say such things ; I thank God neither I nor my son, have ever brought disgrace on the Clancy name.

FATHER MAHONY. You haven't indeed, Mrs. Clancy. You should be proud this day to be the mother of John Clancy. . . . Let us pray for the soul of John Clancy.

[*Curtain.*]

T. C. Murray, who draws equally directly from peasant and farming life, mirrors, at first, in *Birthright,* a world very much like that of *The Land* and *The Clancy Name.* But in *Maurice Harte* his interest is beginning to centre in particular aspects of the peasant's life and mind and the figures he draws in most detail are generally, from then onward, the imaginative or the mystical, highly sensitive minds that, though they are acknowledged in other pictures of this society, are not (except for Colum's *The Fiddler's House* and one or two others) made the centre of study.[1] *Maurice Harte* is one of those rare plays which, if it does not treat precisely of religious experience, comes near it in treating the surrounding experiences of the religious life. The utter sincerity of the play gives it strength and balance ; every one of the characters is a fully realized human being, whose motives and outlook are deeply imagined. The conflict between the devoted parents who have sacrificed everything to make their son a priest and the son who finds on the eve of ordination that he has no vocation grows gradually more intense, the deep underlying sympathy with each other, the fundamental decency of all the five main characters, adding to its pain and to its reality. The inevitable climax draws on relentlessly, bringing frustration to the life-work of the old and to the hopes of the young. Whether it is seen or read, this play leaves an impression of faithful observation ; it is a record of the balancing of implacable forces. Though it has only two acts, the stored-up effort of the past years is as clearly before us as is the climax that is presented directly. The toughness of the contending forces, the unavoidableness of fate, gives the play a compactness that lends strength to each individual part ; the speech of the people is immediate, it forces its way out from their minds, whether it is the agonized protest of Maurice, the slow, half-inarticulate bewilderment of Michael, the father, or the urgent vehemence of Ellen, per-suading her son for their sakes to go back to the priesthood he shrinks from :

MRS. HARTE. Will·you be talking wild, frightening, foolish talk about your conscience, and not think at all of them, nor of us, and all we done for you ?

MAURICE. [*Distressfully*] Mother ! Mother !

MRS. HARTE. You'll go back ? 'Tis only a mistake ?

MAURICE. Great God of Heaven ! .. you'll kill me.

MICHAEL. You'll go back, Maurice ? The vocation will come to you in time with the help of God. It will, surely.

MAURICE. Don't ask me ! Don't ask me !

OWEN. 'Twould be better for you, Maurice. 'Twould surely.

[1] Here, again, we may compare with a play by Rutherford Mayne, *The Turn of the Road* (1906).

MRS. HARTE. [*Passionately*] If you don't, how can I ever face outside this door or lift up my head again ?

MAURICE. [*Piteously*] Mother !

MRS. HARTE. How could I listen to the neighbours' making pity
for me, and many a one o' them only glad in their hearts ?
How could I ever face again into the town o' Macroom ?

MAURICE. Oh, don't !

MRS. HARTE. I tell you, Maurice, I'd rather be lying dead a thousand times in the graveyard over at Killmamartyra——

MAURICE. [*With a sudden cry*] Stop, Mother, stop ! . . . [*There is
a tense pause.*] I'll—I'll go back—as—as you all wish it. [*He
sinks into a seat with an air of hopeless dejection.*]

MICHAEL. [*Drawing a long, deep breath*] God bless you, boy, for
that ! I knew you would.

OWEN. 'Tis the best thing, surely.

MRS. HARTE. [*Kneeling*] Oh, thanks be to the Almighty God
and his Blessed Mother this day.[1]

Here, as all through, there is a finely adjusted balance. Mrs.
Harte, refusing to imagine that her son's welfare can lie
anywhere but in the direction she has determined upon, the
gentler and slightly hesitant urging of the father and brother,
more imaginative and less passionate, the efforts of Maurice,
sensitive and torn between the frantic appeals of two parts
of his divided conscience, are the essential strains and conflicts
of the play. Mrs. Harte, individual as she is, has something
in common with many other studies of strong, devoted,
unimaginative women whose ambition, barred of direct
expression, must realize itself in the life of husband or children
and ruins the more creative and imaginative male whom she
forces towards the destiny she has determined upon for him.
Such portraits as these, the wreckage wrought by the determined devotion of strong-willed women, are common (though
always individualized) in this realistic Irish drama. I do not
believe that the type is peculiar to Ireland, but these dramatists
were among the first to see it clearly and to study both its
processes and its consequences.[2]

[1] End of Act I.

[2] Some of the other pictures, that may be compared with Mrs. Harte, are
those of Mrs. Clancy, Mrs. Crilly in *Thomas Muskerry* and Mrs. O'Regan
in *Aftermath* (T. C. Murray).

CONCLUSION AND PROSPECT

In these three plays and in that body of realistic Irish drama whose beginnings they represent, the first impression left is of honest, direct portraiture. There is no convention for them to follow lazily, no receipt ready at hand for a ' pièce bien faite '. A dramatist must become ' all eye and ear ' if he is to draw upon material that has never before been shaped into artistic form and it was fortunate for the new Irish drama that a standard of severe and yet unassuming accuracy in observation was set by the three writers who initiated it. From this ' objectivity ', this making of the mind into a ' clear mirror ' comes the simplicity and strength of the plays, for event in them grows out of character, and where action is the reflection of direct and vigorous minds the plot as a whole will be simple but balanced and resilient. An unpretentious strength is the hall-mark of the best of these plays and they contrast as sharply with the engineered play of the late nineteenth century in England as did the poetic drama of their own Irish predecessors. To set Jones's *Michael and his lost Angel* against *Maurice Harte* is to receive a lesson in the dramatic treatment of a vital theme ; the English play is unconvincing, hollow, difficult for the imagination to enter and yet full of implications of profundity which seem only to end in fevered confusion. The Irish play— which, incidentally, never attempts to reveal the religious experience itself—is plain and severe, showing with painful immediacy the effect of that experience in a society of which every member shares it to some degree and in which all acknowledge it, however different their estimate of its functions. The same distinction could be drawn between other plays of this later Irish movement and English plays of the nineties that touch corresponding themes. The revolution has been completed. The Irish stage, reversing the process of the contemporary English stage, has come back to realism through the chastening power of the poetic imagination and, reaching it by this road, has made not only the first ' People's Theatre ', but also a clear, astringent and disciplined body of realistic art.

Moreover, in the best of the realistic drama that follows, this poetic imagination never fails. Realism had shown itself soon after the beginnings of the poetic movement to which the imagination of Yeats had given power, but that very realism, when it became in its turn the dominant tradition, kept at its heart the quality which had been the distinctive mark of the earlier period. The ' theatre with a base of realism, with an apex of beauty' seems, it is true, to disappear ; but in fact both elements remain, though in a changed relation. Thus, a few years after Yeats wrote to Lady Gregory in the words with which the present chapter opens, a new dramatist appeared, to inherit the poetry and the realism of his predecessors and to initiate a third phase of the movement.

Sean O'Casey made his name between 1923 and 1928 as the dramatist of the Dublin slums during the Troubles of 1916 to 1922. In certain ways he is closely related to the Irish dramatists who had gone before him ; to his immediate predecessors most evidently, Lennox Robinson, T. C. Murray, St. John Ervine, Rutherford Mayne, but also to those whose material and treatment seem at first glance remote from his, to the founders of the Irish Theatre, W. B. Yeats, Lady Gregory, Padraic Colum and J. M. Synge. His subjects and scenes are different, but his reading of life, like that of all Irish dramatists, is at heart a poet's, even when his method and treatment are clear-cut and satiric. Indeed, it is in these parts of his work that he seems to belong most nearly to a class of writers rare in all literature and very rare in drama, the tragic satirists in whom the comedy of satire points directly to tragic implications. After the first four plays he changed from the realistic treatment of Irish slum life to a partly symbolic or stylised treatment of English life, though he returned to Ireland in *Purple Dust* and to Dublin in *Red Roses for Me*. It is doubtful whether his work gained by that change. Indeed, many of us who watched his early development with hope and interest believe that the loss outweighed the gain. We miss that fine and impartial mixture, of bitter satire with poignant studies of nobility and generosity lurking in unlikely places, that gave their distinctive flavour to the early plays. His first audiences recognised, in the plays between 1923 and 1928, originality in his choice of material and, only in less degree, in his technique.

The material was obviously new in the drama of the twentieth century, and it was the result of genuine originality helped, it may be, by the lucky accident of circumstance and surroundings.

CONCLUSION AND PROSPECT

Very few dramatists, and none of such power as O'Casey, had written realistically of the people of the slums, understanding from their own experience the effects of such a life on character and behaviour and giving us the result of penetrating and sensitive observation without sentiment and without prejudice. Other dramatists in Ireland, from Colum onward, had turned equally unsentimental and unprejudiced eyes on the peasant or the small farmer ; certain English dramatists, notably Shaw and Galsworthy, had given sympathetic studies of the lives of the London poor, but only in plays whose central characters were drawn from other levels of society. Now O'Casey's drama does neither of these things. He seems to look at the north bank of the Liffey with a vision as matter-of-fact in its assumptions as Galsworthy's view of the Forsytes and to see there human beings neither worse nor better at bottom than their fellows, and so entitled neither to more nor to less of disgust or pity. But he sees clearly, (and at first, it would seem, without class-consciousness), what habit of mind and what way of life is produced by crowded slums. He portrays these faithfully. In those early plays, *The Shadow of a Gunman* (1923), *Juno and the Paycock* (1924), *The Plough and the Stars* (1926) and in parts of *The Silver Tassie* (1928), he reveals, almost as though unconscious of the novelty of his picture, the easy, vigorous, expressive speech and action of people in continual and inescapable contact with their fellows ; the mixture of good-fellowship and protective, selfish indifference. His people reveal now the distracted, unstable habits of mind that spring from continual stimulus and a procession of minor excitements, now the seemingly callous detachment, the bleak and lonely obstinacy that is a stronger personality's resistance to this bombardment directed upon its attention and emotion. Minnie Powell, Mrs. Gogan and Norah Clitheroe, Joxer, Clitheroe, Fluther are the natural and spontaneous birth of this soil. But so also, bred of a harder stock, are Davoran and Shields, the gunmen who lead off Johnny Boyle to execution, Brennan, the captain of the Irish citizen army, or Susie and Jessie in *The Silver Tassie*. Admittedly, there are also to be found a Mrs. Boyle and a Bessie Burgess ; but O'Casey rightly knows that spontaneous generosity, courage or nobility, operating without incitement and without reward, are rare at all times ; and his proportioning of the elements here seems just. For what he reveals is precisely what can best be shown by a drama whose material is raw life, whether in the wilds or in the kindred jungle of the slums ; the clash or jostle of untamed and undisciplined forces in communities that have strong passions but few traditions and fewer standards with which to meet the test of war and revolution. It is a world in which the emotions seem to have had no education and the moral sense no training except in those few whom the Church has reached. Apart from this, all is left to instinct and to nature, and, whether or not it is part of O'Casey's conscious intention that we should do so, we carry away at first reading an unformulated conviction that nature has not done too badly and that O'Casey has opened to us in these four plays a world as honestly assessed as that of Dickens, if more limited in scope.

Nor are the events less novel than the characters. The disintegration of standards begun by slum-life is carried further by the impact of revolution or civil war, which even in more disciplined communities tend to throw values back again into the melting-pot. As Denis Johnston was to say, some ten years later, ' The birth of a nation is no Immaculate Conception.' It may be that the freshness has a little worn off this material to-day, partly on account of the actual experience of many of us and partly on account of the occupation of that province by other dramatists. But when O'Casey wrote there had been less use, in recent drama, of the background of revolution, street-fighting, civil war and the professional gunman who is the inevitable product of these. Within twelve years of his fourth play all this material had been used, and used memorably ; by Odets and Anderson in America, with *Till the Day I Die*, *Waiting for Lefty* and *Winterset* ; by Denis Johnston in Ireland itself with *The Moon in the Yellow River*; by Nordahl Grieg and Pär Lagerkvist in Scandinavia with *The Defeat* and *The Man without a Soul*. And the knowledge of much that touched its fringes in these countries, in Russia and in Central Europe between the two wars, had made the circumstances familiar to theatre audiences. But O'Casey broke new ground for his own times and for the English-speaking countries.

Moreover, for Englishmen and Irishmen, there was something

new in his technique. There was, as often at the beginning of a new and original dramatist's career, some confusion in the public mind between what was new in the strictly technical aspects of the plays and what was only in fact the result of novelty in choice of material. But in the first three plays it gradually became clear that the material was making its own demands upon the form, that subject-matter, and still more theme, were beginning by degrees to control the structure of the play, to express themselves in its form. There was, in addition, some actual novelty in the technique of his revelation of character and some in his handling of dialogue. All three could have been paralleled from the work of one or other of the dramatists of the Continent of Europe or of America in the period between the two wars, (notably from the work of Kaiser, Toller, Schnitzler, Pirandello, and Elmer Rice) and the most significant of them from the work of their common predecessors, Tchekov and Strindberg. But there was a strength and firmness in the growth of O'Casey's technique which carried the mark of originality ; here was, clearly, no mere theft of a ready-made instrument.

For the structure of his plays, which was never conventional or orthodox, has at its best, as in the second act of *The Plough and the Stars*, a subtle and original relation to his theme. Here, where disjunction becomes the theme of the play, O'Casey is concerned with the picture of the collapse of a rebellion and the destruction of man's hopes for the birth of a nation and the progress of humanity, and what had once, as in the second act of *The Shadow of a Gunman*, been a brief, comic device for the revelation of character, becomes an integral part of the structure of the play. It becomes charged, therefore, with satiric and tragic implications released from the extension of this device into the very form of the structure.

His place in the Irish Dramatic Movement is of great importance, for he turned into new channels the sharp, fierce or bitter social criticism which had shown itself from time to time in writers as different as Colum, Synge, Mayne, Ervine, Robinson. And in so doing he so added to its strength and force as to bring it to the verge of tragic potency : some would say that he carried it well across the verge. To many of his English readers, O'Casey seemed, in fact, the embodiment of poetry in revolt, and though his was a different poetry and a different revolt, he was thereby akin to many poets of the third decade in England and on the continent.

The Irish drama has been a continuous movement, showing continuous development from its beginnings in 1899 to the present day, and even the most recent drama cannot be sharply detached from that continuum. Just as the work of W. B. Yeats and Lady Gregory, continuing into the 1920's, linked the theatre of the old days of the Lords Lieutenant with the theatre of O'Casey and of independent Ireland, so the later work of such writers as Rutherford Mayne in the north and Lennox Robinson and T. C. Murray in the south, linked the earlier phases of that new theatre with the work of the dramatists of the nineteen-thirties and forties. The most recent drama in Ireland thus includes, alongside the work of the youngest dramatists, such plays as Rutherford Mayne's *Bridgehead* (1934), Lennox Robinson's *Church Street* (1934) and *Killycraggs in Twilight* (1937), T. C. Murray's *Michaelmas Eve* (1934). Some of these, the work of men whose experience has not dimmed their vitality, are among the best things that have been produced in the Irish theatre in the last quarter of a century, and some seem more nearly abreast of the times than the work of younger men. In thought, dramatic technique and the imaging of the manners of a fast-changing civilization, the older men, in Ireland at least, are easily the equals of all but the best of their successors.

But when we speak of recent dramatists we do, in fact, mean something other than recent drama ; we think primarily of the men who have come into the theatre in the last quarter of a century, of their thought, their technique, their image of the modern Irish world. Of the most recent arrivals it is hard to speak, for the opposite reason; because they have not yet declared themselves and it is neither fair nor profitable to attempt to place them. But there is a sufficient group of writers who began work in the twenties or thirties of this century, reaching their full strength somewhere in the the thirties or forties, to form, if not a homogeneous group, at least a connected series of dramatists whose pictures of Irish life are demonstrably painted from similar models. Among these are Brinsley Macnamara, George Shiels, Denis Johnston, Lord and

CONCLUSION AND PROSPECT

Lady Longford, Mary Manning, Teresa Deevy, Lynn Doyle, Micheál MacLiammóir, Patrick Hamilton, Paul Vincent Carroll and others. From these we may choose, perhaps, three who, among them, represent what is most characteristic of Irish drama in the 1930's and 1940's and its image of its world ; Denis Johnston, George Shiels and Paul Vincent Carroll.

The concern of these writers, when they write of the world about them, is with the new Ireland that emerged from the Troubles of 1916 to 1922. The drama can be seen adjusting itself to the new material furnished by the social and political changes that were taking place all over the country, and one of the first things we notice in the plays of this period is just this consciousness, that there *is* a new Ireland and that this is not a matter of statute-books but of the lives of people. There is a new balance of groups and forces ; some of the old restrictions have gone and new powers are, for better or for worse, released ; other controls have taken the place of the older ones, with compensating advantages and disadvantages. All this was matter, first for experience, then for debate, and all the time for observation and comment by journalists, novelists and dramatists.

Yet there is continuity in the picture, even though the task of portraying it passes from hand to hand. Denis Johnston takes over in 1931 what O'Casey bequeathed to him when, in 1928, he turned aside from his pictures of Dublin slum-life to experiment in stylised forms, using English material. Johnston gives us, in his *Moon in the Yellow River*, the first full length study of the mood of those uncertain years that followed immediately after the Revolution and the Civil War, years of uneasy peace and of maladjustment, years of enterprise and expectation for some, but also of reaction, disappointment and occasional outbreak of violence among the defeated parties. When Johnston in his turn moves into a different type of writing, George Shiels, a shrewd and keen observer, an experienced man of the theatre, takes up the tale, giving us increasingly serious pictures, almost photographic in their plain, direct records, of the Ireland of the late thirties ; and what Shiels does not cover, Paul Vincent Carroll makes his special domain. Thus, between them, these four dramatists give us a picture of Ireland from 1916 to 1940, a picture whose title might well be the already quoted words with which Padraic Colum had brought down the curtain on *The Land*, in 1903 : "The Irish nation, which is waiting all this time to be born." And in their work, as always in good drama, the material and the theme determine to a large extent the nature of the treatment and the form.

But to furnish a record is not a dramatist's primary function Indeed, it is only a subsidiary part. Our real concern, when we go to him *as* a dramatist, is to know how far he, having observed, selected and assimilated this material, has made it serve him as matter for his art. His function, when all is said, is to produce drama, not (Ben Jonson's dictum notwithstanding) to 'show an image of the times'. How far and in what ways do these three, the most recent Irish dramatists, do this ? Is the tradition they hand on worthy of the original Irish dramatic movement of the past? And what are they likely to transmit to the future ? To answer this question, we must look at them, not as mirrors of the Irish scene, but as dramatists.

Denis Johnston is a dramatist of originality and versatility whose work has been received with interest in Ireland, England and America. He is equally at home in direct delineation of character, essentially and distinctively Irish ; in the analysis of the conflicting moods of a difficult transition period (the years succeeding the War of 1922–3) ; and in the revelation of the more obscure territories of the mind bordering upon the unconscious, after the manner of Toller, Kaiser and their forerunners. The first of his plays to be produced, *The Old Lady Says No !* (Dublin Gate, 1929), is a satiric review of certain dominant elements in Irish life, thought, political history and literature, and an acute exposure of the sentimentality that may be inherent in some of them. His second, *The Moon in the Yellow River* (1931), earned wide popularity for the preciseness with which the author diagnosed the mood of the middle twenties of this century in Ireland. Though much of the material was so recent as to be used here for the first time, there was a certain mastery and harmony in form and grouping. In *A Bride for the Unicorn* (1933), he produced one of the most original pieces of dramatic technique in the Irish drama and his later plays continue to reveal many of these distinctive characteristics.

CONCLUSION AND PROSPECT

The Moon in the Yellow River gives a picture of the Ireland of the early thirties, with its confusion, at once political, social, moral, psychological and spiritual, but it has at the same time some of the qualities of genuine drama in its rich, varied and yet unconfused groups of characters. Johnston's choice of material is not so profoundly original as O'Casey's discovery that the familiar Dublin slums could be translated into art ; but he is, for all that, a faithful observer and a clear draughtsman. His people reveal themselves by action rather than by talk, or if by talk, then by talk called forth by action and leading to action again. The background figures are slightly drawn but there is often the implication of fuller knowledge behind the sketch. His comedy is neither forced nor unduly irrelevant and his tragic figures, Dobelle and Lanigan the gunman, are sympathetically handled. The mixture of tragedy and half-farcical comedy is not grotesque, though at one point, Lanigan's shooting of Blake, the transition is a little ill-prepared. It was, moreover, a clever stroke that introduced Tausch, the German engineer, at work installing a government power-station, to serve as a commentator and a test of the life about him. His kindly Teutonic logic illuminates unfailingly every twist and inconsistency in the cranky world into which he has dropped.

A different world meets us in *The Old Lady Says No!*, a brilliant piece of satire on Irish thought and letters (including the dramatic movement itself), which tries to force into dramatic form innately undramatic material. The action takes place in the mind of an actor who is accidentally stunned while playing the part of Robert Emmett and thereafter blends in hopeless entanglements his impressions of contemporary Dublin with his memories, now of early nineteenth-century history, now of the late nineteenth- and early twentieth-century drama. The possibilities of satiric exposure for all three are extensive, and Johnston appears to miss none of them. But to savour his effects one must be an Irishman or know Irish history and literature well. The technique of the dream play allows him absolute liberty in space and time, but as so often, this freedom is dangerous. Yet even the Englishman can recognize the brilliance of Johnston's satire, the swift and subtle terms of his analysis.

The material and method of George Shiels is almost as

different from that of Denis Johnston as it is possible for one dramatist's to be from another's given the same setting and time. His style, whether in structure, in choice, grouping or revelation of character, or in dialogue, is simple and straightforward. His characters, like those of T. C. Murray, seem not to be set in motion by the dramatist but to be overheard by him. We might be tempted to call it photography rather than art, were it not that we notice, especially in the later plays, that a problem is set and unobtrusively resolved. The presence of a theme in a play dispels the possibility of mere reporting and we realize that Shiels's simplicity and directness is the end-product of a long training and the index of a specific skill. He made his name in comedy and his early work was realistic without bitterness or harshness, humourous or fanciful without farce and sympathetic without forfeiting that humour or the satire into which it merges. Such comedies, as *Paul Twining*, *Professor Tim*, and *The New Gossoon* were humourous or genially satirical pictures of contemporary life, only the last posing or debating the problems of that society. But at least three later plays revealed Shiels, though still humourously satirical, as a clear-sighted observer and a serious critic of the new Ireland, a man, more-over, who could make of some of its most urgent problems the matter of drama, somewhat as Galsworthy's successors, Hankin, Houghton or Baker, had done before him in England. *The Passing Day* (1936), firm though its grip is on character and theme, is perhaps less fully representative of this new Shiels than the pair of plays on the administration of justice in rural Ireland, *The Rugged Path* (1940) and *The Summit* (1941).

One of the first things we notice in these two plays is the sober, matter-of-fact demeanour of the artist. He resists those temptations to the spectacular, the sensational, the flamboyant into which O'Casey's genius had sometimes led him; all temptations to the high-lighting and the over-colouring that spoil the composition in the work of many of his contemporaries. And there were temptations enough in his material. The Dolis Clan who had lived on their mountain for a thousand years, whose present-day representatives were not noticeably changed from the cattle-rieving murderers who had been their original ancestors, offered almost irresistible opportunities for sensation, melodrama, fantasy or farce. But Shiels has graver work in hand, both as a recorder and as a dramatist. He sees in them one of the unsolved problems of his time, a lawless, shiftless set of gangsters living on the outskirts of prosperous farming communities, terrorising the neighbourhood with their knives and their guns and playing upon the old weakness of the law-abiding Irish citizen, the horror of laying evidence against a criminal lest he himself should be branded as an informer. This superstitious hatred for the name of ' informer ' is, as the younger men admit, a legacy from the days when the law was enforced and adminis-tered by an alien race, when it was a patriotic duty to protect an Irish neighbour from English authorities. It is a wholly illogical sentiment now that Irish law is administered by an Irish Dail, and it needs only a little hardihood to destroy it ; ' That old badge belonged to other days. It should have disappeared with the people who invented it.' Liam Cassidy is right. But behind the inability of the older people to do away with the disgrace of being called informers lies a substantial and quite reasonable fear. The tyranny of the Dolis Clan and their like is far beyond the control of the scattered police, and law-abiding men cannot protect themselves against murder or theft from the vengeful, half-outlawed clan : ' The sergeant lives five miles away,' says John Perrie, ' and the enemy is near at hand. Can the sergeant be sitting with me day and night ? ' As a result, not only will no man lay information, but no jury will convict, even in the face of overwhelming evidence and the clearest leads from the judge. The judge does not have to spend his life with the Dolises as neighbours ; the jury do.

Shiels has made out of this problem and its effects on the lives of a handful of people in a Border community a pair of plain straightforward plays that grip the attention (*The Rugged Path* broke the Abbey records for the length of its run in 1940) and does so without tricks and without resort to theatrical devices. Structure, characters and dialogue alike are genuine ; their honest workmanship is of that serviceable kind which looks artless.

Paul Vincent Carroll's world is again that of Shiels's, but he is in general more concerned with individuals than with groups, with personal than with public problems, though often enough with him also the relations of liberty and law are involved. From the first he took a line of his own, fastening upon and limiting himself to certain characters, analysing them with great perspicacity, and, in some cases, imagination ; the figures of his schoolmasters, intelligent, rebellious, half-cowardly, half-heroic, in confused and bitter conflict with some form of tyranny or oppression, are sympathetically imagined, and his gallery of priests has some fine portraits in it.

His best play, taken all in all, is probably *The White Steed*. Here two priestly characters are drawn in contrast and in conflict, the old, paralysed Canon Lavelle, a wise, lovable man with plenty of foibles, plenty of good sense and vast wisdom, and the young Father Shaughnessy who has come to take his place, a disconcerting mixture of bigot and prig, hero and martyr. Both men are well drawn and the relation between them even better. The final dialogue sums up not only this relationship, but the underlying conflicts and stresses that, as yet only half characterize this new Ireland and give it a theme, far indeed from those of the plays with which the movement began, yet witnessing to a half-hidden relationship. Explicit, where the poetic drama of Yeats achieved all by implication, this is manifestly a picture of the world of Patrick Colum in a later phase of its growth.

CANON. What have you achieved ? You have only succeeded in stupidly dragging into the light the things we old codgers grow in the dark in Ireland.

FATHER S. I will allow nothing to grow in the dark in Ireland.

CANON. Of course you won't, because you're a hot-headed pioneer full of spiritual snobbery. Ten thousand sages of the Church have refused to write certain laws on paper, but you, rushing in with a Gaelic tag in your mouth, scrawl them across a page with a schoolboy's pen. Let me tell you this, that we rule this nation with laws that no one writes but that everyone instinctively accepts. You can cross out a law that's on paper, but you can't cross out a law that's never been written. The day you put these laws on paper in this country, you and I and all we stand for will have to take the field and fight to the death for our continuance.

Can we make any kind of forecast about this new Irish drama ? None, I think, except such as its past abundantly warrants. Few bodies of drama in the Western hemisphere have shown so continuous a stream of vitality for the last fifty years, or a fairer average of craftsmanship than the Irish. Many of the great names are gone now, but fine workmen remain and the indomitable vigour of the Irish race goes far to justify the hope that, when this force has been finally converted to skill and grace it will not, as did much nineteenth century European drama, sink into the sterility of virtuosity without life. When we look back over the long tumultuous half-century of this, the youngest of the European dramas, we realize afresh the justice of the comment of Shiels's Civic Guard: ' I declare to God there's more fine types of Irishmen at large than we could enumerate, and no two of them with the same point of view.'

For there are not lacking signs that even this is not the final phase and that a movement away from realism and towards imaginative fantasy is setting in again in the Irish drama of the present day. It is too early to prophesy whether this will bring back a new poetic movement or whether it represents only the last phase of that which began fifty-four years ago. But that the theatre created then by Yeats and Lady Gregory is alive to-day there can be no question. ' They have won much praise for themselves and raised the dignity of Ireland.'

APPENDICES

CHRONOLOGICAL TABLE OF THE MAIN EVENTS IN THE EARLY YEARS OF THE MOVEMENT (UP TO 1904)

[As the early accounts of these years do not pretend to include all the details and as in some cases they contradict each other when they do, it has seemed advisable to add here a plain, chronological list of events, in so far as I have been able to collect them. There is obviously no place for all these details in Chapter 3, but students of the movement may find, as I have often done, that a complete table of dates is essential for elucidation of the events of the early years. The source I have used is given in each case in the right hand margin, in the abbreviated form shown on p. xvii and some of the other source-books which also refer, or appear to be referring, to the same episode, are mentioned in similar abbreviated form, in the footnotes. I have carried this time-table up to the summer of 1904 when the negotiations for the Abbey Theatre began. After that date the records are generally more detailed or at least more accessible, the ultimate source being the files of the Abbey Theatre programmes, and the history of the company is more straightforward. This is not intended in any way as a substitute for the clear accounts given by Mr. A. E. Malone (*The Irish Drama*) or for the invaluable lists of plays and authors in the Appendices to that work. It is simply an amplification of my own account of the main events of the early years of the company.][1].

Date	Event	Source
1891	W. B. Yeats ' founded in London the Irish Literary Society '.	*D.P.* 13
	W. B. Yeats, George Moore and Edward Martyn meet.	*Autobiogs.* 246. *D.P.* 22.

[1] A more detailed account of certain parts of this summary is to be found in an unpublished doctoral thesis by Alan Cole of Trinity College, Dublin (1952).

Date	Event	Source
June 1892	The National Literary Society founded in Dublin.[1]	Rules of Soc. Dublin, 1897. (Hend. i. 27) *Autobiogs.* 246.
	John O'Leary, the Fenian, first President.	D.P. 14.
	Douglas Hyde, second President. Hyde's presidential lecture ('The De-Anglicization of Ireland') leads to foundation of Gaelic League.	D.P. 14.
	W. B. Yeats discusses a small theatre in London with Florence Farr.	D.P. 15.
April 1894	W. B. Yeats's *Land of Heart's Desire*, performed at Avenue Theatre, London, which was then under Florence Farr's management. 'It ran for a little over six weeks.'	Reviews, e.g., *Sketch* 25/4/94, *Trag. Gen.* 344. *P.C.* 327 (note to *L.H.D.*)
1898	W. B. Yeats and Lady Gregory meet and discuss plays.	O.I.T. 2–3.
Summer 1898	W. B. Yeats, Lady Gregory and Martyn plan to produce *Heather Field* and *Countess Cathleen*, draw up a statement and appeal for subscriptions.	O.I.T. 3, 5–9, D.P. 15, 17.
Jan. 16, 1899	Irish Literary Theatre founded, under auspices of National Literary Society. Promoted by W. B. Yeats and Edward Martyn.	Extract from Minute Book of N.L.S. (Hend. i.7)
Spring 1899	The plays put into rehearsal in London. George Moore intervenes.	O.I.T. 20.[2]

[1] For the account given, in the Rules, of the founding of the Society, see App. 2.   [2] See also *Ave.*, 40–46, 69–94.   D.P. 20, 27, 34–5.

Date	Event	Source
April 17, 1899	W. B. Yeats lectured on 'Dramatic Ideals and The Irish Literary Theatre'.	Hend. i. 101 (Press cutting).
Spring 1899	The pamphlet *Souls for Gold* issued (against *Countess Cathleen*).[1]	*Souls for Gold*, London, 1899.
	Controversy roused. Cardinal Logue wrote to newspapers.	*O.I.T.* 20, 24. *D.P.* 35, 36.
	Martyn disturbed and prepared to withdraw financial support from play.	*D.P.* 35.
	The play submitted to Father Barry[2] and Father Finlay. Both passed it.	*O.I.T.* 21-2, *D.P.* 36. *H.F.* 109.
	Lionel Johnson wrote the prologue for the first performance.	Beltaine. i.[3]
May 1, 1899	First productions of Irish Literary Theatre at the Ancient Concert Rooms, Great Brunswick St.	Beltaine i.[4] Hend. i. 27.
May 8, 8.30	*The Countess Cathleen*. (With police protection. *D.P.* 37-8).	Beltaine i.
May 9, 8.30	*The Heather Field*. (An uncontroversial success.)	,,
May 10, 3.0	*The Countess Cathleen*.	,,
8.30	*The Heather Field*.	,,
May 12, 8.30	*The Countess Cathleen*.	,,
May 13, 3.0	*The Heather Field*.	,,
8.30	*The Countess Cathleen*.	,,
	The committee, on strength of success of *Heather Field*, bespoke Martyn's next (unfinished) play and engaged the Gaiety Theatre for a week in following year for the performances of that and *Maeve*.	*D.P.* 49.

[1] See Appendix 2.
[2] See Appendix 2.
[3] See also poetic works of Lionel Johnson and *O.I.T.* 23
[4] See also *O.I.T.* 23-5, 261 ; *D.P.* 37-9 ; *H.F.* 95-100 and numerous reviews, especially Max Beerbohm's in *Saturday Review*, 13 May, 1899.

Date	Event	Source
Summer 1899	Completion of Martyn's play, *The Tale of a Town*, and re-writing of it as *The Bending of the Bough* by Moore, with help from W. B. Yeats.	D.P. 49, 51–2, 65. H.F. 161, 171, 252, 270–5.
	W. B. Yeats and Douglas Hyde work on scenario of Casad-an-Sugan.	D.P. 65.
Feb. 1900	Second Productions of Irish Literary Theatre at Gaiety Theatre.	
Feb. 19, 1900	W. B. Yeats's address on *Maeve*.	O.I.T. 26–7.
Feb. 20, 8.0	*The Bending of the Bough.*	O.I.T. 26, 261, and Programme. Hend. i. 123.
Feb. 21. 2.30	*The Bending of the Bough.*	Programme. Hend. i. 123.
8.30	*The Last Feast of the Fianna*[1] and *Maeve*.	,, ,, ,,
Feb. 22, 8.0	*The Bending of the Bough.*	Freeman's Journal. Hend. i. 125.
Feb. 23, 8.0	*The Bending of the Bough.*[2]	,, ,, ,,
Feb. 24. 2.30	*The Last Feast of the Fianna* and *Maeve*.	,, ,, ,,
8.0	*The Bending of the Bough.*	,, ,, ,,
October 1901	The third series of Irish Literary Theatre performances.	
	' Mr. F. R. Benson's Shakespearean Company at the Gaiety Theatre.'	Programme. Hend. i. 111.
Oct. 21.[3] 8.0	*Casad-an-Sugan*. (Douglas Hyde).	,, ,, ,,

[1] By Alice Milligan. For text, see Supplement to *United Irishman* (Hend. i. 132).

[2] An alteration was made in the order announced on the first programme of the series. Moore's *Bending of the Bough* was so popular that (as announced in *The Freeman's Journal* for Friday, Feb. 23) it was given an additional production that night in the place of *The Last Feast of the Fianna* and *Maeve*.

[3] ' The cast filled by Members of the Gaelic League Amateur Dramatic Society.' (Programme.) This was the first Gaelic play produced in any theatre (*O.I.T.* 261, 28). Hyde himself acted in it (*O.I.T.* 29).

Date	Event	Source
Oct. 21. 8.45	*Diarmuid and Grania.*[1]	Programme. Hend. i. 111.
1902.		
Oct. 22. 8.0	*Casad-an-Sugan.*	„ „ „
8.45	*Diarmuid and Grania.*	„ „ „
Oct. 23. 2.30	*Casad-an-Sugan.*	„ „ „
3.15	*Diarmuid and Grania.*	„ „ „
8.0	*Casad-an-Sugan.*	„ „ „
8.45	*Diarmuid and Grania.*[2]	„ „ „
Oct. 24–6	[Benson's company completed the week with *Lear*.]	„ „ „
1901	The time now came for a development in the I.L.T. Suggested (by Moore) that a stock company of English-trained actors should be supplied through Benson. W. B. Yeats discovered the amateur productions of Wm. and Frank Fay. Saw them produce Alice Milligan's *Red Hugh*. Gave them his *Cathleen ni Houlihan* to be produced in following April.	D.P. 78.
	Moore then withdrew. (Martyn had already done so.)	D.P. 82. P.C. 3. Note.
	W. B. Yeats and Lady Gregory collaborate in	
	Where There is Nothing[3]	D.P. 83.
	The Pot of Broth	„ 82–3.
Early 1902	A.E. wrote to Lady Gregory that he had finished his *Deirdre*.	O.I.T. 30.

[1] For reviews, see *The Irish Daily Independent and Nation, The United Irishman,* etc. See also, generally, on this season, W. B. Yeats : *Samhain,*

[2] For accounts of Moore's and Yeats's collaboration, see *D.P.* 60–5, 67 and *H.F.* 346 seq. The text of this play is apparently lost.

[3] ' It could not be performed in Ireland ' (*D.P.* 84), but the Stage Society produced it in London in 1904.

Date	Event	Source
Early 1902	A little hall in Camden Street was hired for rehearsals of that and *Cathleen ni Houlihan.*	*O.I.T.* 31.
	The Irish National Theatre Society was founded ... ' to continue—if possible on a more permanent basis—the work begun by the Irish Literary Theatre '.	Leaflet of I.N.T.S. Hend. i. 322.
	' the first performances were in April 1902 '.	,, ,, ,,
	W. B. Yeats made President and A.E. Vice-President.	*O.I.T.* 31.
April 1902	First series of Irish National Dramatic Company's performances at St. Teresa's Hall, Clarendon Street, with W. G. Fay's Company.	Programme. Hend. i. 234.
Apr. 2. Eve.	*Deirdre* (A.E.).	,, ,, ,,
	Cathleen ni Houlihan.	,, ,, ,,
Apr. 3. Eve.	*Deirdre.*	,, ,, ,,
	Cathleen ni Houlihan.	,, ,, ,,
Apr. 4. Eve.	*Deirdre.* ⎫1 *Cathleen ni Houlihan.* ⎭	Programme. Hend. i. 234.
	Standish O'Grady (in *All Ireland Review*) expostulated against the use of the heroic legend. A.E. replied in the *United Irishman.*	*Samhain*, 1902. [*P.C.* 23.]
Oct. 1902	Second series of I.N.T.S.[2] at the Ancient Concert Rooms.	*O.I.T.* 261.

---

[1] For reviews, see *The Leader*, April 12, *The All Ireland Review*, April 19, etc. and for ref. see also *D.P.* 78–80, *O.I.T.* 261.

[2] There is some fluctuation, in the beginning, both in notices and programmes, as to the use of the titles Irish National Dramatic Society (Company) and Irish National Theatre Society. The first was the title of Fay's company and the second that adopted after the amalgamation of W. B. Yeats's and Lady Gregory's schemes with those of the Fays.

Date	Event	Source
Oct. 27. Eve.	Irish concert. Chanting by Miss Farr. Explanation by W. B. Yeats.	*United Irishman.* Hend. i. 211.
„ 28. „	*Deirdre.* *Cathleen ni Houlihan.*	„ „ „
„ 29. „	*The Sleep of the King* (Seumas O'Cuisin). *The Laying of the Foundations* (Fred Ryan).	„ „ „ *Irish Daily Independent.* Hend. i. 208.
„ 30. „	*Deirdre.* *The Pot of Broth.*	„ „ „ *O.I.T.* 261 and *United Irishman*
„ 31. „	*The Racing Lug*[1] (Seumas O'Cuisin). *Elis agus an Bhean Deirce*[2] (Father MacGinley).	„ „ „ *United Irishman.* „ „ *Samhain,* 1901.
Nov. 1. 2.30	Lecture by W. B. Yeats on his theory of chanting. Illustrated by Miss Farr.	*United Irishman.*
Eve.	*The Laying of the Foundations.* *Cathleen ni Houlihan.* *The Pot of Broth.*	„ „ „ „ „ „
Dec. 1902	Third series of The Irish National Theatre Society's performances at the Camden St. Playhouse.	Hend. i. 102. (article).
Dec. 4. 8.0	*The Laying of the Foundations.* ⎫ *A Pot of Broth.* ⎬ 3 *Elis agus an Bhean Deirce.* ⎭	Programme. Hend. i. 246. „ „ „ „ „ „
Dec. 5. 8.0	[Same set]	„ „ „
Dec. 6. 8.0	[Same set]	„ „ „

[1] Published as a supplement to the *United Irishman.* (Hend. i. 209.)

[2] For Mr. Yeats's comment on the ' continual laughter of the audience ', see *Samhain,* 1901.

[3] See also letters from Fay to Lady Gregory, quoted, in part, *O.I.T.* 31, 32 on his project and its success—the takings being £4 15s. 0d. During this transition period it is not always easy to say whether Fay's performances are strictly those of the I.N.T.S. Generally the programme indicates that they are.

Date	Event	Source
1903	A certain number of isolated performances in various places.	
Jan. 9.	*The Laying of the Foundations.* ⎫ Town Hall, *The Racing Lug.* ⎬ Rathmines. *The Pot of Broth.* ⎭	Programme. Hend. i. 168. *Samhain*, 1903.
Jan. 10.	[Same]	
Jan. 24.	*The Pot of Broth.* The Club House, Foynes.	MS. note. Hend. i. 148.
Feb. 21.	*The Pot of Broth.* 44, FitzWilliam Place.	„ „ „
Mar. 14.	Fourth series of Irish National Theatre Society's productions at the Molesworth Hall.	*O.I.T.* 262.
	The Hour Glass.	„ „ *Samhain*, 1903
	Twenty-Five (Lady Gregory)	„ „ „ *O.I.T.* 262.
	Followed by a lecture by W. B. Yeats on ' The Reform of the Theatre '.	Programme. Hend. i. 196.
Mar. 30.	*The Laying of the Foundations.* The Rotunda.	MS. note. Hend. i. 148.
Apr. 13.	*Deirdre.* ⎫ Town Hall, *Pot of Broth* ⎬ Loughrea.	Programme. Hend. i. 246.
Apr. 20.	*The Sword of Dermot* (Seumas O'Cuisin). National Literary Society.	Programme. Hend. i. 253.
	Irish Literary Society of New York, founded this year.	*Samhain*, 1903.
June 3.	*Land of Heart's Desire.*	„ „
	Pot of Broth.	„ „
	Cathleen ni Houlihan.	„ „
June 4.	[Same set]	„ „
May 2. Aft.	*Hour Glass.* ⎫ Queen's Gate *Twenty-Five.* ⎬ Hall, South *Cathleen ni* ⎬ Kensington, *Houlihan.* ⎭ London.	*O.I.T.* 37–8. *Samhain*, 1908. Programme. Hend. i. 64.

Date	Event	Source
May 2, Eve.	⎧ *Cathleen ni Houlihan* ⎨ *The Pot of Broth* ⎩ *The Laying of the Foundations* A prospectus of the I.N.T.S. issued this summer, signed by the Secretary, Fred Ryan, and summarizing the work of the Society to date.	*O.I.T.* 37–8. *Samhain,* 1903. Hend. i. 91.
Aug. 22	*Deirdre,* at Dun Emer, Dundrum. (Private performance.)	Programme. Hend. i. 197.
Oct. 1903	Fifth series of Irish National Theatre Society's productions, at Molesworth Hall.	*O.I.T.* 262. Programme. Hend. i. 198.
Oct. 8	*The King's Threshold,* staged by Miss Horniman, who ' designed and made the costumes'. (*Samhain,* 1904.)	,, ,, ,,
	In the Shadow of the Glen (J. M. Synge).	,, ,, ,,
	Cathleen ni Houlihan.	,, ,, ,,
Oct. 9	[same set]	,, ,, ,,
Oct. 10	[same set]	,, ,, ,,
	The ' Cumann na nGaedhael Irish Theatre Company ' also gave performances this autumn, some of them in English and in one case using *Cathleen ni Houlihan.* E.g. :	
Oct. 31	*Cathleen ni Houlihan.* ⎤ Moles- *Robert Emmet* ⎬ worth (Henry Connell). ⎦ Hall.	Programme. Hend. i. 317.
Nov. 2	*Pleusgadh na Bulgoide* ⎤ (Douglas Hyde). ⎮ *The Sword of Dermot* ⎬ (Seumas O'Cuisin).⎦	,, ,, ,,
Nov. 3	*A Man's Foes* ⎤ (Seumas O'Cuisin). ⎬ *A Twinkle in Ireland's Eye* ⎦ (Joseph Ryan).	,, ,, ,,

Date	Event	Source
Dec. 1903	Sixth series of I.N.T.S. at Molesworth Hall.	
Dec. 3	*The Hour Glass.*	Programme. Hend. i. 255.
	Broken Soil (Padraic Colum).	,, ,, ,,
	A Pot of Broth.	,, ,, ,,
Dec. 4	[Same set]	,, ,, ,,
Dec. 5	[Same set]	,, ,, ,,
Jan. 1904	Seventh series of I.N.T.S. at Molesworth Hall.	
Jan. 14	*The Shadowy Waters.*	Programme. Hend. i. 269.
	Twenty-Five.	,, ,, ,,
	The Townland of Tamney (Seumas McManus).	,, ,, ,,
Jan. 15	[Same set]	,, ,, ,,
Jan. 16	[Same set]	,, ,, ,,
Feb. 1904	Eighth series of I.N.T.S., at Molesworth Hall.	
Feb. 25	*Deirdre* (A.E.).	Programme. Hend. i. 275.
	Riders to the Sea (J. M. Synge).	,, ,, ,,
Feb. 26	[Same set]	,, ,, ,,
Feb. 27	[Same set]	,, ,, ,,
	Two London performances given this year :	
Mar. 26	*The King's Threshold.* ⎫	
	Riders to the Sea. ⎬ The Royalty Theatre.	Programme. Hend. i. 100. Samhain, 1904.
	In the Shadow of the Glen. ⎭	
June 27	*Where There is Nothing.* ⎫ The	
,, 28	[Same] ⎬ Court Theatre	Programme. Hend. i. 287.
August	Negotiations for the setting up of the Abbey Theatre begins.	

MATERIALS

[In this appendix I have included copies, summaries of or extracts from printed or manuscript material which may not be readily available to my readers and which, while not of enough interest to include in the text, may yet be of use to students.]

Hend. i. 27 : (A small pamphlet, pp. 1–19, giving the rules and a brief account of the work of the N.L.S. up to 1897.)
The/National Literary Society/Rules, proceedings, etc./ Rooms : 4 College Green/Dublin/1897.

P. 3.   The list of officers and council.

P. 5–10. The list of nearly 200 members.

P. 11–12. The rules, ending ' N.B. The society is non-political.'

P. 12.   ' This society was formed in June 1892, with the object of promoting the study of Irish Literature, Music and Art (1) by means of the circulation of Irish Literature ; (2) by Lectures and Discussions ; (3) by concerts of Irish Music ; and (4) by the Establishment of Lending Libraries throughout the country, the inaugural address being delivered in August 1892 by Dr. Sigerson, on " Irish Literature, its Origin, Environment, and Influence " at the Ancient Concert Rooms, Great Brunswick Street. . . .'

P. 13 seq. A list of lectures delivered and papers read from 1892 to 1897. Among the names are those of Douglas Hyde, Rev. T. A. Finlay, Standish O'Grady, Count Plunkett, W. B. Yeats, George Sigerson, Lionel Johnson, W. A. Henderson.

A note on *Souls for Gold*

This notorious little pamphlet is conveniently available in Henderson (i. 325).

The t.p. (on the cover) reads :

Souls for Gold !/Pseudo-Celtic Drama in Dublin/' There soon will be no man or woman's soul/' unbargained for in five-score baronies '/ Mr. W. B. Yates [*sic*] on ' Celtic Ireland '/ London : MDCCCXCIX.

The words ' By F. Hugh O'Donnell ' have been added in MS. in the Henderson copy.

P. 3. Half-title :

A Pseudo-Celtic Drama in Dublin/1.Faith for Gold/To the Editor of *The Freeman's Journal*/

[The first letter continues for 3½ pp. and is signed ' F. Hugh O'Donnell, Irish National Club, London.'

P. 9. Half-title :

Blasphemy and Degradation/To the Editor of *The Freeman's Journal*/

[There is a footnote on p. 9 : ' This second letter was refused publication by *The Freeman's Journal*.' .The letter continues from p. 9 to p. 14.]

The contents of the pamphlet are disappointing, the fireworks being chiefly on the title and half-title pages.   The actual passages attacked (some of which were removed in performance and in later editions) were the episode of Shemus kicking to pieces the shrine of the Virgin, that of the demon hunting down and destroying Father John the priest in the very act of reading his breviary and the passages ' The Light of Lights/looks only on the motive,' etc., ' God/smiling condemns the lost,' and the reference to God having ' dropped asleep '. These are the ' Revolting blasphemies and idiotic impieties which sicken and astonish ' the author (p. 11).   In addition, there is, of course, the charge of pseudo-Celticism and there is a good deal of general and less clearly defined attack on Yeats for his impertinence in exploiting Celticism for the English, finding ' a new vein of literary emotion ' . . . ' for his English readers '.

Hend. i. 7 : *The prospectus of the Irish Literary Theatre*

' The Founding of the Irish/Literary Theatre/[Rule]/Extract from the Minutes of the *National/Literary Society* ; January 16th, 1899/ [Rule].

' Mr. W. B. Yeats and Mr. Edward Martyn being in attendance, by arrangement, the project of an " Irish Literary Theatre " was discussed.   Mr. Yeats stated that he wished the project developed and carried out under the auspices of the National Literary Society.   After a long discussion the following three resolutions were drafted :—

' 1. That this Council do hereby appoint a sub-committee to be called " The Irish Literary Theatre Committee ", consisting of Dr. George Sigerson [1] F.R.U.I., W. A. Henderson,[1] W. B. Yeats, Edward Martyn D.L., and Mrs. George Coffey.'

' 2. That the said Committee have power to co-opt additional members, and to take all steps in furtherance of the project of " The Irish Literary Theatre " provided that they shall not subject the Council to any liabilities without first obtaining the express sanction of this Council by resolution.

' 3. That in the event of any surplus of receipts over expenditure accruing from the performances, the amount shall be re tained by the National Literary Society, and renewed for the promotion of the objects of the Irish Literary Theatre.

' Mr. Joseph Holloway moved and Miss Edith Oldham seconded the adoption separately of these resolutions, which was passed unanimously.

' Mr. Martyn voluntarily handed in the following guarantee to be inserted in the Minutes.

' To the President and Council of the National Literary Society :

' Gentlemen,

' I hereby undertake to hold you harmless and free from any financial liability in connection with the promotion of the Irish Literary Theatre,

(signed) ' EDWARD MARTYN.'[2]

Hend. i. 91 : *Prospectus of the Irish National Theatre Society*

This prospectus, of which only a summary need be given, is headed ' The Irish National Theatre ' and begins with the statement ' The Sixth National Theatre Society was formed to continue on a more permanent basis the work begun by the Irish Literary Theatre. . . .'

It goes on to enumerate the plays which the society had produced at the date of publication, listing *Deirdre* (A.E.), *Cathleen ni Houlihan*, *The Pot of Broth*, *The Hour Glass*, *Twenty-Five*, *The Laying of the Foundations*, *The Sleep of the King*, *The Racing Lug*, and adds that the society had given two performances on the previous May at the Queen's Gate Hall, London.

It then announces : ' At the opening performance this season the following new plays will be produced : *The King's Threshold*, *In the Shadow of the Glen*, and, during the ensuing winter

---

[1] In a MS. draft (Hend. i. 20) the titles ' President ' and ' Secretary ' are substituted for the names.

[2] The MS. of this guarantee is preserved. (Hend. i. 17.)

and spring, *Broken Soil*, *Riders to the Sea*, *The Townland of Tamney*, *The Shadowy Waters* and *On Baile's Strand*.' It is signed by the secretary, Fred Ryan, from the offices of the society at 34, Lower Camden Street, Dublin, but is not dated.

This is obviously the 'first prospectus of this Society' that Lady Gregory refers to (*O.I.T.* 262), and she dates the beginning of the I.N.T.S. from March 1903, giving that as the date of this prospectus. But the two references, to the Queen's Gate Hall performances (May 2, 1903) and to the coming production of the *King's Threshold*, etc. (Oct. 8–10, 1903) plainly date the prospectus during the summer of 1903 and the list of plays already produced under its auspices carries us back to April 1902. Moreover the Leaflet of the Society (Hend. i. 322) specifically states that its first performances were in April 1902. I have therefore ventured to differ from Lady Gregory's account here and to refer the society's work back to April 1902 instead, as she does, of beginning it in March 1903.

Hend. i. 322 : *Leaflet of the Irish National Theatre Society, 34, Lower Camden Street, Dublin (n.d.)*

This leaflet states, as usual, that the society 'was formed to continue—if possible on a more permanent basis—the work begun by the Irish Literary Theatre, and it has grown out of the movement which the Literary Theatre inaugurated.' It then goes on to say that 'the first performances with which the society was associated were those of *Deirdre* (A.E.) and *Cathleen ni Houlihan*, produced in St. Teresa's Hall in April 1902 under the auspices of " inginide na hEireann " '. It then conveniently dates itself by stating that at the last Samhain festival the society had produced in the Ancient Concert Rooms, *The Pot of Broth*, *The Sleep of the King*, *The Racing Lug* and *Elis agus an Bhean Deirce* and had produced *The Hour Glass* in the previous March. This dates it as shortly after Mar. 14, 1903.

A copy of the rules of the society will be found in Hend. i. 326.

THE MAIN DATES CONNECTED WITH THE SPREAD OF IBSEN'S WORK AND THOUGHT IN ENGLAND

(a) The publication of Ibsen's most important plays (in Norwegian):
1850, *Catiline* ; 1856, *The Feast at Solhang* ; 1857, *Lady Inger of Ostraat* ; 1858, *The Vikings at Helgeland* ; 1862, *Love's Comedy* ; 1864, *The Pretenders* ; 1866, *Brand* ; 1867, *Peer Gynt* ; 1869, *The League of Youth* ; 1873, *Emperor and Galilean* ; 1877, *Pillars of Society* ; 1879, *A Doll's House* ; 1881, *Ghosts* ; 1882, *An Enemy of the People* ; 1884, *The Wild Duck* ; 1886, *Rosmersholm* ; 1888, *The Lady from the Sea* ; 1890, *Hedda Gabler* ; 1892, *The Master Builder* ; 1894, *Little Eyolf* ; 1896, *John Gabriel Borkman* ; 1899, *When We Dead Awaken*.

(b) Ibsen's work in England ; translation, criticism and production. [These dates are based on the account in Halvdan Koht's *Life of Ibsen*, Vol. II, pp. 114–15 and 266–70.]

1871.   Gosse discovered *Brand* and the poems of Ibsen in Trondheim.

1872.   Gosse wrote an account of the poems in *The Spectator* (April) and of *The Pretenders* and *Peer Gynt* later in the same year.

1873.   Gosse wrote an article for Morley's *Fortnightly Review* (Jan.) on *Ibsen the Norwegian Satirist*, some other articles on individual plays, and translated two poems and some extracts.

1876.   Gosse translated *Emperor and Galilean*.

1878.   A translation was made by A. Johnstone of *Catiline*, Act 1. (This was not put on sale.)

1879.   Gosse expanded the *Fortnightly* essay of 1873 into a book, *Studies in the Literature of Northern Europe*.

1880.   William Archer translated *The Pillars of Society*. (This was not published until 1888.)

1880.   A performance of *Quicksands, or The Pillars of Society* (adapted by William Archer) at the Gaiety Theatre on Dec. 15, is recorded by Clement Scott.

1882. H. F. Lord translated *A Doll's House* and *Ghosts.*

1888. Translations of *Pillars of Society, Ghosts* and *An Enemy of the People* by William Archer and Mrs. Marx-Aveling were published in one volume, with a preface by Havelock Ellis. (This sold well and interest in Ibsen began to spread.)

1889. On June 7 the Novelty Theatre opened with *A Doll's House* (William Archer). It was repeated successfully several times and a controversy on Ibsen began to rise.

On July 17 there was a single performance of *Pillars of Society.*

1890-1. Walter Scott published five volumes of translations containing all Ibsen's prose works from *The Vikings* to *Hedda Gabler*, with a Preface by Edmund Gosse. This was the first authorized English translation and the first collection of Ibsen's works to be published in any country. It was mainly by William Archer.

1890. Two additional translations of *The Lady from the Sea,* a translation of Henrik Jaeger's biography of Ibsen and a new edition of Gosse's *Northern Studies* appeared.

On July 18 G. B. Shaw lectured on *Socialism in Ibsen* to the Fabian Society. Ibsen himself sent to an English paper a statement of his views on Socialism.

1891. [In this year the controversy in England reached its peak.]

Rosmersholm was produced at the Vaudeville in February, and *Ghosts* forbidden by the censor before production.

On March 13 J. T. Grein produced it, nevertheless, for a single performance at his Independent Theatre.

On April 8 Wm. Archer published an article, *Ghosts and Gibberings*, in defence of Ibsen in *The Pall Mall Gazette*, quoting extracts from the most abusive of the attacks that had been made.

On June 6 G. B. Shaw published his lecture of the previous year in an expanded form as *The Quintessence of Ibsenism.*

[There was considerable newspaper controversy throughout this season and various parodies, especially of *Ghosts*, appeared at the revue theatres.]

1892. Wicksteed's *Four Lectures on Ibsen* were delivered and published.

Hedda Gabler was produced by Elizabeth Robins with great success at the Vaudeville.

[From this point onward the controversy became less acrimonious. The status of Ibsen was generally accepted.]

A LIST OF PLAYS PRODUCED IN LONDON BETWEEN
1890-9

[This list is compiled mainly from Clement Scott's lists of plays (1830-99) in the appendix to *The Drama of Yesterday and To-day* and in *From ' tThe Bells' to ' King Arthur '*. No attempt has been made to distinguish the more significant from the less significant plays or the more from the less popular. The standard histories of late nineteenth-century drama and theatre will do this for those readers who consult them. All that is offered here is a brief reminder of the names of plays and authors as a contrasting background to the early history of the Irish movement.]

1890. *Clarissa* (Buchanan from Richardson), *Dr. Bill* (from A. Carré), *A Pair of Spectacles* (Grundy), *Miss Tomboy* (Buchanan from Vanburgh), *The Cabinet Minister* (Pinero), *Dick Venables* (A. Lord), *Fillippo* (Berlyn), *A Village Priest* (Grundy), *The Violin Players* (Berlyn from Coppée), *The Bride of Love* (Buchanan), *Judah* (Henry Arthur Jones), *The New Wing* (H. A. Kennedy), *A Riverside Story* (Mrs. Bancroft), *Theodora* (Buchanan from Sardou), *Kit Marlow* (W. L. Courtney), *Nerves* (Comyns Carr), *Miss Hoyden's Husband* (Daly from Sheridan), *Sweet Nancy* (Buchanan from Broughton), *Sweet Will* (H. A. Jones), *The Deacon* (H.A.J.), *A Million of Money* (Pettitt and Harris), *Ravenswood* (Merivale from Scott), *Bean Austin* (Henley and R. L. Stevenson), *London Assurance* (Boucicault), *May and December* (Grundy), *The Pharisees* (Watson), *Sunlight and Shadow* (Carton), *The People's Idol* (W. Barrett and V. Wignall).

1891. *The Dancing Girl* (H.A.J.), *A Mighty Error* (L. Outram), *The Idler* (Haddon Chambers), *Rosmersholm* (tr. C. Archer), *The Crusaders* (H.A.J.), *Ghosts* (tr. Wm. Archer), *The Henrietta* (B. Howard), *Hedda Gabler*, *Richard Savage* (J. M. Barrie and H. Watson), *Handfast* (Revival: H. and M. Quinn), *Ibsen's Ghost* (J. M. Barrie), *Lady Bountiful* (A. W. Pinero), *The Lady from the Sea* (tr. Mrs. Marx-Aveling), *The Streets of London* (rev:, Boucicault), *Rosencrantz and Guildenstern*

(W. S. Gilbert), *Serge Panine* (C. Scott), *The Sequel* (L. N. Parker), *The Trumpet Call* (G. Sims and Buchanan), *Two in a Bush* (M. Carson), *A Royal Divorce* (W. O.Wills), *A Sailor's Knot* (Pettitt), *The Prince and the Pauper* (Hatton fr. Mark Twain), *The Times* (A.W.P.), *Alone in London* (Buchanan and H. Jay), *Hans the Boatman* (rev:), *The Honourable Herbert* (H. Chambers), *A Pantomime Rehearsal, Quicksands or The Pillars of Society* (Adapted, Archer).

1892. *The Intruder* (tr. Maeterlinck), *The Mountebanks* (W. S. Gilbert), *My Daughter* (Bancroft, fr. German), *The New Wing* (Kennedy), *Lady Windermere's Fan* (O.W.), *Walker, London* (J. M. Barrie), *A Visit* (Archer, fr. Brandes), *The Fringe of Society* (Dumas fils), *The Maelstrom* (M. Melford), *The Magistrate* (A.W.P.), *The New Sub.* (Seymour Hicks), *The White Rose* (Sims and Buchanan), *Agatha* (J. Henderson), *Richelieu* (rev: Lytton), *Virginius* (rev: Knowles), *Hero and Leander* (Bellew), *Mrs. Hilary Regrets* (T. Smith), *The Broken Melody* (H. Keen and J. Leader), *Haste to the Wedding* (W. S. Gilbert), *Haddon Hall* (S. Grundy), *The Prodigal Daughter* (Pettitt and Harris), *The Queen of Manoa* (H. Chambers and O. Tristram), *Agatha Tilden* (E. Rose), *David* (Parker and Clark), *Dorothy* (rev: Stephenson), *Hoodman Blind* (H.A.J.), *The Martyr* (T. Lucas), *My Official Wife* (Gunter), *The Old Lady* (H. Chambers), *Charley's Aunt* (B. Thomas), *Liberty Hall* (Carton), *The Lights of a Home* (Sims and Buchanan), *The Silent Battle* (J. Henderson).

1893. *The Bauble Shop* (H.A.J.), *Charley's Aunt* (B. Thomas), *Hypatia* (fr. Kingsley), *Robin Goodfellow* (Carton), *A White Lie* (Grundy), *Becket* (Tennyson), *The Master Builder, The Amazons* (A.W.P.), *The Black Domino* (Sims and Buchanan), *A Woman of no Importance* (O.W.), *Forbidden Fruit* (Boucicault), *The Second Mrs. Tanqueray* (A.W.P.), *An Enemy of the People, A Woman's Revenge* (Pettitt), *A Life of Pleasure* (Pettitt and Harris), *Sowing the Wind* (Grundy), *The Tempter* (H.A.J.), *The Foresters* (Tennyson), *A Gaiety Girl* (O. Hall), *The Orient Express* (Burnand), *Gudgeons* (Clark and Parker), *Widowers' Houses* (G.B.S.).

1894. *The Charlatan* (Buchanan), *An Old Jew* (Grundy), *The Transgressor* (Gattie), *Dick Sheridan* (Buchanan), *The Cotton King* (Sutton Vane), *Once upon a Time* (fr. German), *Arms and the Man* (G.B.S.), *A Bunch of Violets* (Grundy, fr. Feuillet), *The Masqueraders* (H.A.J.), *Mrs. Lessingham* (O. Fleming), *Lady Gladys* (Buchanan), *A Society Butterfly*

(Buchanan and Murray), *The Wild Duck, Journeys end in Lovers' Meetings* (Hobbes and O. Moore), *The Professor's Love Story* (Barrie), *The Derby Winner* (Harris, Raleigh, Hamilton), *The New Woman* (Grundy), *The Case of Rebellious Susan* (H.A.J.), *His Excellency* (Gilbert), *The Shop Girl* (an.), *The Black Cat* (Todhunter), *Slaves of the Ring* (Grundy), *The Fatal Card* (Chambers and Stephenson).

1895. *Guy Domville* (Henry James), *An Ideal Husband* (O.W.), *King Arthur* (Comyns Carr), *The Notorious Mrs. Ebbsmith* (A.W.P.), *The Girl I left Behind Me* (Fyles and Belasco), *Delia Harding* (fr. Sardou), *The Home Secretary* (Carton), *The Prude's Progress* (Jerome and Philpotts), *A Story of Waterloo* (Conan Doyle), *The Triumph of the Philistines* (H.A.J.), *The Strange Adventures of Miss Brown* (Buchanan and Marlowe), *The Swordsman's Daughter* (B. Thomas and C. Scott), *Bogey* (H. V. Esmond), *Cheer, Boys, Cheer* (Hains, Raleigh, Hamilton), *The Chili Widow* (fr. Bisson and Carré), *Harmony* (H.A.J.), *Her Advocate* (W. Frith), *Poor Mr. Potton* (Mamlyn and Paull), *The Rise of Dick Halward* (Jerome), *Trilby* (fr. G. du Maurier), *Don Quixote* (fr. Cervantes), *The Divided Way* (Esmonds), *The Manxman* (fr. Hall Caine), *The Misogynist* (Godfrey), *The Squire of Dames* (Carton, fr. Dumas fils), *One of the Best* (Hicks and Edwardes).

1896. *Michael and his Lost Angel* (H.A.J.), *The Prisoner of Zenda* (Rose fr. A. Hope), *The Sign of the Cross* (Wilson Barrett), *For the Crown* (fr. Coppée), *Jedbury Junior* (Ryley), *The New Don Quixote* (Buchanan and Marlowe), *A School for Saints* (J. O. Hobbes), *The Geisha* (O. Hall), *Mary Pennington, Spinster* (Walkes), *Monsieur de Paris* (Ramsey and Cordova), *A Mother of Three* (Graves), *The New Baby* (Bourchier fr. German), *A Night Out* (fr. French), *The Rogue's Comedy* (H.A.J.), *The Sin of St. Hulda* (Ogilvie), *The Star of India* (Sims and Shirley), *Magda* (fr. Sudermann), *The Queen's Proctor* (fr. Sardou), *A Bachelor's Romance* (M. Morton), *A Match Maker* (Graves and Kingston), *In Sight of Saint Paul's* (Sutton Vane), *The Strike* (rev: Boucicault), *Two Little Vagabonds* (Sims fr. French), *Under the Red Robe* (fr. S. Weyman), *Little Eyolf, The Late Mr. Costello* (Grundy), *Boys Together* (Chambers and Carr), *The Greatest of These* (Grundy).

1897. *The Sorrows of Satan* (Corelli), *Auntie's Young Man* (an.), *A Bit of Old Chelsea* (Mrs. Oscar Beringer), *The Daughters of Babylon* (W. Barrett), *His Majesty* (Burnand and Lehmann), *La*

Poupée (fr. French), *My Friend the Prince* (J. M'Carthy),
The Mariners of England (Buchanan and Marlowe), *The
Physician* (H.A.J.), *The Princess and the Butterfly* (A.W.P.),
A Marriage of Convenience (Grundy), *Madame Sans Gene*
(fr. Sardou), *The Seats of the Mighty* (Parker), *Secret Service*
(Gillette), *The Silver Key* (Grundy fr. French), *In The Days
of the Duke* (Chambers and Carr), *Francillon* (fr. Dumas fils),
The White Heather (Raleigh and Hamilton), *The Liars*
(H.A.J.), *The Tree of Knowledge* (Carton), *The Vagabond King*
(Parker), *Admiral Guinea* (Henley and R. L. Stevenson),
The Circus Girl (Tamney and Palings), *How London Lives*
(fr. French), *Love in Idleness* (Parker and Goodman), *The
Pilgrim's Progress* (fr. Bunyan).

1898. *Charlotte Corday* (an.), *Peter the Great* (L. Irving), *Sporting Life*
(Raleigh and Hicks), *A Brace of Partridges* (Ganthony),
The French Maid (Hood), *The Conquerors* (Potter), *The Heart
of Maryland* (Balasco), *The Master* (Ogilvie), *Too much
Johnson* (fr. French), *What Happened to Jones* (Broadhurst).
The Belle of New York (Morton), *The Medicine Man* (Traill
and Hichens), *The Runaways* (Aria), *A Runaway Girl* (Hicks
and Nicholls), *The Ambassador* (J. O. Hobbes), *His Excellency
the Governor* (Marshall), *A Greek Slave* (Hall), *Sue* (Bret Harte
and Pemberton), *Lord and Lady Algy* (Carton), *The Gipsey
Earl* (G. K. Sime), *The Elder Miss Blossom* (Hendrie and
Wood), *The Great Ruby* (Raleigh and Hamilton), *Teresa*
(Bancroft), *The Termagant* (Parker and Carson), *Ragged
Robin* (Parker fr. French), *Adventure of Lady Ursula* (A. Hope),
Brother Officers (L. Trevor), *The Manœuvres of Jane* (H.A.J.),
Pelleas and Melisande (Maeterlinck), *When a Man's in Love*
(A. Hope and E. Ross), *The Zest* (Carson and Parker),
The Musketeers (Grundy fr. Dumas), *A Little Ray of Sun-
shine* (Ambient and Heriot), *On and Off* (fr. Bisson).

1899. *A Bachelor's Romance* (Morton), *A Court Scandal* (fr. Bayard),
Matches (Glenney), *My Soldier Boy* (Maltby and Lindo),
What Will the World Say ? (Bancroft), *The Coquette* (an.),
Grierson's Way (Esmond), *The Only Way* (fr. Dickens), *Ours*
(rev: Robertson), *The Cuckoo* (fr. Meilhac), *A Lady of
Quality* (Burnett), *The Man in the Iron Mask* (an.), *The May-
flower* (Parker), *Ambition* (Fomm), *Carnac Sahib* (H.A.J.),
Change Alley (Parker and Carson), *The Gay Lord Quex*
(A.W.P.), *A Good Time* (Sims), *Great Caesar* (Grossmith),
In Days of Old (Rose), *Captain Swift* (rev: Chambers),
Helping a Friend (Denny), *The Upper Hand* (Winthrop

and Lisle), *Wheels within Wheels* (Carton), *An American Citizen* (Ryley), *Carlyon Sahib* (G. Murray), *The Cowboy and the Lady* (Fitch), *A Doll's House, Halves* (C. Doyle), *The Heather Field* (Martyn), *The Jewess* (an.), *Pot Pourri* (Tanner), *The Weather Hen* (Thomas and Granville Barker), *The Guinea Pigs* (Warden), *The Lady of Ostend* (fr. Germ.), *Pillars of Society, The Degenerates* (Grundy), *With Flying Colours* (Hicks and Latham), *The Elixir of Youth* (Sims and Merrick), *The Ghetto* (fr. Heyermann), *Hearts are Trumps* (Raleigh), *The Rebels* (Fagan), *The Silver King* (rev: H.A.J.), *Trip to Midgettown* (an.), *Why Smith Left Home* (Broadhurst), *The Wild Rabbit* (George Arliss), *The King's Outcast* (Mackay), *The Merry-go-Round* (Hicks), *Robespierre* (L. Irving fr. Sardou), *The Tyranny of Tears* (Chambers).

INDEX TO THE CRITICAL OPINIONS OF LADY GREGORY AND W. B. YEATS

[This index only includes the opinions or critical comments of the authors upon dramatic subjects or those persons or topics that are for some reason closely connected with the Irish Dramatic Movement. Unless otherwise stated, the editions referred to are those of Putnam in the case of Lady Gregory and Macmillan in the case of W. B. Yeats (with the exception of *Dramatis Personae* for which reference is made to the Cuala edition). The abbreviations are those given on p. xvii.]

Actors, i. Florence Farr. *O.I.T.* 2 ; *Autob.* 148–51, 229, 344 ; *D.P.* 15, 27, 34–5, 39.
    ii. The Fays. *O.I.T.* 29–32, 46, 79, 107–8 ; *Autob.* 149 ; *D.P.* 75–6, 78, 79.
    iii. Maud Gonne. *Autob.* 151–3, 433–4, 437, 444–8, 450–2 ; *D.P.* 31, 44, 70, 79.
Acting, (see Drama).
Art, Function of, *P.C.* 57–8, 61–3, *Ess. Cutting of Agate : Discoveries*, whole.
    Relation to life, *P.C.* 101–4, 123, 153–9, 160–1, 172, 177, 207–8 ;
    Relation to politics, *P.C.* 53, 59, 65, 160–1.
    Transmutation of life into, *Autob.* 466–7, 469, 476–7, 49. *Ess. Anima Hominis*, whole.
    Poetry and rhetoric, *Autob.* 126–7, 187–8, 190.
Artistic Process :
    Experience of dramatist, Creation of character, *O.I.T.* 80–90, 91–2 ; *S.S.P.* 196, 197 ; *N.I.C.* 159, 160–1.
        Creation of plot, *O.I.T.* 95, 105 ; *P.C.* 290–1 ; *S.S.P.* 201–2 ; *T.W.P.* 214, 215 ; *I.F.H.* ii. 195–6 ; *N.I.C.* 155, 159–61.
    Experiments in playwriting, *T.W.P.* 213 seq. ; *I.F.H.* i. 195–6, 200.
    Genesis of poet, *Autob.* 107, 127.

Methods of work, *O.I.T.* 100–2 ; *S.S.P.* 202 ; *N.I.C.* 158, 159 ; *I.F.H.* i. 200 ; *I.F.H.* ii. 189.

Modification of idea, *Im.* 99–100, 134, 223, 252 ; *N.I.C.* 159–61 ; *T.W.P.* 131, 213–16.

Revisions of text, *O.I.T.* 80–1 ; *Plays* 422–5, 428 ; *L.P.* 360 ; *P.C.* 290–1, 327.

Poet's Mind, The Antithetical self and its function, *Autob.* 234, 241, 255, 289, 305–7, 337–9, 402, 418, 426, 448 ; *Ess.* 336–7, 397–9 ; *Anima Hominis*, whole.

The 'image' and its function, *Autob.* 176–7, 197.

Imagination, *P.C.* 44–5, 56, 57, 96–7, 109, 158.

The 'mask', *Autob.* 188, 305–7, 337–9, 466–7. *Ess. Anima Hominis*, whole.

Saint, poet and hero, *Ess.* 492–504.

Training of a dramatist, *P.C.* 11–12 ; *O.I.T.* 100–2.

Collaboration, *O.I.T.* 26, 28, 80–3, 83–90, 105 ; *S.S.P.* 199 ; *D.P.* 50–2, 60–4, 65–6, 82–4 ; *Plays* vii, 419, 420, 421, 425–6.

Comedy, *N.I.C.* 155, 159 ; *Ess. The Tragic Theatre (passim).*

Criticism, contemporary, *D.P.* 42–4.

Drama : Character, formation of (see Artistic Process).

Character, place of in drama, *S.S.P.* 197 ; *Im.* 252 ; *O.I.T.* 106 ; *N.I.C.* 158–9 ; *Ess. The Tragic Theatre (passim).*

Nature and function of, *P.C.* 416, 418, 434.

Plot, formation of, (see Artistic Process).

Relation to theatre, *S.S.P.* 196 ; *T.W.P.* 214, 215 ; *I.F.H.* i. 205 ; *N.I.C.* 158 ; *Plays* vi–viii ; *O.I.T.* 98–100, 132–3.

to acting, *O.I.T.* 98 ; *P.C.* 20, 48, 132–3, 205, 300 ; *Plays* 420, 423–4 ; *Autob.* 149.

to setting and production, *O.I.T.* 107–8, 141–2, 215 ; *P.C.* 22, 48–9, 68, 133–5, 138–9, 332, 337, 416–17 ; 291, 331–3, 415–18 ; *Plays* 427–8; *T.W.P.* 290 ; *T.L.P.* 119–20.

Types of : Noh plays, *P.C.* 416, *Ess. The Noble Plays of Japan* (whole).

'modern', *P.C.* 155–7 ; *Ess.* 338–43, 372–6.

verse, *O.I.T.* 78–9, 79–80.

Dramatists, their work or opinions :

A.E. (George Russell), *O.I.T.* 30–1, 99 ; *D.P.* 57, 78–80 ; *Autob.* 295–307 ; *Im.* 99 ; *T.W.P.* 214–15, 289 ; *T.L.P.* 164–5.

Boyle, *P.C.* 142.

Colum, *P.C.* 142.

Gregory, Lady, *D.P.* 5, 8–9, 12–13, 27–9, 33–4, 50, 51, 52, 55, 60, 66, 67, 68, 77, 80, 81, 84–8 ; (*White Cockade*) 68 ; (*Cathleen ni Houlihan*) 78, 79–80 ; (*Pot of Broth*) 80, 81 ; (*Where There is Nothing* and *Unicorn*) 83–4 ; *Ess.* 487 ; *O.I.T.* 20–5, 33, 37, 42, 97, 115–17, 140–68, 169, 252 ; *P.C.* 142, 211.

Hyde, Douglas, *D.P.* 14, 65–7, 70, 82 ; *Autob.* 266–71 ; *O.I.T.* 29, 56–8, 73–7, 83–90 ;

Ibsen, *P.C.* 12, 118–19, 122, 155, 157 ; *Autob.* 343–4.

Martyn, Edward, *D.P.* 1, 2–5, 17, 20–1, 34–7, 40, 45, 49–52, 71–4 ; (*Heather Field*) 4, 20, 40, 46, 49, 50 ; (*Maeve*) 4, 49, 50, 54, 55 ; (*Tale of a Town*) 51–3 ; *O.I.T.* 20, 26, 27, 71.

Moore, George (*Bending of the Bough*), *D.P.* 51, 53, 54 ; (*Diarmuid and Grania*), *D.P.* 53, 60, 62, 67, 68–9, 76, 78, 79 ; *O.I.T.* 20, 26, 27, 28, 43, 44.

Murray, T. C., *O.I.T.* 179–80.

Synge, J. M., *P.C.* 44, 120, 142, 211 ; *Ess.* 488–91, *The Tragic Theatre* (whole), Prefs. to *Well of Saints* and to *Poems* (whole), *John Synge* (whole) ; *D.P.* 68 ; *Autob.* 423–7 ; *O.I.T.* 33, 34–5, 109, 111–28, 137–9 ; *I.F.H.* ii. 194.

Shaw, G. B., *O.I.T.* 35–6, 210–11, 267–74, 299–305 ; (*Blanco Posnet*) 140–68, 267–79, 299–305 ; *Autob.* 346–7, 362–4 ; *T.W.P.* 288 ; *P.C.* 40–1.

Yeats, W. B., *Autob.* (*passim*) ; *O.I.T.* 5–7, 22–3, 28–9, 33–4, 37–8, 42–5, 65–8, 78–83, 97–8, 106, 111, 122, 169–70, 193–4, 210–11, 234–6.

Language, 'the living language' and dramatic dialogue, *P.C.* 29–31, 119–20, 162, 169–70 ; *Ess.* (language of Synge) 369–423 (*passim*) ; *D.P.* 64–8 ; *Plays* 419–21 ; *Autob.* 126–7, 187–8, 190 ; *O.I.T.* 124–5.

National movement, some relevant aspects of :
  Gaelic League, *O.I.T.* 29, 76, 83, 135 ; *D.P.* 14, 65.
  Irish Literary Society, and Theatres, *O.I.T.* 8–9, 20–8 ; *D.P.* 13, 15, 17 ; *N.I.C.* 160.
  National Literary Society, *D.P.* 14–15.
  Politics and art in the nineties, *Autob.* 433–4, 437–8, 440–2.
  [see also under Art, relation to life.]

Playwriting [See Artistic Process].

Poets and writers, references to some works and opinions of. [For dramatic works, see Dramatists.]
  Dowson, Ernest, *Autob.* 382–4, 403–4.
  Ellis, Edwin, *Autob.* 197–203.
  Johnson, Lionel, *Autob.* 273–6.
  Morris, William, *Autob.* 172–7, 178–84.

O'Grady, Standish, *Autob.* 271–3 ; *D.P.* 14, 42–3, 47–9.
Symons, Arthur, *Autob.* 394–7 ; *D.P.*, 22, 23, 50, 80–1.
Wilde, Oscar, *Autob.* 160–3, 165–72, 349–59, 362–3.
Style, *P.C.* 46 ; *D.P.* 25–6, 60–2, 64–5.
Subject-matter of drama, *P.C.* 32, 156, 158 ; (heroic material)
    Plays, 417–19, 426–7 ; (' surface of life ') *P.C.* 121, 155–6.
Tragedy, *P.C.* 123–4 ; *Ess. The Tragic Theatre,* whole ; *Plays,*
    423–4, 429 ; *O.I.T.* 106 ; *N.I.C.* 158–9.
Verse, as dramatic medium, *P.C.* 179–86, 458 ; *Plays,* 428, 433–4.

A NOTE ON EDITIONS AND GENERAL WORKS OF REFERENCE

The first edition of this volume contained a short list of general accounts of the Irish Dramatic Movement, a list of a few works on individual dramatists and a note, for the guidance of students, of the standard editions of the principal plays. Much in the first two sections has been superseded by the number of works in this field that have appeared in the interval and they have therefore been reduced to a few references. It seemed advisable to keep the last section, and the standard editions or the publishers of the plays of those dramatists mentioned in the final chapter are now added to it.

I. GENERAL ACCOUNTS OF THE IRISH DRAMATIC MOVEMENT

Readers who wish to make a detailed study of the history of the movement are referred to the manuscript collections in the National Library of Ireland, to the surviving archives of the Abbey Theatre, to theses written for higher degrees of Trinity College Dublin and similar sources. For the general reader, the best introductions are those contained in the prose writings of W. B. Yeats (including the series in *Samhain* and *The Arrow* (1901–9), not all of which were reprinted in the collected works), to George Moore's *Hail and Farewell* (1911–14) (especially the first volume), to Lady Gregory's *Our Irish Theatre* (1914). A. E. Malone's *The Irish Drama* (1929) gives a full survey up to the time of writing, and for more recent descriptions, criticisms or comments, the reader should refer to the critical and autobiographical works of Lennox Robinson and Sean O'Casey. Much information on the history of the movement is also given in J. M. Hone's *W. B. Yeats, 1865–1939* (London 1942).

II. STANDARD EDITIONS OF THE PLAYS

1. Paul Vincent Carroll. Many of the plays are published by Macmillan and the remainder can be found in French's acting edition.

2. Padraic Colum. *Three Plays*, Maunsell & Co. 1917.
3. Lady Gregory. All Lady Gregory's dramatic writings, except *The Golden Apple* (Murray) are contained in Putnam's series : *Irish Folk History Plays* (2 vols.), *New Comedies, Seven Short Plays, The Image, Three Wonder Plays, Three Last Plays, The Story Brought by Brigit*. Putnam's also publish *Our Irish Theatre*.
4. Denis Johnston. Jonathan Cape.
5. Edward Martyn. The plays are published separately by various publishers, chiefly by Duckworth, Maunsell and Fisher Unwin. There is no collected edition.
6. George Moore. The only play of Moore's belonging to the Irish Dramatic Movement is *The Bending of the Bough*, published by Fisher Unwin (1900).
7. T. C. Murray. The plays are published separately, principally by George Allen and Unwin.
8. Sean O'Casey. Principally by Macmillan.
9. Lennox Robinson. Various publishers, chiefly Macmillan.
10. George Russell (A. E.) *Deirdre* (*Imaginations and Reveries*, 258–315). Macmillan.
11. George Shiels. Macmillan.
12. J. M. Synge. Various editions of single works and translations ; collected works as follows :
    1910. *The Works of John M. Synge*. 4 vols. Maunsel & Co., Dublin.
    1911. *Pocket edition of the plays of J. M. Synge*. 4 vols. (*ib.*)
    1915. *The Dramatic Works of John M. Synge*. 1 vol. (*ib.*)
    1932. *The Works of John M. Synge* (Revised collected ed.). G. Allen and Unwin. (1932 *seq.*).
13. W. B. Yeats. Various editions of single works, translations, etc. The standard edition of the collected works is that of Messrs. Macmillan. (1925 *seq.*). This contains the volumes *Early Poems, Later Poems, Autobiographies, Plays, Plays and Controversies, Essays, Wheels and Butterflies*, and *Dramatis Personae*, as well as separate editions of the various volumes of poetry and prose. The separate editions referred to most frequently in the present volume are *Reveries over Childhood and Youth, The Cutting of an Agate*, and *Per Amica Silentia Lunae*, all of which are also included in the volume *Essays*. An edition of the recovered text of *Diarmuid and Grania* is in preparation (W. Becker). For details of the bibliography of Yeats's plays, reference should be made to Allan Wade's *A Bibliography of the Writings of W. B. Yeats* (1951).

INDEX

Abbey Company' (National Theatre Society Ltd.), ix, 42, 47
American tour, 45, 46, 54–7
Patent granted, 46, 47
Abbey Theatre, xi, 47
Abercrombie, Lascelles, xiv, 7
Acting, 70–2
Advice to Playwrights, 64
A.E. (George Russell), 13–15, 40–1, 59, 82, 120, 147, 155, 164, 166, *Deirdre*, 15, 40–3, 66, 72, 181, 182, 185 ; *The Earth Breath*, 100, 164 ; *Homeward, Songs by the Way*, 100, 164
American tour. *See* ' Abbey Company '
Andersen, Hans, 136, 146
Anderson, Maxwell, 198
Archer, William, 6, 20, 32, 134
Artistic Process, records of, 219–20. *See also* Gregory, Yeats

Barker, G., 20
Blake, William, 96
Boyle, William, 7, 188
Bridie, James, 153

Carroll, Paul Vincent, 201, 205–6
Clan na Gael, 46
Collaboration, in Irish Dramatic Movement, 9–11, 81–5, 124–32
Colum, Padraic, xiii, 7, 100, 124, 146, 187, 188, 189–91, 192, 196, 197, 202. *The Fiddler's House*, 188, 193; *The Land*, 188, 189–91.; *Thomas Muskerry*, 189, 191, 194
Critical opinions, Lady Gregory and Yeats, 85–90, 219–22. *See also* ' living language ', tragedy

Deevy, Teresa, 201
Dialect, of Irish peasant, 15, 68–9, 76
Doyle, Lynn, 201
Dunsany, Lord, 188
Drinkwater, John, 7, 153

English Drama, relation to Irish, 2–7, 18, 22, 30. Jacobean Drama, 7, 9–10, 86, 185–6, 187 ; Jacobean dramatists, 9, 10. *See also* Shakespeare. Nineteenth century drama, early, 2–4 ; dramatists, 3, 4, 19, 21. Nineteenth century drama, late, 18–32 ; dramatists, critics, and actors, 20, 28–9 ; lists of plays, 23–4, 214–15. Twentieth century dramatists, 7, 11
Ervine, St. J., 188, 189, 196, 199
Everyman, 108–9

Farr, Florence, 33, 71
Fay, William and Frank, 40, 42, 44, 71–2
Finn, legend of, 155–7
Flower, Dr. R., 172

Gaelic language, 14, 15
Gaelic League, 15, 33
Gaelic plays, xiii–xiv, 15
Galsworthy, J., 20, 197
Gilbert, W. S., 24
Gosse, E., 5, 6, 20, 134, 211, 212
Greek drama and theatre, 11, 12, 86, 114–15, 123, 165–6

Gregory, Augusta, Lady, 2, 13, 100, 101, 176, 183, 187, 196
character, 136–8
work, as historian of the movement, xi, 33–58 *passim*
as manager and director of the Theatre, 33–58, 59, 60
as playwright, 138–62, 200
as translator from Irish, 14
account of her own career, 138, 139
of writing of her plays, 74–81
of collaboration, 9–11, 81–5
technique, structure of comedy, 141–5
structure of tragedy, 66–7, 155, 157–61
treatment of saga and history, 67–8, 75, 152–4
growth of her art, 138–9
use of dialect, 161
critical opinions, 66–7, 86, 88, 219–22
works : *Aristotle's Bellows*, 77, 80, 140, 147, 151 ; *The Bogie Man*, 140 ; *The Canavans*, 80, 140, 152 ; *Coats*, 140 ; *Cuchulain*, 14, 68, 110 ; *Damer's Gold*, 80 ; *Dave*, 140, 147, 151–2 ; *The Deliverer*, 80, 140, 152, 153 ; *Dervorgilla*, 68, 141, 152 ; *The Dragon*, 80, 140, 147, 148–51 ; *The Full Moon*, 140 ; *The Goal Gate*, 66–7, 76, 79, 81, 140, 157 ; *Gods and Fighting Men*, 14, 68, 147, 155; *The Golden Apple*, 147, 148, 151 ; *Grania*, 67, 140, 152–3, 154–61 ; *Hanrahan's Oath*, 80, 140 ; *Hyacinth Halvey*, 140, 141, 152 ; *Irish Folk History Plays*, 15, 67, 152 ; *The Image*, 80, 140, 141, 145 ; *The Jackdaw*, 140, 141 ; *The Jester*, 140, 147 ; *Kincora*, 67, 78, 81, 138, 140, 152–3 ; *Our Irish Theatre*, 18, 33–58 *passim*, 64, 66, 74, 75, 76, 78, 82, 88, 139, 198, 199, 200, 224 ; *The Rising of the Moon*, 140, 146 ;

Sancho's Master, 140 ; *Shanwalla*, 80, 140 ; *Spreading the News*, 76, 139, 140, 141–5 ; *The Travelling Man*, 140, 147, 151 ; *Twenty-Five*, 42 ; *The White Cockade*, 140, 152, 153 ; *The Workhouse Ward*, 82, 140, 141 ; *The Wrens*, 140
Grieg, Nordahl, 198
Gwynn, D., 117, 119, 133, 225

Hamilton, Patrick, 201
Hebbel, H., 8, 59
Henderson, W. A., 207, 208, 209, 210, 223
Hone, J., 38
Horniman, K., 42, 46, 63
Hyde, D., 13, 14, 15, 33, 69, 74, 81, 120, 172. *Casad an't Sugan*, 39

Ibsen, H., 4–7, 8, 11–21, 25, 27, 59, 61, 99, 105, 127, 134–5, 211–13. *A Doll's House*, 5, 212; *An Enemy of the People*, 5, 124, 188, 212 ; *Brand*, 6, 211 ; *Catiline*, 211 ; *Emperor and Galilean*, 6, 211 ; *Ghosts*, 5, 51, 55, 212 ; *Hedda Gabler*, 5, 6, 212, 213 ; *The Lady from the Sea*, 5, 133, 212 ; *Little Eyolf*, 6, 133 ; *The Master Builder*, 5, 98, 133 ; *Peer Gynt*, 6, 98, 108–9 ; *The Pillars of Society*, 5, 20, 211, 212 ; *The Pretenders*, 211 ; *Rosmersholm*, 5, 212 ; *The Vikings*, 212 ; *When we Dead Awaken*, 6, 98 ; *The Wild Duck*, 6, 133
Ireland, ancient, 14, 15
Irish Dramatic Movement, significance, xi, 1–2, 7–12. Early history, 13–16, 33–58, 197–206. Later history, 7–8, 187–207. Relation to English drama, 2, 7, 18, 22, 30. Later dramatists, 7. English view, xi, xii–xiii. Historians xi–xii.

INDEX

Irish Literary Society, 33, 197
Irish Literary Theatre, 13, 33, 41, 198, 208-9
Irish National Dramatic Company, 41, 202
Irish National Theatre Society, 202, 209-10

Johnson, L., 199
Johnston, D., 149, 198, 201, 202-4
Jonson, B., 61
Jones, H. A., 4, 5, 19, 20, 31, 64, 96, 126-7, 128. On history of English dramatic renascence, 21, 22, 25. *Michael and his Lost Angel*, 195 ; *Saints and Sinners*, 20, 128

Knight, W., 73
Koht, H., 20, 31, 211

Lagerkvist, Pär, 198
'Living Imagination', 62-8
'Living Language', 62, 68-70
Longford, Lady, 201
Lowes, J. L., 80

MacLiammòir, Micheàl, 201
Macnamara, Brinsley, 200
Malone, A. E., xii, 18, 22, 33, 54, 58, 154, 197
Manning, Mary, 201
Martyn, E., 13, 15, 33-9, 40, 59, 60, 88, 100, 117-35, 139. *An Enchanted Sea*, 119, 120, 128, 133, 134 ; *The Dream Physician*, 120, 130, 134 ; *Grangecolman*, 120, 127 ; *The Heather Field*, 18, 34, 37, 118, 119-20, 124, 133 ; *Maeve*, 37-9, 118, 119, 120, 122-3, 133, 135, 165 ; *Morgante the Lesser*, 126, 134 ; *The Placehunters*, 120. *The Privilege of Place*, 120 ; *The Tale of a Town*, 38-9, 82, 119, 123-32, 134, 135. On Ibsen, 133-5. On Moore, 130. On English drama, 27

Mayne, R , 188, 196, 199, 200
Meyer, K., 13, 14, 105, 122, 165, 172-4
Moore, G. A., 33, 34, 35, 38-40, 60, 69, 82, 84, 117, 118, 119. *Ave (Hail and Farewell)*, 37, 38, 39, 117, 125, 127, 128, 193, 224 ; *The Bending of the Bough*, 38-40, 82, 119, 124-32 ; *Diarmuid and Grania*, 15, 39, 82, 84, 132 ; *The Strike at Arlingford*, 34, 132. On Irish Dramatic Movement, 33. Share in *The Heather Field* and *Maeve*, 9, 10
Murray, T. C., xiii, 7, 100, 146, 187, 188. *Aftermath*, 194. *Birthright*, 189, 192. *Maurice Harte*, 188, 189, 192-4, 195, 196, 200, 204

National Literary Society, 33, 198, 207
National movement, 13-17. Yeats on, 16-17
National Theatre Society Ltd., *see* 'Abbey Company'
Nō plays, 85

O'Casey, S., 149, 187, 196-200, 201, 203, 204
O'Cuisin, S., 40
Odets, Clifford, 198
O'Grady, S., 13, 14, 122
O'Neill, E., 7

Pinero, A. W., 20, 25
Producing, 43, 45
Purdie, E., xiv, 60

Robinson, L., xi, xiii, 7, 124, 146, 187, 188, 191. *The Clancy Name*, 188, 189, 191-2. *Harvest*, 189, 191, 196, 200
Riots, 49-51
Russell, G., *see* A. E. 49-51

Ryan, F., 41

Setting, 43, 45, 70, 72–3
Shakespeare, W., 153, 154, 156, 160, 163, 166, 171. *Troilus and Cressida*, 112
Shaw, G. B., 6, 13, 20, 21, 22, 25, 28, 31, 48, 49, 52, 53, 57, 107, 133, 212. *Blanco Posnet*, 46, 51–4, 136, 197
Shiels, George, 200, 201, 203–5
Sir Gawain, 111
Souls for Gold, 35, 199, 207–8
Strindberg, G., 8, 199
Symons, A., 119, 122
Synge, J. M., 2, 15, 16, 58, 59, 63, 85, 96, 106, 145, 154, 155, 160, 161, 196, 199. As poetic dramatist, 163–86. As nature mystic, 163–74. His tragedy, 179, 184–6. His comedy, 174–9, 184–5. *The Aran Islands*, 163, 179–80, 182–3 ; *Deirdre*, 164, 171–2, 174, 179–84 ; *The Playboy*, 46, 49–51, 55–7, 70, 77, 164, 170–1, 174, 175–9, 180 ; *Riders to the Sea*, ix, 8, 164, 166, 169–70, 171, 174, 175 ; *In the Shadow of the Glen*, 46, 164, 165, 166, 168–9, 175 ; *The Tinker's Wedding*, 49, 54, 165, 172 ; *The Well of the Saints*, 164, 166–7, 169, 170, 175, 176 ; *In Wicklow and West Kerry*, 163, 165

Tcheckov, A., 8, 199
Theatre and drama, 11–12, 70–3
Tragedy, 86–8. *See also* Gregory, Synge, Yeats.

Verse Speaking, 44, 70–1

Webster, J., 163

Yeats, W. B., xiv, xv, 2, 12, 13, 14, 16–17, 59, 60, 74, 78, 85, 80, 120, 131, 146, 147, 154, 155, 161, 162, 163, 188, 196. As founder and director, 33–58, 91, 196, 207. As historian of the movement, xi, 33–58 (*passim*), 187. As poet and dramatist, ix, 11, 91–115. Development as artist, 91–2, 95–9. Early plays, 99–109. Saga plays, 15, 67–8, 109–14. Last plays, 115. Themes : love, 100–3 ; spiritual growth, 104–9 ; antithetical self, 97–9. On acting, 70–2. On English drama, 27–8. On the function of poetry, 92–4. On ideals of poetic drama, 61–2, 89–90, 94–6, and of an Irish theatre, 60–73. On 'living imagination', 62–8. On 'living language', 12, 15–16, 62, 68–70. On the relation of life and art, 95–9. On tragedy, 65–6, 86–8. On Ibsen, 94–5 ; Lady Gregory, 137–8 ; Martyn 117–19 ; Moore, 84, 132 ; Synge, 164, 174, 186. Critical opinions, 219–22. List of plays and critical works, 116. Works : *Anima Hominis*, 97, 98, 106 ; *The Arrow*, 49, 61, 223 ; *At the Hawk's Well*, 89, 109 ; *Autobiographies*, 16, 61, 90, 162, 164, 186 ; *Beltaine*, 37, 61 ; *Calvary*, 79 ; *The Cat and the Moon*, 115 ; *Cathleen ni Houlihan*, ix–x, 40–2, 70, 82–3, 146 ; *The Countess Cathleen*, 34–7, 78, 91, 99, 101–2, 115 ; *The Cutting of an Agate* (in *Essays*), 28, 61, 65, 88, 89, 164, 186 ; *Dramatis Personae*, 35, 36, 37, 38, 41, 43, 61, 66, 70, 78, 82, 84, 118, 119, 137, 138, 198, 199, 201, 202 ; *Deirdre*, 84, 92, 109, 113–15, 185 ; *Diarmuid and Grania*, 15, 39, 82, 84, 132 ; *Essays*, 99 ; *Essays, 1931–6*, 99, 102–3 ; *The Green Helmet*,,

INDEX

Yeats, W. B.—*continued*
92, 109, 110–11 ; *Hodos Chameli ontos*, 92, 97 ; *The Hour Glass*, 42, 71, 92, 101, 102, 108–9 ; *The Land of Heart's Desire*, 18, 84, 91, 99, 101, 115 ; *The King's Threshold*, 92, 101, 102 ; *The Only Jealousy of Emer*, 109, 111, 112 ; *On Baile's Strand*, 84, 92, 109–10 ; *Per Amica Silentia Lunae*, 61, 92, 98 ; *The Pot of Broth*, 42, 82–3, 140 ; *Purgatory*, 92, 101, 115 ; *Resurrection*, 92, 108, 115 ; *Rosa Alchemica* (in *Early Poems*), 97 ; *Samhain* (in *Plays and Con-*

Yeats, W. B.,—*continued*
troversies, The Irish Dramatic Movement), xiv, 16, 34–51 *passim*, 62, 63, 65, 67, 69, 70, 71, 72, 73, 77, 95, 96, 97, 186, 223 ; *The Shadowy Waters*, 45, 92, 99, 102–3, 106 ; *The Unicorn from the Stars*, 92, 98, 101, 104–9 ; *Where there is Nothing*, 49, 54, 82, 92, 147 ; *The Words upon the Window Pane*, 92, 115 ; annotations to *Early Poems*, 83 ; to *Plays*, 76, 78, 79, 82, 83, 88, 98, 105, 113 ; to *Plays and Controversies*, 17, 58, 61, 101, 187

REPRINTED BY LITHOGRAPHY IN GREAT BRITAIN
BY JARROLD AND SONS LIMITED, NORWICH